Armenians of Jerusalem

ARMENIANS OF JERUSALEM
Memories of Life in Palestine

John H. Melkon Rose

The Radcliffe Press
London · New York

Published in 1993 by
The Radcliffe Press
45 Bloomsbury Square
London WC1A 2HY

175 Fifth Avenue
New York
NY 10010

In the United States of America
and Canada distributed by
St Martin's Press
175 Fifth Avenue
New York
NY 10010

Copyright © 1993 by John H. Melkon Rose

All rights reserved. Except for brief quotations in a review,
this book, or any part thereof, must not be reproduced in any form
without permission in writing from the publisher.

A full CIP record for this book is available from the British Library

A full CIP record is available from the Library of Congress

ISBN 1–85043–596–0

Printed and bound in Great Britain by
WBC Ltd, Bridgend, South Wales

CONTENTS

List of Maps		vii
Acknowledgements		viii
Dramatis Personae		ix
Glossary		xi

Chapter

1	Origins	1
2	The Krikorians	14
3	The Gazmararians	28
4	Malakeh and Margaret, Early Childhood	39
5	Nursing in Hebron then on to Beirut	48
6	Aleppo and the First World War	57
7	Malakeh, Nurse and Midwife	68
8	Isquhie and her Mother in Jerusalem	74
9	The Roses	86
10	The Move to Jerusalem	91
11	Children at Home	97
12	Life in the Greek Colony	106
13	Children at School	115
14	Summers in Ramallah	121
15	The Collegiate Church of St George	132
16	School Days at St George's	139
17	Interests out of School	145
18	The Second World War	156
19	Years of Violence	165
20	England in 1947 and the Return to Jerusalem	173
21	The Dispersal	181
22	1948 War	193

23	Uneasy Calm	202
24	Adapting to Reality	212
25	A Period of Change	224
26	Amman then back to Jerusalem	232
27	Warden of St George's Hostel	245
28	The 1967 War and its Aftermath	260
Maps		277
Index		283

LIST OF MAPS

1. Middle East	279
2. Palestine and Jordan	280
3. Jerusalem and environs	281
4. Jerusalem Old City	282

ACKNOWLEDGEMENTS

I would like to express my gratitude to all those who over the years have helped and encouraged me to write this book. In particular, my thanks go to Bishop Kenneth Cragg, Canon Harold Adkins, Bishop Guregh Kapigian, Bishop Sevan Gharibian (*Desoutch* at Hrishtagabed), Kevork Hintlian (Secretary to the Armenian Patriarch), Arthur Hagopian (Armenian Patriarchate Press Information Office), Nazaret and Marie Chapadarian, Antranig Bakerjian (President of the JABU), Nazaret Banayan, Arshalouise Zakarian, Haig and Isquhie Aghabegian, Garabed Hagopian (*Mukhtar* to the Armenian community of Jerusalem), Sitt Siranoush Ketchejian (retired principal of the school for blind girls), Nubar and Vera Markarian, my sister Gertrude Dorothy Graham, my cousin Vergine Krikorian Darby, Alice and Rizek Abushar, Mona Macmillan, Hugh Macmillan, Marjory Drakeford, Paul Pedretti, Gillian Grant the Archivist at the Middle East Centre of St Antony's College, Oxford, Elia Photo-service in Jerusalem, and my sympathetic editor Dr Lester Crook. Last but not least to my wife Monty for her patience and hard work without which writing the book would not have been possible.

DRAMATIS PERSONAE

THE KRIKORIANS

Krikor Dülger Soghmonian, 1828–78, carpenter – my great-grandfather
Anna Lüleji Minassian, 1832–1924 – my great-grandmother
Minas Minassian, coffee shop owner – Anna's brother

Children of Krikor and Anna:
  Sirpouhie, 1851–80, m. Tavid Genevisian – great-aunt
  Mariam (Mannan), 1854–1943, m. Sapritch Melkon – my grandmother
  Heghnoug, 1856–1964 – great-aunt
  Soghmon, 1860–1926, secretary to Armenian Patriarch – great-uncle
  Horop, 1865–1943 – great-aunt
  Hagop, 1871–1939, shoemaker – great-uncle
  Arousiag, 1873–1955 – great-aunt
  Movses, 1876–1946, commercial traveller, Brazil – great-uncle

  Haiganoush Sarafian, 1883–1918, m. Hagop Krikorian
  Heghineh Hagopjian, 1869–1943, m. Soghmon Krikorian

  Krikor Krikorian, 1893–1960, doctor, deputy Chief Medical Officer for Palestine – cousin

  Nazouhie Krikorian, 1901–79 – cousin

THE GAZMARARIANS

Hovhannes Melkon (Sapritch Melkon), 1835–1910, barber – my grandfather

Garabed Gazmararian, 1825–1911, importer of fancy goods – Melkon's brother

Children of Sapritch Melkon by his first wife, Mariam:
Arousiag, 1866–1925, m. Kevork Stepan – step-aunt
Hagop Haroutiun, 1873–1919, carpenter – step-uncle
Yughaper, 1878–98, m. Hagop Kevorkian – step-aunt

Varbed Christine, 1893–1986 – daughter of Arousiag and Kevork Stephan

Children of Sapritch Melkon and his second wife, also called Mariam:
Macrouhie (Margaret), 1889–1985, m. Harold Rose – my mother
Takouhie (Malakeh), 1891–1986, midwife – aunt
Isquhie, 1893–1989, dressmaker – aunt
Hovhannes, 1895–1898, died an infant

Harold Victor Rose, 1897–1950, m. Margaret Melkon – my father
Sahag Gazmararian, 1903–74, m. Malakeh Melkon – uncle by marriage
Ibrahim Audi, 1890–1960, m. Isquhie Melkon – uncle by marriage

GLOSSARY

(A) = Arabic (T) = Turkish (Arm) = Armenian
(Words used colloquially in Jerusalem)

ab, abu (A): father
adhan (A): Muslim call to prayer
agoomp (Arm): parish club
ajeer (A): apprentice
Antastan (Arm): ceremony of Blessing the Four Corners of the Earth
Arousiag (Arm): morning star (girl's name)

badal (A): exchange
bademe (T): sweetmeat with almonds
badgerhan (Arm): restorer of ikons
bakara (A): pulley
baklaweh (A): sweetmeat
bakraj (A): long-handled coffee pot
balooh (A): city drains
basara (A): fortune-teller
bastoneh (A): walking stick
basturma (T): spiced preserved meat
batieh (A): wooden bowl for kneading dough
bayyara (A): plantation, grove
berber (T): barber
bolsetsi (Arm): person from Istanbul
bournous (A): robe made of towelling
buqjeh (A): cloth bundle, fastened with pins
bustanji (T): gardener

xii GLOSSARY

chabuk (T): quick, nimble

dalha (A): stuffed breast of lamb
dam khafeef (A): lightness of spirit
dar (A): house, household
darbas (Arm): donation
deir (A): monastery, convent
Deir el Zeitouneh (A): Convent of the Olive Tree, local name for
  Hrishtagabed
Der (Arm): Lord
Der voghormia (Arm): Lord have mercy
derder (Arm): parish priest (married)
desoutch (Arm): director, priest in charge
dhikr (A): reminders, recitation from Quran
digeen (Arm): Mrs, Madame
Dirouhie (Arm): ladylike, courteous (girl's name)
dülger (T): carpenter
duq (A): powdered charcoal
durbookeh (A): decorated pottery drum

eed khafeefeh (A): a light hand
efendi, pl. *efendim* (T): man of letters, gentleman
eid (A): religious feast

fanous (A): lantern
fantaziyeh (T): celebration
fass (A): two-pronged pick
firman (T): decree, imperial edict
fteeleh (A): wick, paraffin stove

Gaghant Baban (Arm): personifying New Year
gallabiya (A): loose shirt-like garment worn by men (in Egypt)
Garabed (Arm): The Forerunner (boy's name)
garj (Arm): short
gazmarar (Arm): bookbinder
ghreibeh (A): sweetmeat, shortbread

hab han (A): cardamom seed pod
Hair Mer (Arm): Our Father, the Lord's Prayer
hakim (A): doctor

GLOSSARY

halaq (A): barber
halaweh (A): sweetmeat with sesame
hamleh (A): full (referring to chickpea pods)
hammam (A): bath, Turkish bath
hanoun (A): compassionate
hanqisd (Arm): rest in peace
hantur, pl. *hanatir* (A): horse-drawn carriage
Haram el Sharif (A): the noble sanctuary – Dome of the Rock
Haroutiun (Arm): Resurrection (boy's name)
hastahane (T): hospital (Ottoman *khasta khane*)
hatta & 'agal (A): Arab head dress
Heghnoug (Arm): Helena
hikmeh (A): clinic
hokidoon (Arm): hospices for Armenian pilgrims on the way to Jerusalem
Hovhannes (Ohannes) (Arm): John
Hovhannu Garabedi (Arm): John the Forerunner
Hrishtagabed (Arm): Holy Archangels

imbayed (A): whitener of pots
imsakhan (A): chicken baked with bread, onions, sumach
imsandara (*musandira*) (T): wide high shelf for storage
iritzkeeneh (Arm): wife of the pastor
Isqun nakhadanank (Arm): evensong

jabal (A): mountain
jdad el zeitoun (A): official date for start of olive harvest
Jamerkoutiun (Arm): Sunrise Office of Armenian liturgy
jamgortch (Arm): messenger to waken the *kaghakatsi* for services in the cathedral, a beadle
jarra (A): pottery jar

kabbad (A): fruit of *Citrus medica*, the peel candied and preserved
kabees (A): packed – when Eastern and Western Easter celebrations coincide
ka'ek (A): bread ring with sesame seeds
kaghakatsi (Arm): of the town (Jerusalem), native Armenian
el kahwati (A): owner of a cafe
kaimakam (T): Ottoman local governor
kanoon (A): charcoal brazier used indoors

xiv GLOSSARY

katayif (A): sweet pancakes stuffed with nuts or goats' cheese

kawas (A), *kavass* (T): ceremonial guard of an embassy, consulate or patriarchate

keshkeg (T): broth of pounded meat and burghul

khachkar (Arm): intricately carved stone cross

khatafeh (A): grappling iron

khashlama (T): lamb stew with burghul (cracked wheat)

khawaja (T): gentleman

khubez taboon (A): village bread baked in clay oven

khuffa (A): lightness of spirit

khushkhash (A): *Citrus vulgaris*, Seville orange

kilim (T): woven rug without pile

Kilkhateer (Arm): shrine of St James the Apostle, son of Zebedee, in the Armenian Cathedral of St James (Surp Hagop). Beheaded AD 44. (Lit. 'the decapitated one').

knafeh (A): sweetmeat with goats' cheese and syrup

knisset el mutran (A): St George's Collegiate Church (lit. the bishop's church)

ksoor (A): stone watchtowers in vineyards

kursi (A): chair, also seat at a council

kushan (T): title deeds registering property

kütchük (T): small

laban (A): yoghurt

labaneh (A): curd cheese made by straining laban.

lagan (Arm): large copper basin

libin (A): sun-dried bricks with straw, used for building in Jericho

liwan (T): large reception room

lüleji (T): potter specializing in earthenware pipes and tiles

ma'amoul (A): small cakes made at Easter

mabruk (A): congratulations

mah'oon (A): large cauldron

majnouneh (f) (A): mad

mandeel, pl. *manadeel* (A): women's printed kerchief

mangabardez (Arm): kindergarten

mannan (A): bountiful

maris (A): vegetable plot, allotment

maryazeh (Arm): reception room

massra'a (A): *oil press*

GLOSSARY

matbaqiyeh (A): tiered luncheon-box
maward (A): rosewater
Merilotz (Arm): service of remembrance
Migerditch (Arm): Baptist (boy's name)
Migerdoutiun (Arm): baptismal service
mnajed (A): cotton beater
mouneh (A): stores of food, supplies for a family
mu'allem (A): teacher
mughara (T): cave, storeroom
mughrabiyyeh (A): Moroccan headgear
muhafiz (T): protector of Holy Places
mujaddara (A): dish of rice and lentils
mukhtar (A): appointed leader of a community
Muron (Arm): Holy Chrism
musluk (T): small domestic watertank with tap or spigot

najjar (A): carpenter
nakuz (A): clapper used instead of a bell
namoura (A): sweetmeat with flaky pastry and cheese
na'ib el ashraf (A): head of the noble families
Nijmeh (A): star (girl's name)
nizam (T): order, regularity
nur (A): light

oratsuits (Arm): church almanac
oude (A): lute
oukhtavor (Arm): pilgrim fulfilling a vow
oya (T): crochet edging of tiny flowers on a mandeel, worked in
   minute detail

parisiradz (Arm): benevolence (short for Jerusalem Armenian Benev-
   olent Union)
Pembe (T): rosy-coloured (girl's name)
Pergeech (Arm): salvation, name of Armenian cemetery on Mt Zion

qanawati (A): water channel keeper
qassis (A): clergyman, Protestant minister
qidreh, pl. *qidar* (A): earthenware cooking pot
qirbeh, pl. *qirab* (A): bottle made from whole goatskin

xvi GLOSSARY

qumbaz, pl. *qanabeez* (A): gown worn by men, made of striped cotton from Damascus

rahmeh (A): mercy
rais (A): head, person in charge
rais el baladiyeh (A): mayor
ramad (A): sore eyes, conjunctivitis
rihan (A): basil, *Ocymum indicum*
rotl (A): weight of three kilograms
ruz imfalfal (A): rice cooked and prepared

sabah el khair (A): good morning
sabat (T): round straw tray
sabil (A): drinking fountain
saghlikolsun! (T): expression of thanks
sajeh (A): iron toadstool placed over fire to bake shrak
samneh (A): ghee, clarified butter
sanata (A): wooden stethoscope
sanduq el ajam (A): portable peepshow box
sangari (A): tinsmith
sanjak (T): subdivision of a vilayet (Ottoman province)
sapritch (Arm): barber
sertabib (T): chief doctor
shamiyyeh (A): from Damascus (El Sham)
sharbeh (A): jug holding drinking water
shbeen, *shbeeneh* (f) (A): sponsor, witness, godparent
shrak (A): pancake-thin bread
shurshbay (A): glass-paned outer door
sidriyyeh (A): bodice
Sirpouhie (Arm): saintliness (girl's name)
sitt (A): lady, Mrs
Sittna Mariam (A): Our Lady, the Virgin Mary
skeefeh (A): outhouse
stambouline (T): gentleman's short overcoat
suq (A): market
surp (Arm): saint
Surp Hagop (Arm): Saint James

tabakha (A): clay brazier for cooking
taboon (A): clay oven, floor lined with pebbles

GLOSSARY

tabouleh (A): finely-chopped salad with burghul
taifeh (A): community, congregation
tamarji (T): orderly, male nurse
ta'mireh (A): cultivated plot of land
tanjara, pl. *tanajer* (A): copper cooking pot
Tarkmanchats, Saint (Arm): Holy Translators
tashji (T): stonemason
taub, pl. *twab* (A): Palestinian women's embroidered dress
tawla (A): backgammon
tayara (A): kite
Terempatz (Arm): Ceremony of Unveiling Icons
terzibash (T): master tailor
tsaynavor (Arm): choirmaster

uffeh (A): straw pannier
umm (A): mother
umm umm (A): decorated flask for sprinkling rosewater
ustaz (A): teacher

vank (Arm): convent
varbed (Arm): teacher
varjabed (Arm): teacher, professor
Vartivar (Arm): transfiguration (boy's name)
vernadoon (Arm): gallery

wakeel (A): agent
wali (T): governor of a vilayet (Ottoman province)
waqf pl. *awqaf* (A): Muslim religious endowment
watan (A): homeland, country

ya satir! (A): O Protector!
yerga (Arm): tall
yishadag (Arm): souvenirs
Yughaper (Arm): bearer of the holy oil (girl's name)
yusef efendi (A): a tangerine (named after Mayor of Jerusalem)

za'atar (A): powdered thyme (*Origanum maru*), eaten with olive oil and
   bread for breakfast
zoowar, (A): visitors

To Macrouhie, Takouhie, Isquhie

1 ORIGINS

As a young man I was once described by a friend as 'European with an oriental flourish'. A subtle observation, as indeed my father was an Englishman, my mother an Armenian, and I was born and brought up in Palestine in the cosmopolitan city of Jerusalem. The 'flourish' referred to an emotional reaction to life, to quick sympathy, openness and, above all, to the use of emphatic gestures of the hands in conversation, all characteristic of Palestine Arabs.

From a very early age, while scarcely aware of it, I grew up deeply rooted in two different cultures. At the time of my childhood the drawbacks were many, the suffering seemed great, and I often wished that I was not the child of a mixed marriage. The combination of English and Armenian seemed to intrigue those who did not know me, prompting devious enquiries as to my nationality and origins. At first I found the cross-examination a tiresome intrusion into my privacy, and could not understand why anyone should be interested in my background. To avoid disclosing the fact that I was half foreign, of which at the time I felt somewhat ashamed, I would try to confuse enquirers and keep them guessing. However, as I grew older I came to realize that a combination of cultures was enriching and that my destiny to live in Jerusalem was a great privilege. In time I developed a deep bond with the city, the country and its people – a love which never diminished but on the contrary increased over the years.

My father met my mother in Palestine, in the port city of Jaffa in the aftermath of the First World War. There she had been appointed by the British military administration to be matron of the former Turkish government hospital. After service in Belgium my father had been sent to Egypt and thence to Palestine, arriving in 1917 with the

ARMENIANS OF JERUSALEM

British forces under General Allenby. In 1921 he joined the civil administration of the British Mandate and lived in Palestine for thirty years. He came from Birmingham and was, to say the least, very English in character and remained so even though he had married an Armenian. My father had many talents, was a shy man, spoke very little Arabic, no Armenian, and did not appreciate foreign food. However, he left us children free to develop our own understanding of both eastern and western cultures and to enjoy the best of both worlds. We were surrounded by loving Armenian relatives, Arab friends and neighbours of various nationalities, with all of whom we exchanged frequent visits. They lavished affection on us and contributed to a happy and varied childhood by their continual gentle and loving presence.

From a young age our ears were receptive to many languages. Unfortunately we learned no Armenian from my mother, as she herself had lost the language through being sent as a small child to a German boarding school. My two sisters spoke some Arabic but I grew up bilingual in Arabic and English, which enabled me to feel completely at home with the local people. Life seemed wonderful and I was fascinated and stimulated by Jerusalem, which I loved so much that I had no desire ever to be anywhere else.

At the age of five I was sent to a school in Jerusalem which was exclusively for British and European pupils. There I got the impression that somehow I did not fit in. As time passed I became aware of petty discrimination against my elder sister Margaret and myself. It seemed to us that we were not only treated differently at school, but that we were even excluded from some British children's functions. We were young, at a sensitive age with feelings easily hurt, and we presumed that this was the penalty for being half foreign. There was no getting away from it, the Armenian side of our heritage could be inferred from our appearance; the English side from the pattern of our speech. These days to have parents of different nationalities does not seem to matter at all; in fact people are proud of foreign ancestry.

My mother was an Armenian but an Armenian with a difference. Her ancestors had lived for centuries in Jerusalem, Palestine, and were integrated with and accepted by the local population. Over the years this Armenian community became known as the *kaghakatsi* (of the town) of Jerusalem.

Armenian refugees who came to Jerusalem to escape the Turkish

ORIGINS

massacres in the nineteenth and early twentieth centuries were considered *zoowar* (visitors) by the native Armenian community. These refugees from Turkish Armenia, including many orphans, fled in their thousands to neighbouring Lebanon, Syria, Palestine and East Jordan, where they were welcomed and helped by the Arab population. They arrived starved, sick and homeless. In Jerusalem the *vank*, the Armenian Convent of St James, threw open its spacious pilgrims' hostel and monks' quarters to provide them with free accommodation. The Near East Relief Organization assisted by opening an orphanage for girls in the Greek Convent of the Holy Cross. Boys were placed in the seminary building within the Armenian convent compound. Teachers took charge of the children and *mangabardez* (kindergarten) were organized for the very young. The refugees had to be clothed, barbers were called in to cut their hair, and cooks worked at huge cauldrons to provide meals.

To complicate matters the refugees spoke no Arabic, only Armenian and Turkish. They brought with them different traditions and customs, distinguishing them from those Armenians who had lived in Jerusalem for centuries. As dispossessed newcomers they resented the *kaghakatsi*, finding them more Arab than Armenian and accusing them of having been passive during the massacres – ignoring the fact that at the time Palestine was also under Turkish rule and all the inhabitants were Ottoman subjects. However, many *kaghakatsi* showed the newcomers great kindness and in some cases adopted young orphans into their own families. Over the years some of these refugees established homes elsewhere, some emigrated to other countries, but many remain in the convent to this day.

The Armenian presence in Jerusalem can be traced back to the early Christian era. The Cathedral of St James (Surp Hagop) and the adjoining convent buildings were acquired from the Georgians in the twelfth century. The main shrine in the cathedral is the Kilkhateer; it is believed that the head of St James the Apostle, son of Zebedee, brother of St John, martyred by beheading in AD 44, is buried there under a marble slab. The site, within one of the most beautiful chapels in the cathedral, is much visited and revered by Armenian pilgrims and the local community. Under the main altar of the cathedral is the tomb of St James the Less, brother of Our Lord and the first bishop of Jerusalem.

The Armenians own buildings and land comprising one-tenth of the Old City of Jerusalem, located in the south-west corner of the

4 ARMENIANS OF JERUSALEM

city. The convent buildings, which have developed over many centuries on different levels and during different periods, are difficult to date precisely. The word 'convent' is somewhat misleading to westerners, as the buildings were used exclusively by the patriarch and the Brotherhood of St James, which includes bishops, priests and deacons. Apart from pilgrims and visitors, no lay person was allowed to live permanently within the convent compound. However, this rule had to be changed when those seeking refuge after the Turkish massacres, followed later by those displaced within Palestine by the Arab–Israeli war of 1948, were in urgent need of housing. From then on a lay community was also allowed to live within the precincts of the convent.

It was the aim of successive Armenian patriarchs to buy land and houses that adjoined the convent buildings. After much sacrifice and over a long period this was achieved, and the convent and cathedral were protected by an almost unbroken ring of properties; there were a few gaps, however, where some owners could not be persuaded to sell. Most of these buildings were simple houses dating from the Middle Ages. Many of them were and are still of great character, with charming architectural features. Thick walls were surmounted by arched and domed ceilings enhanced by a central cupola and carved designs embellished lintels, windows and niches. But as with most old stone buildings they were often dark inside, with poor ventilation and incurably damp. To the north these houses extend to the Syrian Convent of St Mark and to the Jaffa Gate area. To the east they back on to the Jewish Quarter of the Old City. The southern and western boundaries are enclosed by part of the Old City walls rebuilt by Suleiman the Magnificent in 1537. Between these walls and the convent a narrow road, once cobbled, runs south from the Jaffa Gate, turns east to Bab el Nebi Daoud (David's Gate) and then on to the Dung Gate, the Wailing Wall and the Haram el Sharif.

It is not known exactly when my Armenian ancestors came to the Holy Land. Armenian pilgrims began visiting Jerusalem soon after they embraced Christianity as a nation in the early fourth century. Many of them returned to their homeland, while some stayed on in support of their churches and monasteries. Information handed down in the family by word of mouth states that my mother's maternal ancestors came from Sis in the Kingdom of Cilicia, Lesser Armenia, whereas her father's ancestors came from Kharpert in Anatolia as religious pilgrims, perhaps as early as the twelfth century. Along with

ORIGINS

many other Armenian pilgrims, tradesmen and their families, they were encouraged to stay in Jerusalem and become part of a permanent secular community supporting the Armenian cathedral. Whereas the Latin and Greek Orthodox churches accepted converts from the indigenous community, the Armenian church did not. Their congregation consisted entirely of Armenians.

Pilgrims who decided to stay on were given the houses already owned by the patriarchate, and gradually what became known as the Armenian Quarter evolved. By the late nineteenth century the community numbered about a thousand. Each family was given the use of a few rooms with a kitchen. These rooms usually opened on to a shared courtyard underneath which lay a water cistern for communal use. Herbs and a variety of plants with heavily scented flowers grew in pots and tins filled with soil brought in from the country. They were placed around the courtyards, on window ledges, up staircases and on roofs, a demonstration of the Armenian love for order and beauty. No rent was paid for these houses and they were handed down from generation to generation, or changed hands by agreement and the payment of modest key-money.

Among other facilities provided was the use of a *hikmeh* or clinic, where medical advice was given and prescriptions issued free. Widows and orphans were given bread and were helped with money at festive seasons. A *mukhtar* (head adviser) was appointed from among the community. His chief duty was to represent them in dealings with government officials and also with the patriarchate. With his official seal he authenticated documents and certificates. Every year the patriarchate issues an *oratsuits*, an almanac listing the names of priests and bishops, saints' days and feasts, public holidays and predictions of the weather. This booklet is much used by the community and forms a bond between them and the convent.

For many generations large families were brought up successfully in cramped conditions; they might not have had a high standard of living but they did have a quality of life. The ancient eastern custom of the extended family was observed, with consideration for the aged who had the rare and now-envied privilege of ending life at home amongst relatives and loved ones. The *kaghakatsi* were known for keeping their houses immaculately clean, fastidious attention was given to hygiene, and they had an inherited tradition of preparing good food; characteristics which contributed to their survival. The quarter became known as *Haret el Arman*, Street of the Armenians,

6 ARMENIANS OF JERUSALEM

and the people as the *taifeh* or community. They were ordinary people with various trades who worked in all parts of the city. Living outside the convent meant that they were not bound by the rules and regulations of the religious community within, such as the closure of the gates at set times. Their religious identity was not lost and they remained ardent supporters of the convent as the heart of their community.

The *kaghakatsi* adopted Jerusalem as their new home, were accepted by the Palestinian inhabitants, and over the centuries conformed to local customs in daily life. Armenian cookery, however, retained its individual character and traditional recipes for special fast and feast day dishes are still in use. In addition to rice, burghul (boiled cracked wheat) was much used as an accompaniment to stews. The burghul is prepared in the quarter by an Armenian family, the Kalaydjians, known as Dar el Burghulji.

Under Turkish rule the *kaghakatsi* Armenians were Ottoman subjects and naturally followed the fashion of the day in outward dress. By the end of the nineteenth century this comprised for the men a European suit with a tarboosh as headgear. A 'stambouline' – a short frock coat – was also frequently worn. Women's styles were not far from those of Victorian England, Paris or Vienna. Influenced by Russia, many children were dressed in sailor suits like the young Tsarevich.

With the passage of time the native Armenians had also adopted for daily use the Arabic language, which they spoke fluently but with a slight dialect. By contrast the classical Armenian language of the liturgy and ecclesiastical learning was maintained in the patriarchate. The one thing that the Armenians of Jerusalem did not change was the Christian faith to which their nation had been converted by Gregory the Illuminator early in the fourth century. They remained totally committed to the Armenian Apostolic Orthodox Church.

For their parish church the *kaghakatsi* were given the use of the Chapel of the Holy Archangels (Hrishtagabed), which lay a short distance away from the centre of the convent. This church was reputed to be on the site of the house of Annas the High Priest, and was known in Arabic as Deir el Zeitouneh – convent of the olive tree. In the courtyard visitors are shown shoots of an old olive tree to which Our Lord was supposedly tied on the night when he was brought before Annas. The little church, built in the twelfth century, perhaps on earlier ruins, is entered through a spacious narthex. At one end is found the baptismal font dating from 1849. By tradition consecrated water is not to be thrown down a household drain: here at Deir el Zeitouneh a clay pipe carries the water from the font to the olive tree in the courtyard outside. A *rais* (in Armenian *desoutch*), a parish priest or sometimes a bishop, is appointed by the patriarch to be in charge of the church. With assistants he conducts services and it is there that christenings, marriages and funerals have taken place over the centuries exclusively for the native Armenian community. For me, the building resounds with the presence of my forebears, who through the generations worshipped there and faithfully served the church, were christened and married there, as well as being buried from there.

A low doorway leading into a short passageway is the only entrance to Deir el Zeitouneh. Above lies a large domed room which serves as a reception hall or *maryazeh*. Here are kept the registers recording births, marriages and deaths of the *kaghakatsi* community. The parish priest has his apartment and office within the courtyard. Around the church, rooms open on to enchanting small private medieval courtyards in which lemon trees, grape vines, roses and other scented shrubs remain, wizened with age. Here a community of nuns used to live, whose many duties included cleaning, the care of church linen, providing and arranging flowers for the altars in the cathedral and various chapels. Most of the rooms are now empty and at the time of writing there is only one aged nun in residence.

In 1988 extensive repairs were begun in the narthex of the church. Layers of old plaster were removed, exposing some fine *khachkars* (medieval Armenian crosses elaborately carved in relief). Scores of small and simple crosses also carved in the stonework mark the visits of pilgrims through the centuries. Close to the font other *khachkars* carved in marble and a hitherto unknown ancient tomb, believed to be that of an Armenian prince, were discovered in the wall. An arched doorway, over which is a faded fresco dated 1626, leads from the narthex into the nave of the church. It is flanked by two spacious grilled windows which enable the congregation to participate in services when there is no more room inside.

A small shrine on the north side commemorates the place where Jesus was imprisoned by Annas. This is decorated with glazed tiles, as is a small chapel on the south side of the main altar dedicated to St Hripsimae, an abbess martyred with 40 other nuns early in the fourth century. The wooden doors of both shrines date from the sixteenth century and are exquisitely carved and inlaid with mother-of-pearl.

8 ARMENIANS OF JERUSALEM

When the church was renovated in 1810 many ancient features were concealed by plaster and tiles. In 1989 restoration revealed a thirteenth-century baptismal font in the wall on the north side of the nave. On each side of the main altar two small stone altars have been uncovered. The pilgrim crosses engraved on the pillars had been concealed by green glazed tiles and are now exposed to view. Some pilgrims had also carved their names to commemorate their visit. The scholar and illuminator of manuscripts, Der Manuel, while living in Deir el Zeitouneh inscribed his name in 1363. Also embedded in small sealed cavities in the stone pillars are prayers and supplications placed there by nameless pilgrims.

The Orthodox churches of the east follow the Julian calendar. However Armenian Christmas in the Holy Land is celebrated on 19 January in order to avoid congestion in the Church of the Nativity on 5 January, the eve of Christmas for the other Orthodox churches. On the night of 18 January the Armenians celebrate the birth of Our Lord (manifestation of the flesh) as well as His baptism (manifestation of divinity). The patriarch with his bishops and clergy celebrates mass at midnight in the Church of the Nativity in Bethlehem, the service attended by many pilgrims. He announces the birth of the Christ child with the words *park y partsouns* (*gloria in excelsis*). The liturgy ends in the early hours of the morning and the congregation is invited to partake of *khashlama*, lamb stew to which burghul is added. This is prepared in large cauldrons in the Armenian convent adjoining the Church of the Nativity.

The *kaghakatsi* by tradition remain in Jerusalem to hold their Christmas liturgy at midnight in St James's Cathedral. The mass is followed by the ceremony of Migerdoutiun, the Baptism of the Cross. While the choir chants hymns, a cross symbolizing the Infant Jesus is laid on an embroidered towel and handed to a robed boy whose parents have taken vows on his behalf. He leads the procession to the font where he holds the cross up to the priest who receives it and plunges it into the water. Out of a small silver vessel in the shape of a dove the priest pours holy oil (*Muron*) over the cross into the font. The service ends at 2 a.m. and the congregation, who have brought their own cups, fill them at the font and drink the holy water before returning home.

Christmas is treated as a solemn religious festival and comes at the end of a week of fasting. New Year's Eve, which falls on 13 January for all the Orthodox communities, is the time for merrymaking,

ORIGINS

feasting and visiting family and friends. An exciting event for children has always been a visit from *Gaghant Baban*, a herald of the new year dressed in Father Christmas costume – going from house to house with a few aides, offering greetings and receiving hospitality. The children of the community to this day are also treated to a party by the Armenian Benevolent Union, the *parisiradz*, at their parish club (the *agoomp*) where each is given a present as well as a *yusef efendi* (tangerine). The Jerusalem Armenian Benevolent Union, a charitable organization, was formed in 1925 by *kaghakatsi* families for the purpose of giving aid to refugees and to the needy.

Easter is celebrated with the other eastern Orthodox Churches, again according to the Julian calendar, the date usually falling one week later than the western Easter, sometimes coinciding with it, sometimes falling up to five weeks later. When the celebrations of Easter coincide the term *kabees* (packed) is used to describe the event. Crowds of pilgrims converge on Jerusalem to spend Holy Week, beginning with Palm Sunday. From the Americas, Europe, India, the Far East and above all from neighbouring Arab countries come Copts, Ethiopians, Assyrians and Armenians, Catholics, Anglicans and other Protestants. Hundreds of Greek pilgrims accompanied by their parish priests regularly come from Greece, Cyprus and the islands. Hotels and hospices are filled to capacity with an overflow into private homes in the Old City.

It was customary in the Orthodox Church to fast during Lent by abstaining from meat and all foods derived from animals. Instead dishes of vegetables and pulses were prepared with olive oil. The Armenians break their fast on the Saturday before Easter, after the Holy Sepulchre bells ring out announcing the emergence of the Holy Fire from the Tomb of Christ. For their first meal after the fast, Armenian families traditionally eat fish fried in olive oil. Possibly this custom goes back to St Luke 24:40–43, where Jesus appears after the resurrection to the disciples in Jerusalem, asks for food and is given cooked fish which He takes and eats in their presence. Other dishes prepared after the fast are parsley omelettes and *ruz imfalfal* (cooked rice). On Easter Day it is usual to have a *dalha* (stuffed breast of lamb) for lunch.

The eastern Easter culminates with the ceremony of the Holy Fire in the Church of the Holy Sepulchre on Holy Saturday. All the Orthodox communities participate in this great ceremony and the church is packed. Invited foreign visitors, consuls and government

10 ARMENIANS OF JERUSALEM

officials are seated opposite the Edicule. Representatives of four *kaghakatsi* families, the Hovsepians, Toumayians, Kankashians and Marashlians, patiently wait close to the Edicule and by ancient right act as torchbearers as soon as the flame emerges from the Tomb of Christ. They rush with their lighted tapers to the *vernadoon* (Armenian chapel in the Rotunda gallery) where the patriarch waits to receive them. The bells ring out and from the gallery he blesses the crowds below, making the sign of the cross over them with his lighted candle. By now the Rotunda and Catholikon are filled with light from flaming candles held by each pilgrim. The other Orthodox communities likewise have representatives waiting outside the Edicule who are the first to receive the flame.

To stand in the Parvis outside the church after the service is over and to witness throngs of joyous pilgrims emerge through the doors clutching their lighted candles is a moving experience. Greeks and Cypriots in their hundreds, usually old, the women dressed in black with *manadeel* covering their heads, dominate the scene. They listen with emotion to the loud pealing of the bells, bowing and crossing themselves as they look up to the belfry. Priests hurry out, protecting their flames in lanterns which in due course they will carry lighted to their churches all over the country in time for the Easter liturgy. The crowd waits patiently to watch the patriarchs and other dignitaries lead their clergy back in procession to their various convents and monasteries. When word is received that the Greek patriarch and his entourage have reached their convent, the bells fall silent and the pilgrims return to their lodgings to prepare for the next event – the midnight service.

The Church of the Holy Sepulchre is crowded for the Greek Orthodox Easter liturgy celebrated at midnight. Throngs of pilgrims attend and watch the processions round the Edicule led by the patriarch, bishops, priests and clergy all robed in richly embroidered vestments. The joy with which people receive the words *Christos aneste* (Christ is Risen) is wonderful to behold. All present embrace and greet each other with these moving words as the bells ring out. The Armenians on the other hand do not hold a midnight service. On the Saturday afternoon, after the ceremony of the Holy Fire, communion is celebrated at the Church of the Holy Archangels. Their main Easter liturgy is sung at the Sepulchre in the early hours of Sunday morning during which *Christos hariav in merelotz* (Christ is risen from the dead) is repeatedly chanted.

ORIGINS

At Christmas and Easter the priest in charge of the *kaghakatsi* community goes round the Armenian quarter and visits each household. On the Christmas visit the family put a loaf of bread, a glass of water and some salt out on a table: dipping his cross in the water the priest blesses the bread, the house and its occupants, announces the birth and baptism of Our Lord and wishes them a happy year ahead. The water, which becomes holy, is poured on to either a tree or a plant. At Easter a plate of coloured eggs symbolizing the resurrection is put out for the blessing. As there were no artificial dyes hard-boiled eggs were coloured in home-made solutions – onion skins for brown, petals of *Chrysanthemum coronarium* for yellow, and an old piece of tarboosh (fez) for bright red. Sometimes parsley leaves were wrapped round the eggs before dyeing, producing a delicate fern-like pattern. With the introduction of instant artificial dyes these old methods were given up. On each visit the priest and his assistant would be given a small sum of money.

Education for boys was traditionally provided by priests in the convent. A seminary for young men was established in 1843, and in 1863 the Gayantiants Girls' School was founded, named after St Gayane, the abbess martyred with St Hripsimae by order of King Trdates in the fourth century. This later developed into the St Tarkmanchats (Holy Translators) School for both boys and girls to secondary level. Here the children of the community receive a good general education with grounding in Armenian language and literature.

By nature the Armenians were industrious and skilled in crafts and trade. Many became jewellers, gold- and silver-smiths, tailors, shoe-makers, carpenters, and latterly photographers by profession. They were trusted by the Ottoman regime and given positions in departments such as customs and the post office, had seats on government councils and in the municipality. A representative of the community was granted a *kursi* or seat at patriarchal meetings. With the ending of Ottoman rule this privilege was dropped by the patriarch. During the massacres of Armenians in 1915, which took place in other parts of the Turkish empire, *kaghakatsi* working in government departments in Jerusalem were merely relieved of their posts; otherwise family and social life continued without interference, except that during the First World War young Armenian men were taken into the army.

It was customary for Armenian family names to end with 'ian' (household of). During the 400 years of Turkish rule in Palestine, the

12   ARMENIANS OF JERUSALEM

Arabic word *dar*, with the same meaning, was adopted by the *kaghakatsi*. Within the community many families were ordinarily known by the Arabic name of their trade: among others are 'Dar el Sa'ati' (the watchmakers' household), 'Dar el Bostaji' (the postman's family), 'Dar el Baitar' (the veterinary surgeons'), 'Dar el Banna' (the builders'), 'Dar el Mukhtar' (the head adviser's household). After the British took over Palestine in 1917 surnames were officially established, usually by adding 'ian' to the Christian name of the head of a family, which was used as the surname from then on by his descendants. For example, Zakar became Zakarian, Krikor Krikorian, Hovhannes Hovhannesian, and Kevork Kevorkian. Others simply added 'ian' to the Armenian name of their trade or profession as in Nalbandian, Krasharian, Gazmararian – households of the veterinary surgeon, typesetter and bookbinder.

From time immemorial Palestine has been subjected to wars and change of rule. Being powerless, the Armenians were compelled to seek protection from the rulers of the day. It is said that as early as the seventh century the Armenian Patriarch Apraham travelled with a large delegation to Mecca, where he sought assurances from the Prophet Muhammad that the Armenians in Jerusalem would be granted protection. The result was an edict protecting the rights and privileges of the Armenians in the Holy Places. Omar ibn el Khattab, who in 637 AD as caliph occupied Jerusalem, was one of the witnesses to this edict and later issued another one of his own. Succeeding caliphs protected the Armenians until the coming of the crusaders and the creation of the Latin Kingdom of Jerusalem in 1099. During this period the crusaders were joined by many Armenian princes and soldiers from the kingdom of Cilicia and the community and convent flourished. Gifts of money and works of art brought by the *oukhtavor* (pilgrims fulfilling a vow) poured into the patriarchate. This priceless collection of treasures includes richly embroidered vestments, gold chalices, crowns and crosses encrusted with precious stones, and a sceptre that belonged to King Hethum I of Cilicia (1215–70), made from a single piece of amber decorated in gold. Many of these exquisite treasures are in use during major feast-day services.

The library in the chapel of St Thoros houses a collection of over 3,000 illuminated manuscripts, many dating from the tenth century. Most of these manuscripts were brought to Jerusalem by pilgrims and donated to Surp Hagop.

When Salah el Din took Jerusalem from the Latins in 1187, the

ORIGINS

Armenians still found themselves in favour. Their rights were reconfirmed in a new and important edict. After Salah el Din's death and with the rise of the Mamluks in 1291, Palestine became a dependency of Egypt for about 200 years. Towards the end of this period the conditions of the Armenians deteriorated and there was general harassment of Christian institutions.

During the 400 years of Turkish rule that began with Sultan Selim 1 in 1517, the Armenians once again enjoyed rights and privileges accorded to them by a new edict. This was followed by similar edicts issued and signed by successive Ottoman sultans. Many of these documents are works of art, with exquisite calligraphy on parchment mounted on silk, and are in the magnificent collection of treasures in the Armenian Patriarchate.

2 THE KRIKORIANS

Anna, my mother's grandmother, was born in Jerusalem in 1832. She was the daughter of Minas el Hindi (Minas the Indian – a nickname, his forebears having been at some time part of the Armenian community trading in Calcutta). By profession he was *lüleji*, a potter specializing in the making of red clay pipes, tobacco-holders for nargiles, waterspouts, chimney pots and also the small pottery cylinders to be used embedded in parapets enclosing roof terraces providing ventilation with privacy. The geometrical arrangement of these cylinders is still a charming feature of the rooftops of the Old City.

Anna's only brother, also called Minas, owned a small coffee shop not far from the Jaffa Gate in a lane close to Christ Church (seat of the first Anglican bishop in Jerusalem). Minas raised a family of three sons and six daughters. The daughters all married; two of his sons died young, while the third left to join the French Foreign Legion and was never heard of again. To his clients and others he was known as Minas el Kahwati – Minas the coffeeman. From his shop he supplied tea or Turkish coffee, as well as nargiles, to surrounding stores and businesses. An *ajeer* (young apprentice) would take round tea or coffee and glasses of water on a polished brass tray suspended from three long bars joined to a decorated handle. To the unaccustomed this seems a precarious way of carrying cups full of liquid, but in skilled hands it is very stable. The apprentice soon learned to weave his way nimbly, swaying his tray, through the crowded *suqs*. Sweet tea is served without milk, sometimes with mint or cinnamon added.

Turkish coffee, very popular all over the Middle East, is offered at all times of day to visitors at home as well as by shopkeepers to their clients. It is made with very finely ground coffee beans to which a

THE KRIKORIANS 15

pinch of *hab han* (cardamom) and sugar is added. The coffee is boiled in a *bakraj*, a long-handled pot varying in size according to the number of cups required. In those days it was boiled over a charcoal brazier. The coffeeman had to cater for people with different tastes: some liked their coffee very sweet, others *sukkar aleel* (medium sweet), others *osmanli* with no sugar. Coffee shops are still found all over Jerusalem and the offering of coffee as a sign of hospitality and friendship continues.

Not much is known about Anna until her marriage, which is recorded in the register of marriages kept in the offices of the Church of the Holy Archangels. Entry 17 reads:

> 25 October 1849 Krikor *dülger* Soghmonian aged 21 to Anna *lüleji* Minassian aged 17. The sponsor, Apraham Soghmonian *tashji*. Officiating priest, Krikor Kharpertsi.

As a means of identification it was the custom to note the profession of the bridegroom, the bride's father and the sponsor. Armenian script was used throughout, even for Arabic and Turkish words. In this entry Turkish has been used, *dülger* for carpenter, *lüleji* for potter and *tashji* for stonemason. 'Kharpertsi' indicates that the priest who married them came from the town of Kharpert in Anatolia. Entries in other registers refer to the bridegroom as *najjar* Krikor, using the Arabic word for carpenter, or Krikor *garj*, the Armenian for 'short' in contrast to another Krikor, Krikor *yerga*, 'the tall'.

Krikor had two brothers, Yeghia and Apraham. Their mother, known to everyone as Umm Yeghia, was a midwife in the old tradition. All her knowledge was gained by experience but though she had no formal training she was much revered in the community. As a sign of respect all married women were addressed as 'Umm . . .' (mother of . . .) followed by the name of their eldest son. The same custom applied to men, using 'Abu . . .' (father of . . .) and this was adhered to throughout their lives. It was disrespectful to call older people by their first names.

Yeghia and Apraham both married and had children; Apraham, however, had one child only, a daughter who in later years was endearingly called Dudu Anna. With no prospect of having more children he arranged to adopt Hovhannes, the young son of a poor Armenian widow who lived in Halab (Aleppo). The Arab community

16 ARMENIANS OF JERUSALEM

found the word Hovhannes difficult to pronounce and they called him 'Waness el Halaby'. Years later his mother came on a visit to try and persuade him to return to Aleppo with her, but he had decided to settle in Jerusalem. Hovhannes trained as a carver working in olive wood and later opened a workshop near the New Gate where boxes, crosses, nativity sets and other artefacts were sold to pilgrims. When he married his family were known as 'Dar el Halaby' (the household from Aleppo), and Hovhannes named his eldest son Apraham after his foster father.

After their marriage Krikor and Anna lived with Krikor's parents in their house in the Armenian Quarter, not far from the Church of the Holy Archangels. This house had been allocated to the family by the Armenian patriarchate centuries before. Three vaulted rooms opened on to a courtyard, one of them below ground level and serving as a kitchen and dining-room. Under the floor lay a large rainwater cistern which with care lasted from one rainy season to the other. At first water was drawn up in buckets but later a hand pump was installed. Two outhouses in the courtyard served as washroom and lavatory, the drains of which were connected to the *balooh*, a network of Roman drains which were still in operation in the city. Over a large carved stone sink in the washroom hung a *musluk*, a small half-moon-shaped tin tank with a brass tap attached which provided running water but had to be refilled frequently.

Around the courtyard tin containers, barrels and urns filled with earth were used as plant pots. In them grew old-fashioned roses, jasmine, basil, geraniums, freesias, amaryllis species and *zambak mar yusef* (Madonna lilies). Most of the flowers were cut and sent to decorate the altars of the cathedral and the Church of the Holy Archangels. Plants of *rihan* (basil) were reserved for the church for use at Eid el Salib (Feast of the Holy Cross) which falls in mid-September and until then, to keep its purity, the growing plant had to remain untouched by human hand. At the ceremony a priest dips a bunch of *rihan* in holy water and making the sign of the cross sprinkles the congregation, reciting prayers and blessings the while.

Anna was a good cook and also had a great love for flowers and gardening, qualities which she passed on to her family. She was a small woman and in later years wore glasses to help her failing eyesight. At the end of a hard day's work she sat amongst her plants and enjoyed smoking a nargile, the purring of which never failed to

THE KRIKORIANS

fascinate her grandchildren. She spoke little Armenian, as she had had no schooling, but was fluent in Arabic as were all the *kaghakatsi*.

Between 1851 and 1876 the couple had twelve children, seven girls and five boys. The eldest child, christened Sirpouhie, was born in 1851. Then came three more girls, Pembe (rosy-coloured) in 1852, Mariam (affectionately called Mannan, 'bountiful') born in 1854, who married Hovhannes Melkon and later became my grandmother, and Heghnoug in 1856. The awaited boy, Garabed, arrived amid great rejoicing in 1859 to be followed by two more boys, Soghmon in 1860 and Krikor in 1864. Then followed two more girls, Horop in 1865 and Isquhie in 1868. In 1871 another son, Hagop, was born, followed by a girl, Arousiag, in 1873. The last child, a boy, Movses, was born in 1876 when Anna was already 44 years old. The family became known as Dar el Samra (household of the dark-skinned), or Dar Kirkoor, a corruption of Krikor. Of these two names the former remains a mystery. When surnames became compulsory the family took the name Krikorian, and remain so-called to this day.

It is amazing that Anna survived the birth of her many children as medical care in childbirth was practically non-existent. Anna's mother-in-law Umm Yeghia acted as midwife. Her only equipment consisted of a pair of scissors and a piece of string with which to tie the umbilical cord. Women gave birth at home while sitting in a specially built wooden maternity chair brought in by the midwife. In the seat of the chair was a large oval hole under which was placed a basin full of warm water. After giving birth mothers were given nourishing food, usually meat or chicken broth. Babies were breast-fed, and when this was impossible a relative or friend who could do so acted as wet nurse. Records show that in a certain year in the 1850s nine out of the twelve young brides from the Armenian community died giving birth to their first child in the year following marriage.

Not all of Anna and Krikor's children survived childhood. Pembe, Garabed, Krikor and Isquhie died in infancy. Epidemics of smallpox, cholera and typhus broke out from time to time, and with little or no medical care available the death toll was high, especially among young children. In 1861 an epidemic of smallpox raged throughout Jerusalem and many children among the *kaghakatsi* succumbed, as is recorded in the register of deaths kept at the Church of the Holy Archangels. Smallpox continued to be a menace for many years. Those of Anna's children who caught the disease and survived were left with faint traces of pockmarks and poor eyesight.

18 ARMENIANS OF JERUSALEM

In 1878 at the age of 50 Najjar Krikor was taken ill and died, leaving Anna responsible for a family of seven. The eldest girl, Sirpouhie, was already married, so the burden fell on Mariam and Heghnoug, then in their early twenties. Employment for women in those days was limited to domestic service, laundry, ironing and sewing. Both Mariam and Heghnoug were very clever with their needles and worked hard to bring up the younger members of the family, whose ages ranged from thirteen to two years. Their sacrifice earned them the life-long love and gratitude of their brothers and sisters for whom they had fended during difficult times.

Mariam and Heghnoug soon acquired a reputation for turning out well-finished sewing. Anna sold a piece of her jewellery and bought a sewing machine, which proved a tremendous help. Work started to pour in. In the city there was an Armenian tailor who specialized in making robes and vestments for monks and priests of the Christian community, as well as for Muslim sheikhs and clerics. He was known as the *terzibash* (head tailor) and his family acquired the name of Dar el Terzibash. Garments from his workshop that needed basting and final touches were packed into a *buqjeh* (a bundle fastened with pins), placed on a *sabat* (round straw tray) and carried to and from the house on the head of an apprentice. Other tailors who specialized in *qanabeez* (silk gowns worn by men) also sent them work to finish. The girls often had so much to do that they sewed well into the night aided by dim lamplight.

As the month of Ramadan drew near, Heghnoug and Mariam would visit Muslim households in the neighbouring Nebi Daoud quarter on Mount Zion. There they accepted orders to sew men's, women's and children's clothes for the feast of Eid el Fitr, the day when the month of fasting ends. From these contacts lasting friendships with many of the Muslim families developed and social visits were exchanged throughout the year.

The family also took in laundry and ironing for foreign consuls and notables living in Jerusalem. They became expert in the starching of their shirts and collars which demanded care and skill. A heavy iron, the hollow of which was filled with red-hot charcoal, was used for pressing clothes. The lid had an insulated wooden handle and was kept in place by a latch surmounted by a proud cast-iron ornamental cockerel. Great care had to be taken, as a splutter of sparks from side ventilators, or an over-heated iron, could permanently damage the cloth. Once starched and ironed, all white laundry was laid out on the roof to be

THE KRIKORIANS 19

aired and bleached on straw trays in the hot sun. Anna helped the girls by preparing and refilling the irons, using charcoal from her store in an alcove in the thickness of the kitchen wall. In addition, as mother of the family, she ran the household and cooked for them all.

As soon as they were old enough, the two younger sisters worked with European families living in Jerusalem. Horop was employed mainly by Templists, a German Protestant sect who had founded their small colony a mile south of the city in 1870. She was appreciated in their households, where she looked after children, saw to their clothes, laundered, ironed and cleaned.

Together with her sister-in-law Heghineh, Horop specialized in the preparation of trousseaux for Armenian and Arab brides and in sewing silk *qanabeez* for men. As she went on with domestic work until she was over 70, relatives and friends would jokingly suggest that her bucket and brush should accompany her to the grave. Her life was one of sacrifice and she died a poor woman in 1943 at the age of 78, having given all her earnings to help the younger generation.

The youngest sister, Arousiag, was taken on as a resident maid in the household of Bishop Blyth, the Anglican bishop in Jerusalem. The other members of his domestic staff were all Arab – a cook from Beit Jala (a village near Bethlehem), a manservant and a garden boy. On learning that her name Arousiag meant 'Morning Star' they preferred to call her by the Arabic equivalent, Nijmeh. She was given a ground-floor room near the kitchen: over her bed hung a portrait of Queen Victoria in an elaborate gold-painted frame.

At mealtimes Arousiag and the manservant waited at table, and she also looked after the rooms, helped with the washing up, saw to the silver and polished the bishop's shoes. Her sisters, Heghnoug and sometimes Horop, came in on a daily basis to do mending, laundry and ironing, including the special task of starching and goffering the bishop's lawn sleeves. Another of their duties was to wash down and scrub the floors of the cloisters and cathedral before Easter.

The bishop, his wife and many daughters lived in the gothic-style square stone house within the precincts of the close. They were very hospitable and the house was always filled with guests, often missionaries working in other parts of Palestine who were regularly invited for meals or to stay for weekends.

The house was surrounded by a well-tended walled garden with flowerbeds laid out by Mrs Blyth around ancient olive trees. The family were keen gardeners and introduced most of the old-estab-

20 ARMENIANS OF JERUSALEM

lished trees and shrubs that one finds at St George's today, including the spectacular yellow *banksiae* roses which adorn the walls of the cloister and are usually at their best around Easter time. In the gardens are jacarandas, heliotrope, lemon-scented verbena, plumbago and jasmine as well as the evergreen spindle-tree, which produces an abundant crop of red berries, used for decorating the cathedral at Christmas time. Cypress and lemon trees were planted and the flowerbeds filled with annuals grown from seed brought out from England. The garden, from which flowers were cut for the cathedral, was ablaze with colour in the summer. It was an English garden, but with its olive, lemon, fig and pomegranate trees retained a Middle Eastern character. The dominating feature was a large jacaranda, a spectacular sight when covered with blue flowers in June.

A deep crusader cistern found in the grounds, fed with rainwater from the street, was reserved for use in the garden. Hassan, a young Arab boy from the village of Beit Iksa, was taken on to help with the digging and watering. He hauled up the water very early in the morning in buckets, aided by a *bakara* (an iron pulley). It was only in 1958 that an electric pump was installed. Hassan stayed at work in the bishop's garden for over 50 years until he reluctantly retired in the 1960s, having served four bishops and one archbishop.

During the summer the bishop and his family would leave for a long stay in England. The house was cleaned and closed up and the domestic staff were given a holiday. Hassan, however, contined to work in the gardens, keeping them at their best for the bishop's return.

Arousiag worked in the Blyth household until the outbreak of the First World War and the departure of the bishop in 1914. From then until 1917 the house was occupied by a Turkish general (*kütchük* Djemal pasha) and it was there, on the bishop's desk, that the surrender of Jerusalem was signed in 1917. For family reasons Arousiag did not go back to St George's when Bishop Blyth's successor, Rennie MacInnes, took up residence in 1918.

Only two of Anna's daughters were to marry; Mariam to found a small happy family, and Sirpouhie with less fortunate results. Sirpouhie at the age of 22 married Tavid Genevisian. The name Genevis is said to indicate that the family were descendants of Genoese traders, many of whom settled in Cilicia about the year AD 1100. Locally the family were known as Dar el Sawabini (household of soapmakers) since they made and sold scented soap. They also made rose and orange blossom-water, arak, pickles and *basturma* (dried preserved salt

THE KRIKORIANS

21

meat heavily flavoured with garlic). Tavid was unstable and bad-tempered; he worked Sirpouhie to death in his enterprises. They had one son, Bedros, who was still very young when Sirpouhie died as a consequence, it was thought, of her unhappy life. Her unmarried sisters, Heghnoug, Horop and Arousiag, vowed that they would never marry, seeing as a warning what marriage had done to their sister. Bedros was brought up by his grandmother, Anna, and later by Tavid's new wife, Dirouhie, who produced eight more children and was also over-worked by Tavid.

Soghmon, Anna's eldest son, joined the Armenian seminary in 1872 at the age of twelve. He was tutored by priests and proved to have the makings of a scholar. He had a good voice and later became *tsaynavor* (choirmaster) in the cathedral of St James. By then he had become a teacher of Armenian and Turkish in the seminary. Besides Arabic he also had a knowledge of French and German. His qualities fitted him ideally for the post of secretary to the Armenian Patriarch, where his knowledge was indispensable in dealing with the Turkish authorities. This position of trust, which he held until 1926, earned him the title Soghmon efendi, the Turkish style for a man of letters, a gentleman.

In those days authority for any official business had to come from Istanbul in the form of a *firman*. This centralized bureaucracy of Ottoman rule often caused much delay in the business of the patriarchate in the distant *sanjak* of Jerusalem. On the sultan's birthday telegrams of congratulations would be sent to Istanbul and a *fantaziyeh* or festival would take place in Jerusalem, the entrance to the convent decked with lights and bunting for the occasion. Another of the secretary's duties was to send a telegram to the sultanate in Istanbul describing events at the Feast of the Holy Fire on the Saturday before Easter. The authorities were always eager to learn that the event had passed peacefully, as trouble often broke out between the Christian communities at this ceremony.

In 1886, when he was 26, Soghmon married Heghineh, the daughter of Nigoghos and Soghmeh Hagopjian. Heghineh was seventeen, very beautiful and had already had many proposals of marriage. Her family had come from Istanbul to Aleppo and then to Jaffa, where they had settled generations before. Her father was a trader and one of her brothers, Hovhannes, was caretaker of the lighthouse and the site believed to be the house of Simon the tanner (Acts 9:43).

After their marriage the couple went to live with Soghmon's widowed mother, Anna, and her children in the family house in

22   ARMENIANS OF JERUSALEM

Jerusalem. As a sign of respect for her husband, Heghineh never used his first name; instead she called him *varjabed* (teacher). Their first child, Krikor, was born in March 1888 but he died of a fever two months later. The parents were devastated, and it was not until 1893 that a second son, also named Krikor, was born. He was followed by four more children, Anna in 1897, Nazouhie in 1901, Kegham in 1904 and Yerevant in 1910.

Parents sometimes vowed a boy to the church for the first years of his life if the marriage had been childless for many years, if they had already suffered the loss of a child, or if their child had recovered from a severe illness. The outward sign for Armenian boys was long hair, which after a few years was cut for the first time by a priest at a special service in the cathedral. During the ceremony the child would be taken to the entrance of the Kilkhateer where the priest cut a few locks of hair in the shape of a cross from the crown of the boy's head. The child was then taken home in procession, and a barber completed the hair-cutting to normal length in the presence of friends and relatives. This was a happy occasion and the guests were offered coffee and sweetmeats before leaving. Soghmon and Heghineh, who had lost their first child, followed this custom and took vows on behalf of each of their three sons. Other communities had similar customs; for example children would be dressed in monk's clothing for a period: Orthodox in black robes with pepperpot hat, Latins in a brown Franciscan habit.

After Soghmon was appointed secretary to the Armenian patriarch, the family were given a house on the road between the Jaffa Gate and the convent. This consisted of two large domed rooms up a flight of stairs, with kitchen and washrooms below. Two other families lived in rooms around the same large courtyard, the door of which opened on to the street. As was the custom, no rent was paid for these rooms.

Soghmon wished to educate his children at foreign schools in Jerusalem, but the fees were high and his pay from the patriarchate was inadequate. To make ends meet Heghineh had to work day and night at dressmaking; as a result little attention was paid to housework and more often than not the cooking burned unattended. However her sister-in-law Heghnoug, who was very fond of the family, would try to come in daily in her limited spare time to help with the sewing and to wash up accumulated piles of pots, pans and dishes. Heghnoug, whose company was much sought-after, was very sociable and loved receiving and imparting news. She usually stayed with the family until

THE KRIKORIANS

midnight, then she would walk home by herself, the clap of her footsteps on the cobbled stones echoing loudly in the by-now deserted alleys and streets of the Armenian Quarter – but the way home was safe.

Krikor, Soghmon's eldest son, graduated from Bishop Gobat School for boys and in 1910 went on to study medicine at the Syrian Protestant College in Beirut. When he returned to Jerusalem it was wartime and he was obliged to join the Turkish army, which he did as a medical officer. Later he was appointed deputy chief medical officer for Palestine, a post he retained until the end of the British Mandate in 1948. Of the girls, Anna was slight, with blue eyes and fair hair, and counted as a great beauty. She married Dr Najib Abujoudeh, a Lebanese who was working in Palestine, and they raised a family. Nazouhie by contrast was very tall, athletic, and of strong character, not lightly to be crossed: she was quick-tempered, though this concealed kindness and affection. Her complexion, with much-envied rosy cheeks, required no makeup. Because she was so imposing Nazouhie was referred to privately among friends as 'the major'. Usually dressed in expensive costumes and low-heeled shoes, she would deck her bosom with a corsage – a hydrangea flower or a full-blown rose – and often wore a fox fur. She was a good tennis player, and was regularly to be seen walking Krikor's two mastiffs, Knut and Kundri. Neither Nazouhie nor Krikor married, but their two brothers, Kegham (who emigrated to the United States) and Yerevant, both did so and raised families.

One of Soghmon's younger brothers, Hagop, was apprenticed to Ashour, the Muslim owner of a well-known shoe-shop in the Old City. On completing his training he moved to Beirut to learn new techniques and become familiar with the fashionable shoe-styles for which the city was famous throughout the Middle East. His sister Horop accompanied him to keep house and they stayed for two years. When he returned to Jerusalem Hagop opened a small shop near the Grand New Hotel inside the Jaffa Gate.

Prior to the 1860s there were almost no residential buildings outside the Old City. However, from 1875 onwards many Jerusalem families who had been confined to living within the sixteenth-century walls gradually acquired land for building in what became fashionable and fast-developing suburbs. In about 1890 Hagop, helped financially by his two sisters Horop and Arousiag, himself purchased a piece of land in the Upper Baqa'a on the old Bethlehem road about one and a

24 ARMENIANS OF JERUSALEM

half miles south of the city. The plot was not far from the German Templist colony and close to the Jerusalem-to-Jaffa railway line completed in 1892. Later other *kaghakatsi* families acquired land in the vicinity and a small Armenian neighbourhood sprang up.

Soghmon bought land a short distance away in the Wa'ariyeh, an Arab quarter named after a notable Muslim family, Dar el Wa'ari. However, when land became available next to Hagop's plot Soghmon disposed of his previous purchase and moved alongside his brother. The plots were walled and the grounds planted with young trees: cypresses and Aleppo pines as well as pomegranates, grape vines, lemons, *kabbad* (*Citrus medica* from which delicious candied peel is made), plums, pears, *khushkhash* (Seville oranges), all grew to maturity as the building progressed. At first there was no source of water on the premises with which to water the young trees and it had to be fetched laboriously in earthenware pots from the *sabeel*, the drinking fountain above Bourqet el Sultan (the Sultan's pool) about a mile away.

Many bushes of *maward* roses (*Rosa damascena* from which rose-water is made) were planted around the garden walls. Very early each morning, while the dew was still on them, the family collected the rose petals and with the aid of a simple retort made by a tinsmith, distilled rose-water to give away to relatives and to keep themselves for the whole year. Rose-water was used as a perfume, a flavour for desserts, and to resuscitate anyone feeling faint. Rose blooms were also sold by weight in the *suq* where in early summer baskets-full were brought in by women from the Arab village of Malha south-west of Jerusalem. There for centuries this shrub rose (which needed no watering) had been cultivated to provide quantities of petals for the Greek and Armenian convents in Jerusalem and other customers. Alas, as a consequence of the Arab–Israeli war of 1948 the inhabitants of Malha were displaced and few traces of the original village remain.

Hagop and his sisters worked very hard and sacrificed all their earnings to put up their solid family house. It was to be modelled on houses the German Templists had built in their colony nearby. Methods of construction had moved on and vaulted stone roofs so characteristic of the Old City had been abandoned. Cement, timber and iron were now in use and red tiles, imported from Roux Frères in France covered gables and lofts. The beginning was humble, and the building grew by stages, the third storey only being completed in 1930. A large cistern was excavated first, with a cellar on each side of it. The Old City house was kept on, but part of the family moved to the new property when it consisted only of the cellars and a small outhouse used as a kitchen. By camping on the site they were able to supervise the builders and cut the cost by labouring themselves. Visiting relatives were obliged to help remove rubble and debris left on the premises. My mother and her two sisters, Hagop's nieces, always amusingly complained that whenever they visited their aunts as children they were given an *uffeh* (straw basket) in which to collect stones, often too heavy for them to lift.

Another achievement arduously accomplished by the womenfolk was the polishing of large limestone floor tiles in the central hall of the downstairs flat. These came in natural colours ranging from russet through shades of pink. They were quarried locally then shaped into flagstones, some as large as two feet square and four inches deep. The tiles were laid in a design as effective as any carpet and then painstakingly rubbed by hand over many months with sand and water until they shone like mirrors. The result was a floor of utmost elegance and character, capable of lasting for centuries. Unfortunately, manufactured cement tiles later became fashionable and many lovely floors of that date and earlier were torn up.

In 1905 at the age of 34 Hagop decided to marry and settle down in his new house in the Baqa'a. Eligible young *kaghakatsi* bachelors often sought, for prestige, to marry Armenian women from Syria, Egypt or Lebanon and Hagop was no exception. An Armenian priest who was a friend promised to arrange a marriage between him and Haiganoush Sarafian, a doctor's daughter whose family came from Istanbul but were now living and working in Damascus. She was 22 years old, had a Russian mother and was very good-looking. Haiganoush's parents made extensive enquiries about Hagop before allowing their daughter to marry him. When all was settled Heghineh, his sister-in-law, acting as *shbeeneh* (sponsor), accompanied Hagop to Damascus where the wedding took place.

Since Haiganoush had been brought up in Istanbul, she was better educated and had a different outlook from that of her mother- and sisters-in-law with whom she was now to live. She spoke classical Armenian perfectly and Turkish, but little Arabic, which proved to be a drawback and the cause of much misunderstanding within the family. Arousiag and Horop would come home tired after their day's work and find fault with her housekeeping. Further difficulty was caused when Hagop was taken away for long periods by the Turkish

26 ARMENIANS OF JERUSALEM

army to work as a shoemaker at a camp in Beersheba, in lieu of military service.

Haiganoush and Hagop had six children, Araxie, Aram, Vahan, Yevkineh (who died aged three months), another Yevkineh always called Vergine, and Sirpouhie. As a baby the fourth child, Yevkineh, was taken on an outing by her mother to watch an aeroplane piloted by two Turkish fliers land in Jerusalem. A large field in the German Colony not far from the house had been made ready and decorated for the landing on the afternoon of 16 March 1914. Hundreds of people gathered to witness the event, which turned into a grand *fantaziyeh* with flags, bands, scouts, and school students participating. Unfortunately the crowds got out of control and many people were hurt by stampeding horses, among them Yevkineh who died a few hours later. Next day the plane, heading for Egypt, crashed near Jaffa and both pilots, Nuri bey and Isma' in bey, were killed.

In 1918 Haiganoush developed pneumonia and on 25 August died at the age of 35. She had been under the care of Dr Kalebian, one of the best Armenian doctors in Jerusalem, and my mother, by then an experienced nurse, was called in to look after her, but nothing could be done. Two weeks later her baby daughter Sirpouhie, born while Hagop had been away in the Army the previous year, died of dysentery. The remaining four children, the eldest of whom was only eleven, came under the care of their two aunts, Horop and Arousiag. Hagop built a tomb for his wife in the Armenian cemetery of Pergeech on Mount Zion, carrying the words:

Haiganoush Sarafian *bolsetsi* (of Istanbul) 1883–1918. Your good and holy spirit guide me straight to salvation. Mother of four young children.

At the time of his wife's death Hagop was only 47, but he never remarried.

Hagop gave his children the best possible education. He bought the girls an upright piano and they were given music lessons. Araxie and Vergine went to the Jerusalem Girls' College, while Aram and Vahan began their education at St George's School. From there they moved to the Collège des Frères in the Old City, which was closer to home. When they graduated both boys went on for higher education at the Jerusalem Men's College; afterwards Vahan went into banking and

THE KRIKORIANS

Aram qualified as a surveyor at the American University in Beirut. All four of Hagop's surviving children married and raised families.

Movses, the youngest child of Anna and Krikor, tried his hand at the making of wine and spirits but without much success. He then emigrated to Brazil, hardly communicated with the family in Jerusalem, never married, and was not seen again. Years later came news of his death.

Anna, who had worked so hard and endured much grief, faded and died at the age of 92 in her Old City house surrounded by her daughters. She had been a widow for 46 years, and had gallantly seen her family through times of hardship, war and death: she had also witnessed happy occasions – marriages, births and christenings. She was laid to rest in the family plot in Pergeech, her tomb simply inscribed:

Here lies *digeen* Anna Krikorian of Jerusalem 1832–1924. May her soul rest in peace.

3   THE GAZMARARIANS

My mother's father was born in Jerusalem in 1835 and was given two Christian names, Hovhannes Melkon (John Melchior). He had one elder brother, Garabed (the Forerunner), but no sisters. The family, then known as the household of Kevork, had come to Jerusalem from Kharpert in Asia Minor centuries before. Some time after settling in Jerusalem, members of the family had been employed as bookbinders in the Armenian Convent. It was then that they were referred to among the Armenian community as Dar el Gazmarar (household of bookbinders). When surnames were introduced, Melkon's brother Garabed took the name Gazmararian for himself and his descendants. Melkon, however, converted his first name into the surname Hovhannesian. His children used his second name and took the name of Melkonian for themselves. Later, in European circles, the name was shortened to Melkon – my mother and aunts were known as the Miss Melkons. Similarly, some of Garabed's descendants who had emigrated to the United States of America changed from Gazmararian to Gazmarian.

The only education the boys, Garabed and Melkon, received was through priests in the Armenian convent, where they learned to read and write Armenian and also acquired a knowledge of Turkish and Arabic, both necessary for daily life.

From my mother and aunts I learned that their father, Hovhannes Melkon, was tall and good-looking. He did not tolerate gossip or interference in other people's affairs and was well respected in the community. He attended church regularly and read a psalm and portions of the bible daily at home. Hovhannes Melkon had a good singing voice and played the *oude* or lute, which made him popular at weddings and other festivities. His clothes were simple, a silk *qumbaz*

THE GAZMARARIANS

made out of material imported from Damascus, a stambouline, and on his head a *mughrabiyyeh* (short soft fez with tassel, surrounded by a muslin kerchief).

Young Armenian men of the day usually took up a trade: building, stonemasonry, carpentry, blacksmithery, tailoring and so on. At an early age Hovhannes Melkon was apprenticed to a barber and he later opened a shop of his own. It appears that in his professional life he did not use his first name: various entries in records held at the Church of the Holy Archangels identify him as a barber in three languages – Armenian, Turkish and Arabic – *sapritch* Melkon, *berber* Melkon, or *halaq* Melkon. True to the custom of the day, the household was called Dar Melkon el Halaq.

Melkon's brother Garabed traded in household goods and owned a shop below the Grand New Hotel inside the Jaffa Gate. As his business required him to travel as far as Istanbul, he became more Europeanized than his brother and wore suits and a fez. From his shop he sold imported goods: *manadeel* (printed headscarves worn by women of the time), embroidered slippers, corsages of artificial flowers, henna for hair-dyeing, snuff, sets of towels, as well as copper and brass bowls for use in the Turkish baths. Among other wares were tiny bottles of perfume and ivory combs.

Garabed married and had five sons. His wife, Heghineh, was a great help to him; she acted as his saleswoman, carrying samples to the womenfolk in Muslim families where her husband could not enter. Of their sons, the three eldest all married and raised families in Jerusalem. One worked in the Austrian post office, one as a jeweller and the third as an engineer involved in the construction of the new road from Jaffa to Jerusalem. The two youngest sons, still bachelors, one a tailor and the other a civil servant in Jaffa, twice avoided joining the Turkish army by payment of *badal* (a sum of money in lieu of military service). Eventually they were unable to pay yet again and were obliged to join up. In the army they both contracted fever, from which they returned home to die.

Melkon opened his barber's shop in a building owned by the Armenian patriarchate at the top end of David Street, facing the Citadel. Over the shop Thomas Cook & Son had their travel agency. To help pay the rent he allowed a Jewish watchmaker to have working space within the shop. As an assistant he employed Kevork Stepan, who later became his son-in-law. Most of his clients came to the shop for a haircut or shave, but Melkon would attend to foreign consuls

30 ARMENIANS OF JERUSALEM

and other notables in hotels and in their homes. He also extracted teeth, stocked and applied leeches to remedy high blood pressure, had skills as a bonesetter, and as a herbalist made up many traditional medicines and gave advice on their use. In May 1888 Melkon applied to Bishop Yeremiah, vicar of the Armenian patriarchate of Jerusalem, for the honorary post of medical adviser to the community, stating, 'though I am engaged by profession as a barber, I have enough knowledge and light surgical training to fill the position of the late Zakar Baba'. It is not known whether Melkon was offered this vacant post.

By the end of the nineteenth century the Jaffa Gate area developed into a shopping and commercial centre. It became a meeting place for the old city, surrounding villages and the fast-growing suburbs of the new city. At night the city gates were shut and the keys handed to the office of the governor. However, for a small fee the gatekeeper would oblige latecomers and let them in through the wicket gate. Those arriving on camel or horse back were obliged to tether their animals outside until morning.

Foreign tourists had begun to visit Jerusalem in large numbers, and to cater for them hotels and souvenir shops opened inside the Old City. Around the Citadel, villagers were allowed to hold a market of fresh fruit, vegetables and poultry. The womenfolk, who came from all over the country, were charmingly dressed in traditional *twab* (long dresses of handwoven linen). These beautiful garments were richly and colourfully embroidered in cross-stitch, work which took many months to complete at home. Each dress had a distinctive regional pattern readily identifying the locality from which its wearer came. The market would start at day-break, the villagers bringing in their produce on donkeys, mules and camels. This busy and picturesque scene, where much haggling took place, continued until mid-morning.

Just outside the Jaffa Gate stood a fleet of horse-drawn *hanatir*. These carriages were available for hire, ready to drive travellers to the suburbs and outlying towns and villages. Abu Shakir was in charge of the fleet of carriages (which were also known as 'delaisances', a corruption of the French 'diligences'). His office was near a large coffee house where passengers were able to partake of refreshments while waiting. This system of transport survived until the 1930s when it was gradually replaced by buses and taxis.

In 1858 at the age of 23, Melkon married Mariam, the fifteen-year-old daughter of Boghos Genevisian. Unlike most of the *kaghakatsi*

THE GAZMARARIANS

community, the young couple went to live outside the Old City in a small house which Melkon had inherited from his father. It was a fifteen-minute walk from the Jaffa Gate, at the far end of Mamillah opposite the Muslim cemetery. Their first surviving child, a daughter, Arousiag, was born in 1866, followed by Hagop Haroutiun in 1873, in 1875, Apraham, who only lived for a year, Yughaper ('bearer of the holy oil') in 1878 and in 1880 another Apraham, who also died in infancy. In 1884, when the children were still young their mother died, aged 41.

After his wife's death Melkon found it increasingly difficult to leave his three young children on their own in his isolated house while he was away at work in the city. He petitioned Patriarch Yessayi to give him rooms in the Armenian Quarter, writing on 10 June 1885: 'It is impossible for me to live outside the Old City and leave my children in the hands of Turks and troops and other strange people.'

In 1886 the patriarchate agreed to let him have two rooms and a kitchen in a building in the street below the east wall of the convent. Initially he was required to pay three Ottoman pounds annually, since he was receiving rent for the house he had vacated in Mamillah. Bishop Yeremiah's dragoman recorded that:

> According to the decision of the Reverend Fathers, *berber* Melkon has been called to the office and for his dwelling rooms I demanded three pounds as rent. The abovementioned promises to pay the rent from the beginning of Muharram after having paid his debts and the interest thereon.

Muharram, the first month of the Arab lunar new year, was the time when people moved house and made new rent agreements.

The rooms were on the ground floor of a two-storey house in which two other Armenian families also lived. Melkon's elder daughter, eighteen-year-old Arousiag, looked after the household for her father until, two years after his wife's death, he decided to marry again. As his second wife Melkon asked for the hand of Mariam, daughter of Anna and Krikor the carpenter. She was 32 years old and known for her domestic skills and good nature. He was 51. She accepted him, albeit reluctantly, as he was a widower 19 years older than herself, with three children. Later on, when she was tired or depressed, she used to say, 'It is enough that I married a widower, and an old one at

32 ARMENIANS OF JERUSALEM

that.' The marriage, which took place on 4 August 1886 at the Church of the Holy Archangels, is recorded thus:

> Sapritch Melkon, widower, to Mariam dülger Krikorian, spinster. Sponsor, Apraham Samra Soghmonian (the bride's uncle). Officiating priest: Vartabed Nigoghos.

Mariam joined Melkon and his family in their house which was close to the one in which she herself had been brought up. From then on a happy and lasting relationship developed between Mariam and her step-children.

In November 1889 Melkon and Mariam's first child was born, a daughter who was christened Macrouhie (purity) and later called Margaret. She was to become my mother. In April 1891 another daughter arrived, named Takouhie, the Armenian word for 'queen'. At home her pet name was Taktak but throughout her life she was called Malakeh, the Arabic translation of her name. In November 1893 a third daughter, Isquhie (truth), was born. She was followed in April 1895 by the long-awaited son, Hovhannes (John). This event was a cause of great joy to the family. In the Middle East the birth of a girl was often greeted with tears, but not that of a boy.

It was the custom for Armenians to christen their babies within a few weeks of birth. At this ceremony the child is fully accepted into the church and receives Holy Communion. The parents would choose a *shbeen* (godparent), who would then act for each of their children from first to last. A godparent and his family were treated as close relatives from then on. Melkon and Mariam chose their friend Christos Dur, who was a carpenter working in Jaffa.

Christenings were recorded in a register kept by the parish priest in the offices of the Church of the Holy Archangels. Birth certificates were not issued, and thus age beyond early childhood was always a matter of guesswork. No one ever discussed age, and birthdays as we know them were not celebrated. Sometimes children would have the year of birth tattooed on their wrist. Exact dates were not kept, but every child was told by its parents that it was born near the time of a certain religious feast. Macrouhie and Isquhie were told that they were born about the time of Eid el Mughara, the feast of the finding of the Cross by St Helena, which falls in November; Takouhi and Hovhannes in April, close to Sabt el Nur, the day of the Holy Fire on the Saturday before Easter. After death, relatives referred to the book

THE GAZMARARIANS 33

of records and it was only then that approximate ages were revealed: to look during a person's lifetime was ruled out by courtesy or perhaps superstition. Registration of births and deaths had broken down towards the end of Turkish rule and was only re-started and made compulsory under the British Mandate. From then on official birth certificates were issued, but the ancient system of registration at the Armenian patriarchate continues to this day.

Instead of birthdays it was the custom to celebrate name days. These coincided with saints' days and often included people with different names. The feast of the Virgin Mary was not only the name day for women called Mariam but also for six other names, Macrouhie, Takouhie, Isquhie, Azniv, Dirouhie, and Sirpouhie. All these names represent the virtues of the Virgin Mary – purity, queenliness, truth, nobility, courtesy, saintliness. Hovhannes Melkon and his brother Garabed celebrated their name day on the Feast of John the Baptist, Hovhannou Garabedi (John the Forerunner). Men with such names as Kaprel (Gabriel), Mikail, kept their name days on the feast of St Michael and All Angels. All others with names of Armenian kings and princes such as Haig, Vahe and Vahan, celebrated on the feast of Vartanantz. This was the day of remembrance of Vartan, an Armenian saint, a prince killed in defence of his faith at the battle of Avarayr in AD 451.

On name days friends would call on each other to wish the family well in the coming year. Liqueurs, Turkish coffee and *ghreibeh* (home-made shortbread) or *bademe*, made from ground almonds and icing sugar, were offered to the guests. If a member of a family was absent or had emigrated, it was usual for his parents to continue with this custom. Visits between friends and relatives also took place at Christmas and Easter. Again liqueurs and Turkish coffee, accompanied by *ma'amoul*, were served. These home-made Easter cakes, whose outer casing was made of semolina and butter, were filled with a mixture of crushed walnuts, sugar and spices or with pounded dates. The ones filled with walnuts were formed into rounded shapes like small sponges and decorated by pinching with a pair of special tweezers. Those filled with the date mixture were formed into small crowns and decorated in the same way. Before serving they were sprinkled with icing sugar. These two cakes symbolized the sponge and crown of thorns used at Our Lord's crucifixion. The making of *ma'amoul* was a sociable event. Neighbours and friends would get together to help each other, some filling the cakes, others decorating

34 ARMENIANS OF JERUSALEM

them in preparation for baking. It remains a good opportunity for friendly gossip.

Chocolate had not yet been introduced but most households made their own delicious preserved fruits, amongst them cherries and apricots. These were served in delicate glass goblets imported from Bavaria. On the same tray would be silver spoons and a glass of water into which they were plunged after partaking of the preserve. Turkish coffee followed. When manufactured sweets were introduced no one bothered to make home-made preserves any more.

Melkon's wife, Mariam, and her young family lived happily with the children of his previous marriage, Arousiag, Hagop and Yughaper. Soon her three step-children married and started households of their own. Both Arousiag and Yughaper were good-looking and Hagop was tall and handsome. Characteristics of good looks in women were fair skin, large expressive eyes, a long neck and above all *dam khafeef* (lightness of spirit or *allegria*).

In 1889, at the age of 23, Arousiag married Kevork Stepan, her father's assistant, who was 35 years old. A house called Dar el Ajayez (the house of the old ladies) near the Syrian Convent of St Mark became their home. They had four surviving children, the eldest boy having died of diphtheria: two girls, Heghineh and Christine, and two boys, Apraham and Stepan. When the youngest child was only 40 days old Kevork died. To provide for the family, Arousiag offered her services as wet nurse for the baby of English missionaries who lived at Christ Church near the Jaffa Gate. When her father, Melkon, learned of this he was furious and ordered her to stop at once, fearing that it would affect the health of her own baby. From then on he sent the family a weekly supply of provisions to make sure that they had enough to eat. Arousiag continued to work by taking in laundry and sewing. She also joined other Armenian workers repairing tents for Thomas Cook & Sons at their storage depot in Mamillah. These had to be checked in readiness for the tourist season. The work was hard and she often returned home with swollen and painful hands. In 1925 while on a visit to Mariam her step-mother, Arousiag was taken ill. She was helped back to her house where she died, aged 59, as the result of a stroke.

Arousiag's children grew up and went their different ways. Her elder daughter, Heghineh, who was of great character and beauty, started work as a teacher in the Armenian school. She later married Haigazoun Voskerichian, a priest. From then on he became a *derder*

THE GAZMARARIANS
35

(parish priest) and Heghineh assumed the title of *iritzkeeneh*. Married priests were recognized by the Armenian church, but it meant forfeiting promotion. The couple moved to Alexandria in Egypt, where they founded Institut Haigazoun, a high school in which Armenian and French were taught to brevet supérieur standard.

Of the two boys, Stepan emigrated to America; Apraham, following his father's and grandfather's profession, became a barber in Jerusalem, where he married and had many children.

Christine, Arousiag and Kevork's youngest daughter, took up dressmaking and earned the name *varbed* (teacher). She was very clever at cutting out patterns and was admired for never hesitating when using her scissors on precious material. Although she had many proposals she did not marry. While still young she formed a close friendship with one of the notable Muslim families in Jerusalem, Dar el Husseini. Ibrahim efendi el Husseini, whose title was *Na'ib el ashraf* (head of the nobles of this ancient and eminent family) was a widower with four young children. He invited Christine to be governess and companion to his daughters Effat and Saffa who were still students at the Sisters of Sion Convent school for girls. Christine was treated as one of the family and spent most of her time in their house on the Mount of Olives, although she carried on with her dressmaking.

During the winter months Christine accompanied the Husseinis to their house and garden in Jericho, where the family regularly lived from October until the end of April, enjoying the mild climate. Their grove covered 30 dunums (about eight acres). In the garden banana trees and vegetables grew in one part. To add to the beauty of the scene impressive groups of date palms towered above the smaller trees. The larger part of the garden was planted with citrus, including oranges, lemons, grapefruit, pomelos and *yusef efendi* (tangerines). The latter were named in honour of Yusef efendi el Khalidi, a long-serving reforming *rais el baladiyeh* (mayor) of Jerusalem, appointed in 1867, who for a few years also represented the Sanjak of Jerusalem in the parliament in Istanbul.

The house itself was built of *libin* (bricks of sun-baked clay and straw) in traditional Jericho style with a sloping roof supported by wooden beams, and its interior was tightly lined with canes of bamboo. The single-storey building formed three sides of a square. A flight of steps led to the only room on the second floor, a grand reception room. From there one had a commanding view over the whole oasis of Jericho, the mountains of Moab, and Jabal el Quarantal (the Mount

36 ARMENIANS OF JERUSALEM

of Temptation). The two wings of the building enclosed a formal garden with a small raised pool, which was separated from the main grove beyond by a row of heavily-scented *fitna* (frangipani) and *tamr henna* (*Lawsonia alba*) trees. In the flower beds grew many bushes of old-fashioned roses, amongst others huge floppy pink blooms of *ward juri* (*Rosa indica*), so popular in gardens all over the Middle East. In one corner a white jasmine clambered over a chicken house. In the cool of the evening delicious scents would fill the air, especially when the citrus trees were in full bloom. A path shaded by a pergola smothered in grape vines led from the house through the garden to an open space where friends and relatives could pass their time. At this point there stood a very old and magnificent *dom* tree (*Zizyphus spina-christi*), the tallest in Jericho and a landmark for miles around. Its shade provided an ideal cool picnic place, especially for children, and a haven for various song birds including bulbuls (Syrian nightingales), whose tender whistle delighted the ear as they flitted from one branch to another seeking out ripe berries.

Here a cemented channel flowed the length of the garden, day in and day out taking water to various neighbouring orange groves from nearby Ain el Sultan (Fountain of the Prophet Elisha). Each garden in turn had exclusive use of the water weekly for a fixed period. Water rights were part of the property, bought and sold with the land. The *qanawati* (municipal water watchman) was in charge of opening and shutting sluice gates controlling the flow to individual gardens according to their rightful share.

At the far end of the garden near the house of the *bustanji* (gardener), a gate opened on to a lane leading to Ain el Sultan below the *tel* of ancient Jericho. This perennial spring provided water for many households, the womenfolk collecting it in earthenware jars or tins. It was also a favourite meeting place for the inhabitants of the town in the late afternoon. They came to enjoy the cool air and the sound of rushing water as it burst forth through tunnels, the cavernous sides of which dripped with maidenhair fern. The stream which flowed away from it, in which grew many water-loving plants, provided a home for toads and frogs whose croaking filled the air after sunset.

The Husseinis were very hospitable and Christine's relations enjoyed their friendship. They were constantly invited to visit and stay at the house in Jericho. Mariam, my grandmother, who used to spend part of the winter there, was much loved by the family and their friends. As a child I was often taken there by my aunt Isquhie to spend

THE GAZMARARIANS 37

a few days. Outings were organized for us to the Jordan River, the Dead Sea, the Mount of Temptation and to visit Husseini relatives, Dar Mihy el Din, in their house and garden at the mouth of the Wadi Qelt. Christine continued to live with the Husseini family until her death at the age of 93. Alas all that remains is a memory now, as the *bayyara* where we spent so many happy days has been sold and the house pulled down in the name of modernization.

Melkon's younger daughter, Yughaper, was to live a very unhappy life. She became deeply attached to Nigoghos (Nicholas), a young man who lived with his parents across the courtyard from their rooms. Nigoghos was handsome and very much a ladies' man, reputedly teasing the girls by saying: 'Give me a kiss. Why are you preserving your cheeks for the worms?' – a very shocking request in those days. Yughaper and Nigoghos wished to marry but her father would not allow it and Yughaper had no say in the matter. Melkon adhered to church laws that forbade *badal*, (exchange): a man was not allowed to marry the sister of his brother-in-law. At the time Yughaper's brother, Hagop Haroutiun, was already engaged to marry Nigoghos's sister, Shogheeg.

In 1894 when she was sixteen it was arranged that Yughaper should marry Hagop Kevorkian, a blacksmith; but this led to disaster. Nigoghos, her thwarted admirer, still tried to flirt with her, and to tantalize the newly-weds would stand late at night below the windows of their house in the Armenian quarter, serenading them with his accordion. This continued for some time until it was decided that the couple should move from Jerusalem to the seaside town of Jaffa, there to make a fresh start. The move was useless as Hagop took to drink and began to ill-treat Yughaper. Soon she developed tuberculosis and died, young, beautiful and childless at the age of twenty in 1898, so ending four unhappy years of marriage. Melkon blamed himself for his daughter's misery and early death and built an elaborate marble tomb for her at Pergeech.

Hagop Haroutiun, Melkon's only son by his first marriage and a carpenter by profession, was of a mystical nature and loved the open air, the wilderness and the countryside. He readily gave up life in Jerusalem and went to work in the Wadi Qelt (the biblical Brook Cherith) at a flour-mill owned and run by the Husseini family. There he lived in a cave enjoying the noise of rushing water, animals and birds. The dramatic atmosphere of the wadi, with its changing colours, cliffs and ravines, seemed to suit his temperament. He rode up to

38   ARMENIANS OF JERUSALEM

Jerusalem on horseback only when necessary, travelling very early in the morning or late at night to avoid the heat. On the way he would water his horse at Bir el Miscob, a well built by the Russian church for the use of pilgrims walking to the Place of Baptism at the River Jordan. The pilgrims would carry shrouds with them to dip in the river waters; then take them back to Russia to be used at the time of death.

After a long engagement Hagop Haroutiun, as arranged, married Shogheeg, sister of Nigoghos, in the spring of 1905. He was 32 and she was 30, and initially she tried her best to live in the cave but she was scared by all nocturnal sounds. The primitive accommodation which her husband had provided was not to her liking. After much nagging they moved to Jerusalem, where Hagop found work as a carpenter in the German Colony. They moved into a house in the Armenian Quarter where they raised three daughters, Mariam, Yughaper and Asanet. In 1914, when her youngest child was only four years old and her husband was away in the Turkish army, Shogheeg died of cancer. Her brother Nigoghos made all arrangements for her burial. On his return Hagop Haroutiun, who was devastated, brought the girls to his stepmother Mariam, and said, 'These are yours, please take them into your charge'. She gladly looked after them for a while and then they were sent off as boarders to Talitha Cumi, the German school for girls, where they were unhappy and would not settle down. Later they were sent as boarders to a school in Bethlehem founded by The Society for the Promotion of Female Education in the East and run by the Church Missionary Society. There they learned very good English and had a reasonable education.

Hagop Haroutiun drank far too much after his wife's death and in 1919, at the early age of 46, he too died. The orphaned children then became the responsibility of their uncle Nigoghos. When they grew up it was arranged that the eldest girl, Mariam, should marry a rich Armenian living in Chile, whom she had never met. A photograph of him as a handsome young man was sent to Jerusalem and she accepted him. On arrival in Chile she found he was much older than she had expected, but with no alternative she had to marry him. This was a trap that many prospective young brides fell into when marriage was arranged by correspondence. Many years later she was joined in Chile by her sister, Yughaper. Asanet remained in Palestine, married Sarkis Shahinian and went to live in Jaffa.

4 MALAKEH AND MARGARET, EARLY CHILDHOOD

Melkon, Mariam and their young family continued to live in the house allocated to them by the Armenian patriarchate. Although strict and a disciplinarian by nature, Melkon was also kind and generous, and saw to it that all household needs were adequately provided for. Fresh fruit, vegetables and meat purchased in the *suq* or market were always of the highest quality and delivered daily by a basket-boy. Mariam had a simple kitchen but produced delicious meals cooked over a charcoal fire; she made sure that all was ready for her husband's daily return home for lunch. The family took their meals on a low, round wooden table, sitting on cushions on the floor. As an aperitif Melkon usually had a small glass of arak. Food was served straight from the *tanjara* (tinned copper pot) in which it had been cooked. Before starting the meal Melkon would recite *Hair Mer* (the Lord's Prayer), the customary Armenian grace.

On his return in the evening Melkon would bring the day's takings from the barber's shop in a linen bag, empty the contents on the table and make a count. He then attended to the large glass jar containing sand and water, in which he bred leeches for use in his medical cures. The children were in awe of him and as soon as they heard the tap of his silver-handled *bastoneh* (walking-stick) on the cobblestones outside they scuttled indoors and put on their best behaviour.

From a very early age the children were encouraged to attend services in the Armenian Cathedral as well as at the Holy Sepulchre. At weekends and on the eve of feast days the community were reminded of forthcoming services by a *jamgortch*, who in the early hours would go round the quarter, calling with a loud voice and banging on courtyard doors with his stick. Tucked away under their covers, the children were quite frightened by the noise he made.

40 ARMENIANS OF JERUSALEM

For the daily Sunrise Office (*Jamerkoutiun*) the congregation would be at Surp Hagop at half past six in the morning. Every Saturday the *kaghakatsi* attended the Armenian liturgy held in the Church of the Holy Sepulchre, celebrated by their parish priest. In the early hours the children and their mother would leave the house and join a small group of friends and neighbours to make their way through the Old City to the church. Their aunt Horop would often come from the Baqa'a, spend the night and go with them. They always felt perfectly safe, although the streets were dark and empty at that time of the morning.

On their return the city would be coming to life, awakening to the noisy hustle and bustle that the day brings. As dawn breaks the call to prayer echoes from one minaret to another, a reminder to Muslims of their duty to God. A glimmer of light appears over the Mount of Olives to the east; dawn light gradually bathing the city in warm shades of yellow and pink; light which cannot be compared with that in any other part of the world. The customary greeting, *sabah el khair* (good morning), is exchanged with those met on the way, be they friends or strangers. When they reached home again the family would all sit down to an early breakfast.

In 1896, when Margaret was about seven years old and Malakeh five their parents, seeking a good education for their daughters, decided to send them to one of the foreign schools in Jerusalem. They chose a German school run by Protestant Kaiserswerth Diakonissen.

The Kaiserswerth Diakonissen came to Jerusalem in 1851 at the request of Samuel Gobat, Anglican bishop from 1846 to 1879, to help with his charitable work among the people of the Old City. In the same year Bishop Gobat, with the Church Missionary Society, established the boys' school on Mount Zion which was named after him. The German sisters had been trained at a Protestant benevolent institution, Diakonissen Anstalt, founded by Pastor Theodor Fliedner in 1836 in the town of Kaiserswerth near Düsseldorf. From there they were sent to work as missionaries in many parts of the world.

In addition to their other duties, the Diakonissen taught a few young Arab girls in the Old City who had no other opportunity of schooling. It was soon realized that there was need for expansion and in 1868, under the direction of the architect Konrad Schick, buildings for a school were erected on a large plot of land about a kilometre to the west of Jaffa Gate. Like most institutional buildings of that date it was vast, with thick walls, basements, and floors covered with large

MALAKEH AND MARGARET, EARLY CHILDHOOD   41

flagstones. Originally it was out in the country but it was later engulfed by expanding western suburbs. Over the main entrance were inscribed the words 'Talitha Cumi', the name given to the school to signify hope for raising the aspirations of young women in Jerusalem. In Aramaic this means 'girl, arise' (Mark 5:41; 'and he took the damsel by the hand and said to her Talitha Cumi; which is, being interpreted Damsel I say unto thee, arise'). The order's emblem – a dove in flight carrying an olive branch – was carved into the lintel.

This was to become the first modern girls' school in Jerusalem, with accommodation for a hundred pupils, mostly Arab, a few Armenians and others, including orphans who had been brought to Talitha Cumi from all over the Ottoman empire. The fee for those who could afford it was one gold pound a year per child. In addition to their regular school classes, the girls were trained in sewing, cooking and domestic work. Local girls, or those of 'oriental origins' as they called them at the time, who wished to become Diakonissen, were given special training to enable them to join the sisterhood. A few followed this path and remained with the school for the rest of their lives.

During the eight years that Malakeh and Margaret were boarders the school had two superiors. The first, Schwester Charlotte Pilz, born in 1819 and a deaconess for 50 years, was suceeded in 1903 by Schwester Dorothea Reichau known as Schwester Dorchen. I had often wondered why the school was referred to by the local population as 'Shalotta': I realized it was a corruption of the name Charlotte. Malakeh and Margaret were pitifully young when they joined the school, and they needed help even with dressing themselves. A *kaghakatsi* pupil Takouhie, who was a few years older, took them under her wing and fended for them. They never forgot her kindness and over the years they constantly mentioned her with great affection. The girls spent their time at school under a regime of austere discipline. They were taught in Arabic and German and in consequence did not learn Armenian.

The day started at six a.m. with the girls emptying chamber pots used in the dormitory, and also the ones used by the nuns. There were no lavatories inside the building. A roster for work allocated them in turn to the sewing room, laundry, bakery, kitchens, gardens, and the cleaning of the vast stone floors of the corridors and rooms. Gardening included regular watering of many plants, especially the hundreds of roses growing in green-painted four-gallon paraffin tins.

42   ARMENIANS OF JERUSALEM

In season fruit, almonds and vegetables had to be picked, some for use in the school and the rest to be taken on donkey-back for sale in the market in the Old City. Before work began there were daily prayers in the Kapelle.

On the day in the spring of 1905 when the girls had been granted permission to go to their half-brother Hagop Haroutiun's wedding, it was their turn for duty in the laundry. No reprieve was granted and they were made to get up at midnight in order to finish their work by the morning. This example of inflexible rules was never forgotten by Margaret and Malakeh.

Singing lessons were part of the curriculum. The pupils were trained to sing German and Arabic folksongs and hymns, their conductor starting them off with 'Eins . . . Zwei . . . Drei . . .'. Both girls had good voices; Margaret sang soprano while Malakeh was given alto parts. It was customary for the choir to sing to the patients at the German Hospital, and for the lepers in their home Jesushilfe run by the Moravians. The kaiser's birthday was celebrated and the children sang for that occasion. When Kaiserin Augusta-Viktoria visited the school in 1898 they gave a concert and welcomed her, singing 'Gott grüsse Dich'. Every Sunday morning they were taken to sing in the Erlöserkirche (Lutheran Church of the Redeemer) at the German service, then at a service for the Arabic congregation conducted by Qassis Iskander and Qassis Said who came from Beit Jala.

Long walks in the country were the only form of recreation. The pupils were sometimes taken to Bir Ayoub (Job's well) in Silwan, usually in the spring when after a wet winter water gushed into the Kidron valley. Other places visited on foot were the Musalabeh (Convent of the Cross), the Mount of Olives and the Tombs of the Kings. After Schwester Charlotte Pilz's death in 1903, groups of girls were taken to the Protestant cemetery on Mount Zion to visit her grave. Wild flowers were collected on these walks in the spring, pressed, dried, and later mounted on cards. These together with various knitted garments, embroidery, lace and needlework, all made by the girls, were sold to visitors in aid of school funds.

Food in the school was ample but very unimaginative and poor. For breakfast the girls were given black coffee and slices of bread with olives and goats' cheese. Lunch always consisted of rice and a vegetable stew, with meat only included on Wednesdays and Sundays. Two dishes recalled as exceptionally unpleasant were pumpkin stew

MALAKEH AND MARGARET, EARLY CHILDHOOD 43

and a soup of flour and weak broth. For supper plenty of bread was given, to be eaten with olives, raisins, dried figs or *halaweh*, a nourishing sweetmeat made of sesame seed oil and sugar. The Diakonissen had their own dining room where they ate better food. At noon and in the evening the girls saw large platters of roast meat and vegetables carried in there. During the afternoon the Schwesters entertained parents and other guests to tea.

Malakeh and Margaret were not to be denied a few luxuries. Their father had ordered them a wooden tuck-box with a lock in which to keep food sent from home. The key to this box was always worn around Margaret's neck. They were visited frequently by their youngest sister, Isquhie, as well as by their mother, who would walk over from the Old City with a basket full of cooked food, fruit and sweetmeats. Together they would picnic under the trees until the gatekeeper, Schwester Jamileh, of whom they were terrified as she had a glass eye and a wooden leg, rattled her stick and ordered them to go back to work. If Malakeh and Margaret misbehaved at home during the summer holidays, their mother would threaten to report them to Schwester Jamileh. Later on robbers broke into the gatehouse, gagged and beat up the Schwester; thereafter she had to be moved into the main school building and to relinquish her post to a man.

Winters in Jerusalem were very cold but no heating was provided in the school, at least not for the pupils. There was no electricity and water was pumped up by hand from large cisterns which lay under the buildings and in the grounds. The school broke up for two months during the summer. There was no break for Christmas or Easter but monthly visits home were permitted.

Punishment was frequent and took the form of a stroke with a ruler on the hand. Girls who wet their beds were humiliated and made to stand in a corner with a wet sheet over their head while their classmates were brought in to look at them. This rigid German upbringing to which Malakeh and Margaret were exposed from a very young age did not go to waste. On the contrary, it formed their characters and strengthened the self-discipline and integrity which were to mark them for the rest of their lives. They were educated in German and Arabic, and could read, write and speak both languages fluently. Isquhie, who had stayed at home with her parents and attended the Armenian convent school, was in consequence the only one of the three sisters who learned Armenian well.

On 7 October 1898 the family were dealt a sad blow. Dar

Nigoghos, their neighbours in the shared courtyard, were adding extra rooms to their house. To keep out of the way of the building work Mariam had begged Melkon to hire accommodation for them in Bethlehem for the summer months, but he stubbornly refused. One afternoon while Hovhannes was playing, he slipped and fell into an uncovered pit of quicklime. He was rushed to the Jewish clinic near the Convent of St Mark, but the doctor was unable to save him as he had been so badly burned and blinded. Mariam's only son, aged three years and six months, was dead – an event she was never to recover from. The little boy was buried in the Armenian cemetery of Pergeech on Mount Zion and his parents built him a marble grave on which is inscribed:

Hovhannes son of Melkon the barber who in his fourth summer fell into a pit of quicklime and was burned to his death. 1898.

Mariam paid regular visits to the grave and planted a small garden around it in which she grew asters, irises and other plants. To ensure that the Sudanese watchman at the cemetery looked after the grave, she supplied him with tea and sugar.

After this tragedy Mariam found it difficult to continue to live in the house where her son had met his death. She blamed the neighbours for negligence in keeping the lime pit uncovered and an unpleasant atmosphere was created between them. The solution was to move. Melkon wrote to the patriarch's office to ask if they could offer him different accommodation.

Near the Armenian Cathedral, in what is now known as No. 1 St James's Road, lived three families around a common courtyard. One of them was constantly quarrelling with the other two. To settle the matter the convent authorities decided that this troublesome family should exchange houses with Melkon and Mariam.

Melkon and Mariam's new house also consisted of two rooms and a kitchen, which opened on to a shared courtyard. During the day it was customary, and safe, to leave the heavy wooden door of the courtyard shut but unlocked so that visitors could come in from the street at any time. A strong piece of string which dangled through a small hole in the door unfastened the latch when pulled down from the outside. The string was drawn back inside by the last person coming home at night: any other caller had to knock for admission. The other two families living in the courtyard, Dar Simoun and Dar

MALAKEH AND MARGARET, EARLY CHILDHOOD   45

abu Zeron, were also quarrelsome but Mariam never interfered and always shut the door of her room firmly until the air cleared.

Mariam was very house-proud, forever washing, cleaning and cooking, and found no time to mix with her neighbours. In the kitchen there was a deep alcove with a built-in grate where cooking was done over charcoal. Tin-plated copper pots and earthenware (*qidar*) were used for cooking, with hand-carved wooden spoons for stirring the food. In one corner over another grate stood a huge cauldron or *mah'oon* in which water was heated up for baths and for laundry. In one of the main rooms a large wooden shelf (*imsandara*) had been installed between two of the arches. This was out of reach of the children and was used for storing provisions – rice, sugar, olive oil, cooking fat, cheese, home-made jams and so on, for the rest of the year. A white muslin curtain was drawn across it.

The two doors from the courtyard into the rooms each had a *shurshbay*, a glass-panelled outer door, which during the day let in the light and kept out the cold. The larger room, which was used as a sitting-room by day, was converted into a bedroom at night. Mattresses were rolled out on the floor and the girls and their mother slept under quilts covered by a large woollen *kilim*. Melkon had the privilege of sleeping in a bed. During the day bedding was tidied away on a stone ledge in a large alcove in the thickness of the wall, over-hung by a rose-patterned linen curtain.

Laundry was hung out on the roof where Mariam also had rows of earth-filled containers in which grew Madonna lilies, freesias, sparaxis, amaryllis and roses. In the intense heat of summer these had to be watered every day. A sweetly scented white jasmine grew in a large barrel standing in their part of the courtyard. In the early morning the open flowers were picked, placed in a plate of water and taken indoors where their fragrance filled the room. A pot of pink zephyranthes, which lay dormant through the summer, produced a mass of leafless pink trumpets in the autumn.

The family did not possess a clock, but could readily tell the time by various familiar city sounds that wafted through the air. The call of the muezzin and the pealing of monastery and convent bells conveniently spanned the hours of day. Bells rang out, and still do, at regular times: five a.m., at noon and at six in the evening. As the house was only a street-breadth away from the convent walls, they could also hear the sound of the clappers (*nakuz*) used there instead of bells (which had been banned under Turkish rule until about

46   ARMENIANS OF JERUSALEM

1840). These resonant clappers, one made of wood, the other of metal, hang from thick chains in the porch outside St James's Cathedral. Their gong-like note when struck still announces the start of services. Melkon himself possessed a gold watch which he carried in the pocket of his stambouline.

For warmth in the winter a *kanoon* was used, a brazier made of polished brass with a chafing dish over which sat a filigreed domed lid capped by a crescent. The chafing dish was filled with very fine charcoal, *duq*, ignited with a few sticks and a drop of paraffin and then placed in a draught outside until it took light. The *kanoon* was then carried into the centre of the room to be heated and every now and then stirred with a pair of iron tongs, momentarily exposing the red hot particles of *duq* underneath. Before retiring to bed the *kanoon* had to be put out of doors for fear of carbon monoxide poisoning. *Duq*, charcoal and wood were fairly cheap. They were delivered in sackfuls by mules or camels and kept in the *mughara*, a cave-like storeroom close to the main entrance.

There was no electricity, and paraffin lamps were the source of light. Elaborate ones were made of decorated Bavarian glass, others of brass. They were surmounted by an opaque glass shade fitted into a frame deeply fringed with green beads. Small lamps which could be carried around and hung on a wall had an oval mirror at the back of the chimney to enhance the light. Great care had to be taken not to knock over a lamp as the result could be disastrous.

A cistern beneath the courtyard provided water for domestic use. It was shared between the three families and always ran dry by the end of the summer. When this happened water had to be bought. Bashir, the milkman, who lived in Silwan, also supplied the family with water which he sometimes brought in *qirab* (large bottles made of whole goat skins), or in empty paraffin tins carried on chains attached to a yoke across his shoulders. One full *qirbeh* cost half a bishlik – about a penny. To keep track of how many tins he had delivered, Bashir, who was dumb, as were his many children, used a piece of charcoal to mark up the number on the whitewashed wall outside the kitchen door. The marks were only rubbed off when he had been paid. The water was stored in the kitchen in large earthenware pots. Drinking water for the household had to be obtained elsewhere. It was kept in a *sharbeh* – a porous pottery jug which held it ice-cold. This was placed on a cool window ledge, and had to be replenished frequently.

A woman from the village of Ain Karim sometimes brought them

MALAKEH AND MARGARET, EARLY CHILDHOOD 47

pure spring water in a *jarra* (pottery jar), which she sold along with fresh fruit and vegetables. At other times Mariam and Isquhie would go out through the Zion Gate and walk down to the *sabil*, the beautiful and ornately carved drinking fountain built by order of Suleiman the Magnificent in AD 1536. This fountain, at the head of Bourqet el Sultan (the Sultan's Pool) on the main road to the south, was fed by water which flowed through a pottery aqueduct built in the time of Herod the Great. The source of the water was ancient reservoirs at Arroub near Hebron.

The Sultan's Pool (also known as the Lower Pool of Gihon) served as a catchment for rainwater in winter. In early summer it seethed with frogs and toads. Porters, as well as the poor from the Old City, would come to bathe in it and wash their clothes. When it dried up in the summer it was used as a cattle market.

The Old City was full of ancient cisterns, the largest lying under the Dome of the Rock. Some of these reservoirs, found in the compounds of monasteries and convents, were only put to use at the end of summer when water was short or during the influx of pilgrims. At various points in the city, taps connected to the Roman aqueduct were unlocked early in the morning for about an hour, and anyone who wanted to fill a water pot could do so at no cost.

A Turkish bath, a *hammam* near St Stephen's Gate, was also supplied with Arroub water. Mariam would often take her daughters there, joining other family friends. Women bathed during the day and men had their turn at night. Most families in Jerusalem made use of these baths as they had no facilities at home. Accommodation for relaxing after bathing was provided in a large cool *liwan*, where friends would meet and share food, sherbets and lemon juice before going home.

The *hammam* was always reserved in the morning on the day before the wedding of an Armenian bride, for a ladies' party given by her mother. In her trousseau the bride was given three brass bowls, a *bournous* (bathrobe), towels, soap and perfume, a small carpet, and three pairs of clogs, all for use at the baths. The bridegroom and his friends also gave parties at the *hammam* on the night before the wedding.

5 NURSING IN HEBRON THEN ON TO BEIRUT

When Malakeh and Margaret left school they parted company for a short time. Margaret returned home but Malakeh joined the staff of the German hospital in Jerusalem to train as a nurse. The hospital, run by Kaiserswerth Diakonissen under the direction of Schwester Theodora, had been built in 1893 on the corner of the Street of the Prophets not far from Talitha Cumi school. Over the main entrance is carved a quotation from Isaiah 53:4, 'Er trüg unsre Krankheit und lüd auf sich unsre Schmerzen' (Surely he hath borne our griefs and carried our sorrows). Above it is the order's emblem of the dove carrying an olive branch.

The hospital had a hundred beds, and clinics for out-patients. Malakeh worked hard in the hope that she would soon become a Krankenschwester (hospital nurse). As a probationer she had to wash bandages and utensils that had been used in the operating theatre. Her fingers became infected, and she was advised to leave work and rest at home for a time. She rejoined the family in the Old City house, but soon a fresh opportunity presented itself to both Malakeh and Margaret.

In addition to their charitable work in Jerusalem, a group of Kaiserswerth sisters had established a clinic on the outskirts of the ancient city of Hebron (el Khalil) where they worked among the local population. In 1893 the Mildmay Mission, whose headquarters and hospital were in Bethnal Green, London, took over the work. In July that year the Free Church of Scotland appointed Dr Alexander Paterson and his wife May to run the clinic in Hebron. Dr Paterson was born in Madras where his father had been a medical missionary. He qualified as a doctor in Edinburgh in 1885 and after working for a

NURSING IN HEBRON THEN ON TO BEIRUT

few years in the Mildmay Hospital in London served as a missionary doctor in Cairo and Aden.

In September 1888 boats carrying a group of Galla slaves captured in Abyssinia were intercepted by the British warship HMS *Osprey* while on their way to Mocca. The slaves, all young boys and girls, were rescued and landed in Aden, where they were first housed by the authorities, then moved to the Keith-Falconer mission of the Free Church of Scotland. It was later decided to send this group of children, numbering 22 girls and 42 boys, to the mission's school at Lovedale in South Africa. Alexander Paterson was put in charge of the group and they reached their destination in August 1891. He stayed at Lovedale for a year, during which time he married May Muirhead, daughter of the headmistress of the girls' section.

Dr Paterson was in his thirties when he and his wife came to Hebron. He spoke fluent Arabic, and his previous experience in the Arab world gave him an understanding of the people. In addition to enlarging the clinic Dr Paterson was to open a small hospital. In 1901 the Mildmay Mission relinquished responsibility and the work was transferred to the United Free Church of Scotland, under the direction of their Jewish Missionary Committee. Dr Paterson, who remained in charge, bought a small plot of land on behalf of the committee on which to build the new hospital. In the meantime a house outside the town was rented and used as a hospital, since no Christians were permitted to live in the centre of Hebron. This spacious house, surrounded by vineyards, had been built for the Kaimakam (local governor) Farid beg. It was known locally as Khair el Din and had at one time been used as a hotel, the Kamnitz. The Patersons rented another house nearby in which to live themselves. Farid beg helped them and was in full support of the medical work they had come to do among his people.

The hospital was often in need of local staff and Mrs Paterson, with her previous experience at Lovedale, was made responsible for recruiting them. On a visit to Talitha Cumi she asked the Diakonissen if any of the girls who had recently finished their schooling might be interested in training as nurses. The deaconesses at once thought of Malakeh and Margaret and sent Mrs Paterson to the Old City house to speak to them.

In those days it was not customary for women to work away from home, but after much thought and consultation with their parents Margaret and Malakeh decided to go to Hebron. As their father,

50 ARMENIANS OF JERUSALEM

Melkon, was himself a herbalist and practitioner of local cures he encouraged his daughters to enter the nursing profession. Mrs Paterson suggested that Margaret should start her training immediately, while Malakeh was offered domestic work in the doctor's house until she was older.

The hospital had twenty beds but they were not often fully occupied, as except in the most desperate cases most patients preferred to return home after treatment to be cared for by their families. The outpatients' department was attended by thousands of people each year. Dr Paterson treated those who came in, and also rode out for long distances to surrounding villages on his horse, Lulu, to visit the sick who could not come to him.

Many quarrels and feuds took place between villagers in the Hebron area and as a consequence the doctor had to attend to stab wounds. *Ramad*, sore eyes, were common among children in summer, especially during the fig-picking season when it was caused by contact with milky juices exuded by the ripe fruit. Malaria, dysentery and other stomach ailments were common. Burns, caused during the making of gunpowder (used for blasting and quarrying stone), were frequent. In 1902 a cholera epidemic broke out in Hebron and many died. Paterson, affectionately called by the inhabitants *el hakim* (the doctor), was trusted by all who knew him in south Palestine, where he was to serve for 29 years.

Margaret joined the hospital staff in the autumn of 1905 to start her nursing training. Miss Bell, a Mildmay deaconess who had joined the Patersons in 1903, had succeeded Miss Vartan as matron in 1906. Miss Reid, who came from Scotland, was staff nurse; the dispenser was Miss Marian Wilson. A Christian Arab, Mr Salim Bawarshi, was general factotum and helped in the clinic. He later became a qualified anaesthetist. His son, Najib, was on the staff as a young orderly, and one of his duties was to help Margaret wind bandages on a wooden spool. He was attracted to her and asked for her hand in marriage, but she did not agree to his proposal.

Margaret had grown into an attractive young woman, due not only to her looks but also her light spirit. In the east the saying goes that no matter how beautiful you are, if you lack lightness you are worth nothing. An Egyptian proverb illustrates this, suggesting that a beautiful woman sell some of her beauty and exchange it for *khuffa* – lightness. Malakeh, too, was handsome in her own right. She had good bone formation and a well-formed chin which did her proud in

NURSING IN HEBRON THEN ON TO BEIRUT   51

profile photographs. Both of them had inherited large, expressive brown eyes.

Malakeh joined her sister in Hebron as a maid in the Paterson household. The doctor's house was furnished in oriental style and boasted a fine collection of Persian carpets and ornaments which had been brought from Cairo. On arrival Malakeh was put in the charge of Miss Grace Kerr Walker, who had been the Paterson's housekeeper since 1895. She was shown around, told what duties would be expected of her and given a tiny sparsely furnished attic room to herself. Miss Grace did all the cooking – lovely scones and pies, which were always available for visitors who came from Scotland to see the work of the hospital. She was rather bossy, and spoke with a strong Scots accent which Malakeh at first found difficult to understand. Miss Grace was very fond of cats, and accumulated a large number of strays who waited for her outside the kitchen door where she usually fed them on tinned sardines – an extravagance which Malakeh found deeply shocking in a country where there was such poverty.

Malakeh's duties included cleaning, polishing silver and brass, ironing, and waiting at table. Both women wore black dresses, white starched caps and aprons, as was the custom in European households. Badawi, a young *khalili* (Hebronite) looked after the gardens and was in charge of the doctor's horse, Lulu. He also went shopping for both the household and the hospital in the main *suq* in Hebron. Plumbing was inadequate in the buildings and there were no indoor lavatories. Badawi had the unpleasant task of emptying the sand closets daily into pits which he dug in a vineyard near by. Among the daily staff were two Jewish women who came out from the town on Mondays to do the laundry for the house and the hospital.

The Patersons lived in style and frequently entertained other missionaries and visiting foreigners. They always dressed for dinner and Dr Paterson's red cummerbund, which he wore every evening, and the swishing sound of the ladies' long silk skirts made a lasting impression on Malakeh. Their work over in the dining-room, Malakeh and Miss Grace would sit down to a meal in the kitchen. Badawi was not allowed to join them: he collected his food and ate it by himself in the corridor outside.

The Patersons and the Scottish staff often went for weekends to Jerusalem, where they stayed at St George's Close with Bishop Blyth and his family. Malakeh and Margaret were allowed home once a month. For the return to Hebron they would join the Scots nurses at

52 ARMENIANS OF JERUSALEM

Jaffa Gate and be driven in a diligence holding five persons, drawn by three horses. Seats had to be booked in advance and the journey took over four hours with stops on the way. In the winter when it was bitterly cold the foreign missionaries had blankets and hotwater bottles provided by the hospital to keep them warm – but Malakeh and Margaret were not included, perhaps because 'local' nurses were supposed not to feel the cold. This slight was never forgotten and the story was repeated for many years. Three stops were made on the way to Hebron: the first at the khan near Solomon's Pools, where a rest was taken and the horses watered; then on to a roadside spring at Arroub. The last stop was made at St Philip's Fountain, the supposed site of the conversion of the Ethiopian (Acts 8:36–39).

Whilst at Hebron Margaret and Malakeh saw each other frequently, although at first they did not live in the same building. Hebron was a Muslim town; women wore the veil and never ventured out alone. There was a small ancient Jewish quarter, the inhabitants of which co-existed harmoniously with the Arab population and remained unmolested throughout Ottoman rule. Margaret and Malakeh spent most of their time in the hospital and did not visit the centre of town, except on one occasion when they were invited by the Jewish washerwomen to a Passover *seder*. They sometimes joined other members of staff on walks to Abraham's Oak at Mamre and to the gardens of the Russian monastery and hospice nearby.

On Saturdays Mrs Paterson conducted a choir practice of the metrical psalms and hymns to be used the following day. On Sunday mornings an Arabic service was held in the house of a blind Lutheran evangelist, Mu'allem (teacher) Elias. On Sunday afternoons Dr Paterson conducted an English service in the hospital for the Christians on his staff. No services were held in the wards or outpatients' clinic.

During their training at Hebron Margaret and Malakeh's father Melkon, by then aged 68, had had a slight stroke. When in Jerusalem Dr Paterson frequently called to see him at the Old City house, which the family greatly appreciated. Melkon was obliged to give up his work as a barber and from then on the household had to rely on their savings. These had been deposited with the Armenian Convent, which acted as bankers for members of the *kaghakatsi* community. Melkon had to sell the rooms and plot of land which he owned opposite the Muslim cemetery in Mamillah and his barber shop at the top of David

NURSING IN HEBRON THEN ON TO BEIRUT

Street was taken on by Karnig, an Armenian watchmaker who remained there for many years. It is now a souvenir shop.

Malakeh and Margaret were fluent in German and Arabic but had little English. Mrs Paterson gave them lessons and they quickly learned to speak, read and write. Later Margaret went on an intensive course with Mrs Theophilus Smith in Jerusalem, who gave her a lesson each day. Mrs Paterson recognized that Margaret and Malakeh had potential and were willing to progress, so she decided to apply for scholarships for them at the nursing school of the Syrian Protestant College in Beirut.

The college was founded in 1866 by an American missionary, Dr Daniel Bliss, who came to teach English, philosophy and history to a group of Arab students. The work grew, land was bought outside the city in Ras Beirut and college buildings put up as money came in. In 1920 it was renamed the American University of Beirut. By then both Dr Daniel Bliss and his son Howard, who succeeded him as president of the college in 1903, had died. In their honour Omar Da'uk, the administrator of Beirut who had been appointed by the departing Turks, named the road leading to the university 'Rue Bliss' – and so it remains to this day.

On the strength of Mrs Paterson's recommendation both Margaret and Malakeh were accepted, and it was hoped that after graduation they would return to nurse in Hebron. Meanwhile Malakeh had moved from the Paterson household to become a trainee nurse in the hospital. As she was a year and a half younger than Margaret, she had to wait until she was over seventeen to start at the nursing college. Theirs was a bold decision and they were the first women of the *kaghakatsi* to go abroad to a university. They remained on the list of alumni of the American University of Beirut to the end of their lives.

Margaret bade farewell to her colleagues at Hebron, packed her belongings in a large wicker trunk made by blind students at Schneller's orphanage and prepared to leave for Beirut. On the day of her departure her mother went with her in a carriage to the railway station to see her off to Jaffa. There she stayed for two days with her cousins the Gazmararians, until *The Khedive* arrived from Egypt to take passengers on to Beirut. Movses Gazmararian, son of Garabed, lived with his family in a lovely old house right on the sea front in the Armenian quarter of Jaffa close to the port.

Jaffa port was not deep enough for ships to tie up at a quay, the sea was usually very rough and small boats were used to ferry passengers

54 ARMENIANS OF JERUSALEM

to and from waiting vessels. The voyage from Jaffa to Beirut took one night, most passengers preferring to spend the time on deck. On arrival Margaret was met by a member of the college staff sent by Mrs Dale.

Mrs Mary Bliss Dale, widowed daughter of Dr Daniel Bliss, was the first superintendent of the college hospitals. Her brother, Dr Howard Bliss DD, was president of the college at the time. There were three nursing pavilions, one for women's diseases, which came under Miss Jane E. Van Zandt RU, who was principal and tutor of the nursing school. The second, for eye diseases, was directed by Miss Minor; the third, for children, by Miss March. Franklin J. Moore, MA, MD, was the secretary. All the students, Arab, Jewish or Armenian, were on probation for six months. Only when it was felt that they could continue with the course were they issued with nurses' uniforms. Students moved from one pavilion to the other for fixed periods to widen their knowledge of nursing. The course comprised three years' study plus one year of practical work; attendance at surgical operations was part of the curriculum. There were no expenses apart from the cost of books; a *majeedy* (silver Turkish coin issued during the reign of Sultan Abdul-Medjid 1839–61), worth a quarter of a gold pound, was given to them monthly as pocket money.

In 1910 Malakeh joined her sister at the nursing school in Beirut. Margaret was already an intermediate when Malakeh started her six months' probation. 1910 also brought the news, in a letter bordered in black, of the death of their father. He had been bedridden for the past two years, nursed devotedly at home by his wife, Mariam. Her cousin Minas el Kahwati was of great help and stayed with Mariam and Isquhie until the end. Minas made the arrangements for the funeral, which was attended by many friends and relatives. Melkon was buried in the family plot in the Armenian cemetery of Pergeech on Mount Zion. Inscribed on his gravestone are the words:

Here lies the body of *berber* Melkoni Hovhannesian of Jerusalem who came to rest in the Lord in his 75th year. Peace to his soul. 1910.

Since early childhood Malakeh and Margaret had been away from home in schools and institutions and had never known their father well. Isquhie, on the other hand, had lived at home and was a devoted daughter.

NURSING IN HEBRON THEN ON TO BEIRUT 55

The two sisters enjoyed life in the cosmopolitan city of Beirut. Time was spent visiting friends in the Hamra, walking to the Manara and then along the coast to view the Pigeon Rocks. There were lectures, debates and social events in the main college buildings in which Malakeh and Margaret and the other nursing students joined. With their friends they often left the heat of Beirut and spent their free time in the *jabal* (mountains) where the air was cool. Picnicking under the umbrella pines with the sound of cicadas in their ears, eating *tabouleh* and other Lebanese foods, was much enjoyed, the pleasure enhanced by the view of St George's Bay and the sea beyond. During the summer vacations, which lasted for two months, the sisters returned home to Jerusalem. Their cousin Krikor, who was studying medicine in the college at that time, used to join them on *The Khedive*.

In her last year Margaret became a senior, and at the end of the academic year passed her final exams and graduated. These exams were oral and practical, with no written work. It was now 1913. As was the custom her certificate was later framed and hung in the Old City house for all to see. Malakeh, in the meantime, went on with her studies in the nursing school.

After leaving the college Margaret volunteered to work for a short time in the tuberculosis hospital at Azounieh in the mountains above Beirut. She then returned to Jerusalem where she was offered a position as staff nurse in the Church Missionary Society's hospital in Jaffa. She accepted but did not stay long as the missionaries in charge were strict: the staff were not allowed to go out alone and frequent attendance at prayers and services was compulsory. Margaret felt that this was not the place for her and decided on a change.

An old friend, Victoria abu Fadil, who with her husband ran a large book and stationery store in Cairo, invited Margaret to come and stay while she looked for a nursing post. Margaret accepted and left for Egypt, travelling on *The Khedive* once again. There were many hospitals in the Middle East, some run by religious orders, others by European societies with their own foreign staff. In Cairo there was a large German hospital, also run by Diakonissen, under the direction of Schwester Maria Graff. She was glad to find in Margaret a qualified German-speaking applicant and offered her a position as staff nurse. Margaret's first duties were in the isolation section, where she looked after extreme cases of smallpox, the like of which she never came across again. She found this work intolerable, but her problem was soon solved when Mrs Dale wrote from Beirut to ask if she would

56 ARMENIANS OF JERUSALEM

come back to help nurse her aged mother, Mrs Daniel Bliss, who was by then an invalid. Margaret agreed, returned, and undertook the night duty. The two sisters were pleased to be together once again in Beirut.

Malakeh graduated at the end of her course and was awarded a certificate, as her sister had been the year before. This was headed 'Syrian Protestant College Training School for Nurses' and signed by Howard Bliss, Franklin J. Moore, Jane E. Van Zandt and Mary Bliss Dale:

> This certificate witnesses that Malakeh H. Melkon has satisfactorily completed the studies prescribed in the curriculum of the Training School for Nurses of the Syrian Protestant College including the practical ward work assigned to her during the course of her studies. Given at Beirut, Syria, the 16th day of June AD 1914.

Attached to it was a gold seal embossed with the cedar of Lebanon.

Both Malakeh and Margaret were now qualified nurses, and were soon to be presented with an exciting new challenge.

6 ALEPPO AND THE FIRST WORLD WAR

It had been brought to the attention of the wali (governor) of Aleppo by the administrator and doctors that the town's municipal hospital, Ghooraba Khasta Khanasi, was run down and needed reorganization. In the summer of 1914 the wali was advised to apply to the Syrian Protestant College in Beirut for graduate nurses. His request came to Mrs Dale, who with other members of the faculty agreed that Malakeh and Margaret would be suitable candidates. She called them into her office to ask if they would consider going to work in Aleppo, telling them that it would be a challenge to introduce modern nursing standards in the municipal hospital. She encouraged them and was confident that they would be able to cope. Malakeh and Margaret were taken aback by such a daunting proposal and asked for time to think the matter over. After much discussion they accepted and Mrs Dale, always keen to find positions of responsibility for her pupils, was delighted.

The last few days in Beirut were hectic and sadly there was no time to return to Jerusalem to see their mother and sister. There were many farewell visits, and shopping and packing to do before departure. Mrs Dale and Miss Van Zandt were there to see them off very early in the morning at the railway station. At Rayak junction they changed trains, leaving the main Beirut–Damascus line to join the line running north through Homs and Hama, reaching Aleppo twelve hours later. The wali had sent Kamal beg (the *sertabib* or senior doctor) and Ja'afar beg, the administrator of the hospital, to meet them at the station: so began a new life in Aleppo.

A vilayet, or province, of Asiatic Turkey, Aleppo was a fascinating city with unusually large covered bazaars, spacious khans and gardens. It owed its prosperity to its position on the caravan route to Baghdad,

58 ARMENIANS OF JERUSALEM

Persia and India. Orchards extended for miles along the river Kweik where residents of Aleppo were allowed to pick freely, as long as the fruit was eaten on the spot. Aleppo was a centre for trade in fruits, cereals and various nuts, especially pistachios (*fustuq halabi*), the Aleppo nuts famous throughout the Middle East. Other products on display in the vast *suqs* included carpets, leather goods, copper and brass, lengths of silk to make *qanabeez*, bales of cotton and woollen textiles all produced and woven locally. It was in this town, situated on the borders of the desert and surrounded by a belt of green, that Malakeh and Margaret were to spend the years of the war which was about to begin.

The hospital, housed in an old building, was administered by the municipality. It was situated in the centre of the town opposite the imposing Citadel of Aleppo at the eastern end of the *suqs*. Margaret was appointed matron and Malakeh staff nurse. They were the only two women nurses in the hospital. Their wages were four and three gold pounds a month respectively, with full board and uniforms provided. They shared a spacious bedroom and had a large sitting-room where they were able to entertain friends. Doctors and other members of staff would join them there for coffee. They also had their own dining-room and kitchen. An elderly temperamental Armenian lady, Umm Asadour, cooked for them and prepared both Arab and Armenian dishes. Kamal beg inspected the kitchen daily and made sure that the food was of the best quality.

Malakeh and Margaret took over the running of a hospital that, as Mrs Dale had predicted, was run-down and disorganized. There were about 50 beds in the wards, some for men and some for women, but the number of men admitted far exceeded the number of women. Surgery was not performed except in an emergency. Most of the patients suffered from various endemic illnesses. An isolated section housed women with venereal diseases, where quarrelling patients often had to be separated and pacified. Equipment, medicines, beds and bedding, pillows, sheets and blankets were in short supply and many patients had to sleep on mattresses on the floor in large, draughty, vaulted corridors. Plumbing by modern standards was virtually non-existent. Cash to pay expenses and wages was often as much as three months overdue. The hospital accountant, Murat, whose duty it was to fetch money from the *saraya* (headquarters), would frequently be told that funds earmarked for the hospital had not been received from Istanbul, and he would return empty-handed.

ALEPPO AND THE FIRST WORLD WAR 59

Criminals and lunatics, many of whom were chained to the walls, were kept in a separate building within the hospital compound. This sad place was maintained by a Syrian Arab employee, Abu Addour, who was responsible to Margaret. She herself made a daily inspection of the premises and saw to it that the patients had enough to eat. This was the worst part of her work. The sight of mentally confused and violent people in chains staring through an iron grill was a harrowing experience which she was never able to forget.

Dr Iskander, an Armenian, ran the out-patients' clinic. Dr Kamal, who was Turkish and came from Istanbul, visited the wards in the evening with Margaret and a pharmacist, who would take the prescriptions and later bring back the medicines. Dr Aram Altounyan, a noted Armenian physician who ran his own private hospital in Aleppo, came in occasionally for consultations.

After their first few weeks in the hospital Margaret and Malakeh, wearing their uniforms and Beirut caps, were taken by Kamal beg to meet the wali and his wife at their residence. They were warmly greeted by the wali, who conversed with them in fluent German. His wife spoke in Turkish, which Malakeh and Margaret understood, although Syrian Arabic was generally spoken in the hospital. Before leaving they were served with Damascus sweetmeats and small cups of Turkish coffee. A month later the wali was invited by the doctors and Kamal beg to inspect the hospital and see the improved conditions for himself. He was very impressed and turning to his entourage said: 'It is obvious that there are trained women nurses in this building now.' Malakeh and Margaret were pleased. They had worked hard to put the hospital in order, helped only by untrained nursing colleagues but with the full support of the medical staff. A surprise visit from Miss Van Zandt, who had come from Beirut to see them also gave great pleasure. She was shown round and told of the difficulties they had encountered. Messages and greetings were sent to Mrs Dale and colleagues at the College Hospital in Beirut.

During their stay in Aleppo both Malakeh and Margaret made many friends. While training in Beirut they had met a young medical student who came from Aleppo. After he qualified Dr Kayyali returned to his home town, where he opened a private clinic. He and his family befriended both Malakeh and Margaret, who were frequently invited to meals at the Kayyali home. During the month of Ramadan they were sometimes privileged to join the family in breaking the fast after the cannon sounded at sunset. These meals consisted of

60 ARMENIANS OF JERUSALEM

a variety of nourishing Arab foods served on round tin-plated copper trays. Rice smothered with meat and fried golden-brown pine nuts, marrows and vine leaves stuffed with rice and ground lamb, *karshat* (tripe) stuffed with a mixture of rice, chickpeas and ground meat cooked in broth – these were among other delicious dishes served. After the meal the sweetmeats for which Syria is noted were handed round, amongst them *katayif* – round pancakes stuffed with ground walnuts or white cheese, then fried in *samneh* (clarified butter) and covered with syrup. The meal ended with Turkish coffee.

Abu Addour, who had taken a great interest in the welfare of the ladies from the day of their arrival, always escorted them when they were invited for an evening outside the hospital. He had already told them that, as women with no relatives around, they were now under his protection. He would put his hand on his chest and refer to them as *banati* (my daughters). All three would set out in the cool of the evening through darkened streets, Abu Addour carrying a *fanous*, a hurricane lamp hanging on a stick, to light the way. He walked a few paces in front of them and at intervals called out '*ya satir!*' – an indication that women were on the scene and men should make themselves scarce. When they reached their destination Abu Addour too would be given a meal while waiting to take Margaret and Malakeh back to the hospital.

The Kayyalis had a lovely house with a central courtyard off which opened many rooms. The surrounding walls were draped with jasmine, roses and other climbing plants. In tubs grew a popular sweet-scented shrub-jasmine, *fileh* (*Jasminum sambukum*), which added to the delicious scents that filled the evening air. In the courtyard stood a pool full of brilliant goldfish which had as its centrepiece an antique carved stone column surmounted by a small basin. Through it ran a fountain; the dripping water cooled the air and the murmuring sound provided a pleasant background to gentle conversation. The hospitality shown to them was unsurpassable: both Malakeh and Margaret were invited to visit many Muslim families, where they were treated like relatives and made to feel at home. Among other hostesses the wali's wife invited them to receptions on special days. They did not, however, mix much with other Armenians who were living and working in Aleppo at the time. Perhaps the fact that they were attached to a Turkish hospital was resented.

Hardly had they taken up their duties in the hospital when the 1914 war broke out in Europe and Turkey was soon to ally herself with

ALEPPO AND THE FIRST WORLD WAR

Germany. For the first few months life continued normally and the town did not lack anything in the way of food. It was not long, however, before all able-bodied men were called up to the Turkish army. Citizens were reminded of their duty to enlist by the nightly beating of a drum through the streets of Aleppo.

Postal services were erratic and Margaret and Malakeh were unable to communicate with their mother and sister in Jerusalem, nor were they able to take leave and return home. One day much to their surprise they were told that a soldier in the Turkish army had called to see them. They were delighted when he turned out to be Hovhannes, son of Zeron, one of their neighbours in the courtyard at home in Jerusalem. He brought them news of Isquhie and their mother and as he was returning next day they sent back a letter and a small box of *baklaweh*.

The wali had achieved his objective – the smooth running of the municipal hospital. Now that the country was at war it was decided that Malakeh and Margaret should be moved to a military hospital, where there was greater need for trained nurses. This hospital was a few miles north of the city, cut off from the bustle of civilian life. They were both very sorry to leave Abu Addour and their many friends in the town and were apprehensive of the problems they might find ahead.

The military hospital also needed reorganization. Malakeh and Margaret were the only two qualified women on the staff, although there were many *tamarjis* (male nurses). The doctors were all military men of Turkish and German origin. Conditions in this hospital were primitive to a degree – there was a lack of medical equipment, not enough beds for the patients, and sick soldiers had to lie on mattresses on the floor in huge rooms. Medicines, bandages, gauze and cotton were in short supply. The food, which was badly cooked, was sent in pails from an army kitchen some miles away.

To add to their problems, Armenian women who had fled the genocide of 1915 arrived at the doors of the hospital in a pitiful condition as a result of their horrifying experiences at the hands of the Turks. Those who survived the long trek across the desert had swollen ankles, and were exhausted and starving. Margaret and Malakeh tried to be of help whenever possible by giving out surplus food and attending to sores and injuries.

Many fleeing Armenians took refuge in the Arab provinces of the Ottoman empire, where they were not molested. In Aleppo deportation of Armenians was not strictly enforced by the Turkish authorities for fear of criticism from the numerous diplomats and foreign residents in the city. Little was it realized at the time that these displaced people were never to return to their towns and villages again.

The influx of refugees brought in disease, smallpox, cholera and typhus. In 1916 an epidemic of typhus broke out and thousands, Turks, Arabs, soldiers and civilians, died. The hospital could hardly cope and every available space was converted into makeshift wards. Mortality was high, as most patients were only admitted in the last stages of the disease. Both Margaret and Malakeh rose to the occasion and worked devotedly, witnessing the ordeals and suffering of many. Margaret herself caught the fever and was very ill. She was isolated, treated by a German-Jewish doctor, nursed by Malakeh, and eventually recovered to start work again.

Years later the two sisters relived their experiences at the military hospital in Aleppo when they saw the film *Lawrence of Arabia*, which was shown in Jerusalem in 1965.

Towards the end of 1916 the two sisters informed the wali that they could no longer go on working in the military hospital. As war continued conditions had become much harsher and they felt their isolation. Malakeh and Margaret, who had been together since their childhood at Talitha Cumi school, were now destined to part.

Margaret applied for work with the German Red Cross and was immediately accepted. She was to travel south to field hospitals in the Gaza and Beersheba area of Palestine. Malakeh was taken on as staff nurse in a hospital in Aleppo which had been newly opened for German officers. This hospital was staffed by German doctors and nursing sisters, and the sick and wounded were brought in from the southern front. At the time there was a great concentration of Turkish forces in Aleppo. It was now about January 1917. Malakeh and Margaret parted, and they were not to see each other again for several years.

Before leaving Aleppo Margaret deposited her savings in a safe at the Baron Hotel which was owned and run by an established Armenian family, the Mazloumians. Arrangements were made for her to travel south by rail and she was to join members of the German Red Cross at the railway station in the Selimiyeh quarter. The group spent a few days in Beirut,then continued south to Ramleh where they had to wait for medicines and stores which they were to collect and take with them to the front. They finally arrived at their destination, a large field

ALEPPO AND THE FIRST WORLD WAR

hospital in the vicinity of Gaza. The sick and wounded were housed in tents scattered over a wide plain. Margaret was given Red Cross uniform and her meals were taken at the officers' table. To enable her to go from tent to tent she had to ride on horseback, which she did sitting side-saddle wearing a specially provided riding skirt.

By January 1917 the British forces under Sir Archibald Murray had come up from Egypt and reached Rafah on the Palestine frontier. Their aim was to capture Gaza, but the first attack failed and both sides resorted to trench warfare. The sound of heavy gunfire was easily audible in the German field hospital and was a strain on the staff's frayed nerves. Many wounded soldiers were brought in daily in addition to those who had fallen sick with malaria, dysentery and exhaustion. As summer approached water became scarce and conditions deteriorated.

In July 1917 Murray was replaced by Sir Edmund Allenby, and by the autumn preparations were ready to launch a new attack. In the German field hospital the staff were given orders to be ready to move north at a moment's notice. Beersheba was attacked first and fell to the British on 31 October 1917. This opened the way to Gaza, which was bombarded from air, sea and land, and found abandoned when British troops entered on 7 November. All that remained of the town were the cactus hedges surrounding heaps of rubble. The campaign was so successful that the British advanced much further north and had captured the town of Jaffa by mid-November 1917. In the face of the advancing British army Margaret retreated with the officers and staff of the German Red Cross as far as Jerusalem. It was there that she decided to leave them and rejoin her mother and Isquhie at home in the Old City.

Conditions for civilians in Jerusalem during the 1914–18 war were harsh and there was much poverty. Food was scarce, fuel was almost unobtainable, there were no matches, and to overcome this problem charcoal was ignited by reflecting the sun's rays through a piece of glass. The flame was then shared among several neighbours. Few households could afford lamps; the city went to bed at sunset and rose at dawn. Turkish and German army officers came first and all available supplies were kept for their use. Civilian families were issued with a small loaf of bread daily, barely enough to feed four. Trees were ruthlessly cut down and converted into fuel for running trains. It is said that in the hills surrounding the village of Artas near Bethlehem about 3,000 established oaks were felled. During their retreat the

64 ARMENIANS OF JERUSALEM

Turks removed money from banks, government records and registers, drugs and surgical instruments from hospitals and pharmacies, furniture and stocks of food. Before the end of the war the patriarchs and high officials of the ancient churches were exiled to Damascus, leaving priests and laymen to carry on as best they could.

In the meantime General Allenby had reached the outskirts of Jerusalem. In order to avoid fighting within the city he ordered his troops to surround it. On 9 December 1917 the city surrendered. Two days later Allenby made his solemn entry on foot through the Jaffa Gate, and at the entrance to the Citadel made the following proclamation:-

To the inhabitants of Jerusalem the blessed and the people dwelling in its vicinity:

The defeat inflicted upon the Turks by the troops under my command has resulted in the occupation of your city by my forces. I therefore here and now proclaim it to be under Martial Law, under which form of administration it will remain so long as military considerations make it necessary.

However, lest any of you should be alarmed by reason of your experiences at the hands of the enemy who has retired, I hereby inform you that it is my desire that every person should pursue his lawful business without fear of interruption. Furthermore, since your city is regarded with affection by the adherents of three of the great religions of mankind, and its soil has been consecrated by the prayers and pilgrimages of devout people of those three religions for many centuries, therefore do I make known to you that every sacred building, monument, holy spot, shrine, traditional site, endowment, pious bequest or customary place of prayer of whatsoever form of the three religions, will be maintained and protected according to the existing customs and beliefs of those to whose faiths they are sacred.

Margaret, Isquhie and their mother, whose house was just a stone's throw from the Jaffa Gate, were able to join the crowds to witness this great event. Hundreds of people from all walks of life, Christian, Muslim and Jewish, priests from religious communities, porters, the rich and the poor, crammed the Jaffa Gate area. Many climbed on to roofs, some on to the balconies of the Austrian post office building opposite the Citadel. The Arabs of Jerusalem and Palestine were

ALEPPO AND THE FIRST WORLD WAR 65

delighted to be rid of 400 years of Turkish rule. There was one immediate disappointment however, the announced introduction of martial law.

The Arabs of Palestine felt that they had contributed to the eviction of the Turks by bravely assisting the incoming British troops, by gathering intelligence, and by mass desertions from the Turkish army. They had been suppressed by the Turks over centuries, they were poor, demoralized and lacked leadership. At last they seemed to have a chance to build up a social and political structure of their own. In their simplicity they now hoped for a better life under temporary British rule, believing that this would lead to the independence that had been promised to them. At the time they did not know that duplicitous and contradictory promises had been made to both Arab and Jewish leaders concerning the land which they each claimed. In England on 2 November 1917 the Balfour Declaration had been made public, but Allenby refused to allow it to be published in Palestine lest it should upset the Arab population.

The war in the rest of the country continued for some time longer. There was a lull after the capture of Jerusalem, and all attempts by the Turks to recapture the city were ineffectual. Allenby's army advanced slowly on all fronts, and one by one the towns in the north were taken. Haifa and Acre fell on 23 September 1918, and the capture of Samakh and Tiberias on the shores of the sea of Galilee, after a fierce battle on the 25th, ended organized Turkish resistance in Palestine. In Syria, Damascus fell to the Allied forces on 1 October and Aleppo on 26 October. A few days later, on 31 October 1918, the Turkish Armistice was announced. The Ottoman Empire in Syria and Palestine had crumbled after four centuries.

A new era had begun and there was relief amongst the population. On 12 November 1918 a service of thanksgiving for the end of the war was held at the Church of the Holy Sepulchre. Margaret, Isquhie and their mother attended amongst hundreds of other Jerusalemites. The galleries were packed with people who showered those below with flowers. A prominent position was given to the military governor, Colonel Ronald Storrs, who sat on a golden throne placed on a dais. Afterwards a reception for the new administration was held at the Greek Orthodox Patriarchate.

Five days later on 17 November 1918 a liberation day service took place at St George's Anglican Cathedral. The church was crammed with religious dignitaries from all denominations, representatives of

66 ARMENIANS OF JERUSALEM

the Syria and Palestine Relief Fund, the American Red Cross, the YMCA and YWCA. Bishop Blyth's successor, Rennie MacInnes, who had been consecrated Bishop in Jerusalem at Westminster Abbey in 1914, was in Egypt at the time and unable to attend. The text used for the sermon was taken from Psalm 126:

> When the Lord turned away the captivity of Sion: then were we like unto them that dream. Then was our mouth filled with laughter: and our tongue with joy.

Margaret stayed at home in Jerusalem until the situation calmed down. When she heard of the fall of Aleppo to the allies, she decided to travel back there to collect her savings deposited at the Baron Hotel. The family were also anxious about Malakeh, as nothing had been heard from her since the end of the war. Margaret obtained a travel permit from the British military authorities and returned to Aleppo, where she was told that Malakeh had already left for Istanbul with other nurses on a German hospital train. Margaret collected her money, but in the train on the way back to Jerusalem her purse holding all her savings was stolen. On return home she was confronted with another decision: Abu Zeron's second son, Migerditch, who was studying in Paris, proposed marriage. Margaret's family were not keen on the match and neither did she wish it herself, so he was refused.

To be of help to her mother and Isquhie Margaret needed to look for a nursing position to earn money. She was advised to see Colonel Scrimgeour who was the military medical administrator with OETA (Occupied Enemy Territory Administration). His office was in the old Fast Hotel. When they met, she asked him if Dr Paterson was returning to reopen the hospital in Hebron: if so, she would like to rejoin his staff.

Dr Paterson and the remaining foreign staff had left Hebron at the end of October 1914 and his house and the hospital were ransacked by the Turks directly after their departure. Luckily their personal belongings had already been stored at the Moravian leper home in Jerusalem, and the mission archives were safely deposited with the American consul, Dr Otis A. Glazebrook. Dr Paterson and the staff were confined to the Olivet Hotel in Jerusalem until the end of December, when Dr Glazebrook arranged for them to leave via the port of Jaffa on the US battleship *Tennessee*. Dr Glazebrook was of utmost help to British nationals during his term as consul from 1914

ALEPPO AND THE FIRST WORLD WAR

67

to 1920, and at his farewell dinner in appreciation he was presented with a silver tray by the British community.

On arrival in England Dr Paterson had joined the British army, and in June 1917 he was sent to the Egypt Expeditionary Force hospital in Kantara. When Palestine was liberated he returned to Hebron and was appointed principal medical officer of the district, where he organized relief work. He was to reopen the mission clinic in 1920 and he continued to work there until May 1922. Then, as a consequence of deep disagreement with the home board of his mission, he resigned. The work was handed over to the Church Missionary Society and the following year was taken on by the Anglican bishop in Jerusalem. Before leaving for good Dr Paterson was handed a signed and sealed testimonial from the sheikhs of the mosque and the people of Hebron, expressing their appreciation for all his humanitarian work amongst the people of south Palestine over 29 years.

Colonel Scrimgeour told Margaret that Dr Paterson had returned but was now engaged in relief work. Instead he offered her a position in Ramallah at the Friends' Boys School, which had been converted into a British military hospital. She accepted, but only stayed there for a few months before she was transferred to the municipal hospital on the Jaffa road in Jerusalem.

Her next move was to be the last in her professional nursing career. Early in 1919 she was appointed matron of the former Turkish government hospital in Jaffa, now under British military administration. She remained there as matron for over a year and left the hospital to be married.

7 MALAKEH, NURSE AND MIDWIFE

Malakeh continued to work at the German hospital in Aleppo which, in contrast to the Turkish municipal and military hospitals, was well run by qualified nursing sisters. There she made many friends among the Germans, both lay and religious. For most of the time she nursed patients with ear complaints, worked in the outpatients' clinic and in her spare time volunteered to help in a military canteen. After Aleppo fell to the allies at the end of October 1918 the hospital had to close. Orders were received that the German staff, together with the sick and wounded, were to be repatriated. A hospital train would take them north as far as Istanbul. The railway between Istanbul and Aleppo had only been opened by Turkey early in October 1918, just before the war ended. Forced labour was used, the arduous tunnelling through the Taurus mountains completed by Armenian captives.

Malakeh's next step was to set the course for her future. She wanted to specialize in midwifery and felt that an opportunity had come her way. After consulting Dr Seige and others on the staff, she asked whether she might accompany her colleagues to Germany for further study. They encouraged her and advised that when she reached Berlin she should apply for a place in the university medical school. In appreciation for her loyal and efficient nursing Dr Seige and other doctors gave her references, which she placed in a large brown envelope with her certificate awarded in Beirut.

The train journey seemed endless: there were stops for days in the middle of nowhere as there was no wood to fire the engines. The nurses were all crammed together in one carriage while the rest of the train was full of soldiers, sick and wounded. During the journey the nurses had to look after the patients as best they could. A particular problem for the small number of women amongst so many men was

MALAKEH, NURSE AND MIDWIFE 69

lack of privacy and of lavatories. With ingenuity they resorted to scooped out water melons which they used when necessary as chamber pots. This amusing side of the journey was related by Malakeh to close friends in a hushed voice when she eventually returned to Jerusalem. Food was rationed, medicines were in short supply, and the absence of toilet facilities added to the discomfort of the journey. These problems were minor compared to the cloud of depression that hung over the passengers. They were retreating in defeat and were uncertain of the conditions of civilian life at home in Germany.

The train crossed the Taurus mountains and on reaching Konya stopped for two days to replenish supplies. Winter had set in, it was bitterly cold and snow lay everywhere. After another tiring journey they eventually reached Haidarpasha, the rail terminus for Istanbul. There the group was split up and placed in two internment camps, one at Kadiköy and the other at Üsküdar (Scutari) on the shores of the Sea of Marmara. Malakeh, with some of the other nurses and patients, was interned in a large tented camp at Kadiköy, where they waited for one month. While there she was summoned to military headquarters at Haidarpasha to be interviewed by two officers, one German and one English. Both men asked Malakeh if she would like to return to her home in Jerusalem, which was now under British military administration. If so, the English officer would take charge and ensure her safe passage. Malakeh's reply was that she wished to travel on to Berlin for further study. The German officer asked her how she proposed to do this and she assured him that she had sufficient resources and contacts in Berlin. It was agreed that she should rejoin the other nurses at Kadiköy who were waiting for repatriation.

Eventually orders came that the internees were to pack up and be ready to travel to Istanbul, where they would embark on a ship to sail the 350 miles to Odessa on the Black Sea. However, when they reached Odessa they were refused permission to land and after much arguing and delay the boat turned round and sailed back. It was an anticlimax – the return to wait indefinitely in the camp at Kadiköy. Permission was at last received, and once again they boarded the ship to sail through the Bosphorus and into the Black Sea. At Odessa they landed and were put on a train to start the long journey north-west across the Ukraine and eastern Europe to Berlin.

While in Aleppo Malakeh had made friends with a German Diakonisse, Schwester Louiseh, who was extremely helpful to her all

70 ARMENIANS OF JERUSALEM

through the long journey. On arrival at Berlin they stayed at the Brevitz Pension to have a few days rest. Next Malakeh made contact with Frau Hantscheck who lived in Charlottenburg. Frau Hantscheck's son Gunter had been one of her patients in Aleppo, where she had nursed him back to health after a serious operation on his ear. When he learned that she intended to go to Berlin he gave her the address of his parents in token of his appreciation. He had already written to them and hoped that they could assist her when she arrived. Frau Hantscheck was expecting Malakeh and offered her accommodation until she settled her affairs. Times were very hard in Berlin in 1919. Food was scarce and the first thing Malakeh had to do was to get a ration card. She had brought a knapsack full of tinned food which had been issued by the army, and she gave it to the Hantscheck household.

After a few days Malakeh went to the Charité Hospital in Luisenstrasse and asked for an interview with Professor Stickel. This was arranged and she went in an optimistic mood armed with her references and certificate. Her acceptance, however, was not to be straightforward, as she was told that before thinking of specializing she must take a general nursing course all over again in German. The certificate she had received in Beirut was not recognized. Undeterred she went through the course again and passed her exams in six months. She then had to prove that she was proficient enough in the German language for specialized study. For her this was no problem, and the last hurdle having been overcome she was accepted in the department of midwifery, Berlin University, for the academic year starting in the autumn of 1919.

Before leaving Aleppo Malakeh had deposited part of her savings, a thousand Marks, with Dr Seige. On his return to Berlin he paid it over to the university towards her fees. The time came for her to move from the Hantschecks' to the university campus, where she was given a basement room. There she studied late into the night and was often disturbed by the noise of rats running to and fro in the gaps between the ceiling of her room and the upstairs floor.

There were only four other students on the course and they looked upon Malakeh with slight suspicion, referring to her as 'die kleine Türke'. None of them knew from where or how she had come to Berlin, and Malakeh kept them guessing. She was so studious that there was no time to form close friendships. Once postal services resumed, Malakeh received occasional letters from her sisters, Mar-

MALAKEH, NURSE AND MIDWIFE
71

garet and Isquhie, who sometimes enclosed money to help with her expenses.

The course took eleven months to complete, after which came exams, written, oral and practical, supervised by professors from other medical institutions. The students had to examine a pregnant woman and prove their knowledge in dealing with labour cases. All five of them passed and were awarded certificates. Malakeh was now a qualified midwife.

On leaving the university Malakeh asked if she might practise midwifery but was told that foreigners were not permitted to do so. However she was allowed to join a group of private nurses who were sent out to look after patients in their homes whenever the need arose.

During her spare time Malakeh was able to go to the opera, theatre and concerts. While at the university she attended readings of the poetry of Goethe and Schiller. She particularly enjoyed a production of *Die Fledermaus* by Johann Strauss, themes from which she later sang to us as children. With friends she visited Potsdam and Sans Souci, Koln-am-Rhein and other parts of the country.

As soon as she had saved sufficient money Malakeh decided, as she had always intended, to return to Palestine, the land of her birth. There she could use her professional skills among her own people, where the need was greater. Professor Stickel was of help again and in the autumn of 1921 found her a place on a cargo ship – *The Eider* – which was one of the first commercial ships to leave Hamburg for Palestine. She was the only passenger on board amongst a crew of sixteen. The ship took a month to reach Jaffa as it stopped many times on the way to discharge cargo. She had written to Margaret giving the name of the ship so that she could be met at Jaffa.

She arrived in November 1921. The sea was very rough and the small boat in which she was brought to land nearly capsized. New regulations were enforced by the British authorities and she was put into quarantine at the port for three days. During that time she was visited by her new brother-in-law, Margaret's husband, Harold Rose. Upon her release he took her back to their house in Jaffa, where she stayed for a few days exchanging news with her sister and enjoying their three-month-old baby daughter, Margaret. Then she left for Jerusalem to rejoin her mother in the Old City house.

In order to pursue her profession Malakeh had to obtain a licence to practise as a midwife and nurse. This was granted without any difficulty and shortly afterwards a notice board went up on the wooden

72 ARMENIANS OF JERUSALEM

door to the courtyard and another one in the street between the Jaffa Gate and the Armenian Convent. In English and in Arabic were painted the words: 'Miss Malakeh Melkon, qualified Midwife'. The one in the street hung in mid-air on an iron bar, and could be seen by passers-by going and coming between the Armenian Quarter and the Jaffa Gate. It was in place for many years until one day a passing bus tore it down. A career in nursing and midwifery that was to last a lifetime had begun.

Mariam, now living alone as both Isquhie and Margaret had recently married, was pleased to have Malakeh with her in the Old City house. This was not to be for long, however, as Malakeh was soon asked to go to Gaza and organize the midwifery section of the public health department. It was there that she earned a reputation for skill and reliability. On her return to Jerusalem doctors in both the private and public sectors held her in high esteem and never hesitated to recommend her to their private patients. She was always in demand as nurse, and more so as midwife, among Arab families, both Muslim and Christian, among Armenians and the expatriate community.

From Germany she had brought a midwifery bag containing all the equipment she required, including a wooden stethoscope (which she referred to as a *sanata*) with which she examined expectant mothers. To us as small children it looked like a trumpet and provided much amusement. We would take turns to lie down on her examination couch and pretend that we could hear noises inside each other's bodies.

Midwifery had come a long way since the time of Umm Yeghia and Umm Nazar. It was customary for women to have their babies at home, but Malakeh was often called by Dr Orr-Ewing to the English Mission Hospital, by Dr Gemalin to the German Hospital, and by Dr Roux to the French Hospital to attend difficult cases.

Twice Malakeh was asked to nurse women patients who needed care while travelling. First she accompanied Lord Curzon's daughter to Piraeus. Later an American, Mrs Pierson, engaged her as nurse on a journey to London. It was a new experience for Malakeh to travel first class and to stay at the fashionable Piccadilly Hotel. In London she went sight-seeing and shopping and acquired some of the latest fashions of the 1920s. The Piersons invited her to go on to America with them, but the urge to return and serve the community in Jerusalem was far stronger and she refused.

Malakeh was expert at giving painless injections and had a reputa-

MALAKEH, NURSE AND MIDWIFE

tion for *eed khafeefeh* (a light hand). The charge for an injection was a shilling a time. For attending the birth of a child, which included a week's nursing care at the patient's home, a fee of three Palestine pounds was paid, less by poor women and nothing at all by those who could not afford it. She was always ready to respond to a call whatever the time of night. A knock on the courtyard door was enough to awaken her and bring her out, bag in hand. She would then be escorted by men from the expectant mother's family to the house where her services were needed. In the early dawn she would be given a good breakfast. During the day she was always to be seen about the town visiting her patients.

As the years passed she earned the courtesy title Sitt Malakeh, a sign of respect acknowledging her skill and devotion as a midwife. She was well-known all over Jerusalem and many would tell me with a smile that she had acted as midwife at their birth. Friends and relatives with gynaecological and other health problems would always seek her advice, and in all confidence referred to her as *nus hakimeh* (half a doctor).

In 1929 Malakeh married Sahag, her second cousin, son of Movses Gazmararian who had lived in Jaffa. After leaving the Armenian school he was educated in the Collège des Frères in Jaffa where he learned fluent French and Arabic, which he always wrote neatly and in elegant style. Sahag was short, fair, with blue eyes inherited from his mother. Her family, known as Dar el Badgerhan, was so-named for their profession, the restoration of ikons and church paintings. Sahag started work with the Singer Sewing Machine Company, and later became area manager. At the time of his marriage he was on his own, since his widowed mother, two brothers and only sister had all died in a short space of time from that dreaded disease, consumption, for which there was then no cure.

Malakeh and Sahag were married in the Armenian chapel in the Church of the Nativity in Bethlehem. Their only child, Movses (always called Morris), was born in 1931. However, marriage did not prevent Malakeh from pursuing her profession, and she went on working well into the 1960s. After a career of 40 years she retired, but even then people still sought her advice and admiringly continued to consider her *nus hakimeh*.

8 ISQUHIE AND HER MOTHER IN JERUSALEM

While Malakeh and Margaret were away pursuing study and work, Isquhie continued to live at home with her parents. As a child she was sent to the Convent elementary school, St Gayantiants, where she learned to speak, read and write Armenian. Later on she acquired a knowledge of English, some Russian, and of course she spoke Arabic fluently. All the classes were conducted in a large hall, each teacher responsible for a group of girls seated round separate tables. Mariam would prepare food for Isquhie to take to school, usually rice with a stew which she carried in a *matbaqiyeh*, a three-tiered tin-plated copper lunchbox secured down the sides with hooks.

In those days there was little in the way of entertainment for children of Isquhie's age. She was expected to help her mother in the house; the rest of the day was spent working at embroidery and cross-stitch. To hang about the courtyard door or to play in the street was not allowed. In the afternoons she would accompany her mother on visits to relatives and friends. Sometimes they would go for a walk through Bab el Nebi Daoud and on to the Taleh, the west-facing slope of Mount Zion, a popular place to escape to from the cramped confines of the Old City. Families with their children would go there to meet friends, enjoy the space, the sun, the fresh air and the view to the Bethlehem hills beyond. The fields around were planted with cauliflowers and other vegetables. Before returning home Isquhie would run down to the *sabil* (fountain) above the Sultan's Pool where she filled an earthenware jar with fresh drinking water to carry home.

The Russian Compound, about half a mile to the north of the city, was another favourite place to visit. The gardens surrounding the Cathedral of the Holy Trinity were wooded, and at weekends and on public holidays a Turkish military brass band played there from a

ISQUHIE AND HER MOTHER IN JERUSALEM

raised stand. Soft drinks, sweets, toffee-apples, cakes, chickpeas, as well as melon- and pumpkin-seeds were on sale, and an added attraction for children was the *sanduq el ajam* (a portable peepshow).

Visits to Jerusalem by heads of state and other dignitaries also gave the inhabitants something to look forward to. People turned out in large numbers to watch the many processions which usually came in by way of the Jaffa Gate. Her father's barber shop on the corner of David Street provided a good vantage point for Isquhie. Melkon always prepared an upturned wooden crate which served as a dais for her to stand on.

At the end of October 1898 Kaiser Wilhelm II and Kaiserin Augusta-Viktoria were invited by the Turkish authorities to visit Jerusalem. The imperial couple and their large entourage arrived at the port of Haifa on the *Hohenzollern*. Messrs Thomas Cook & Sons were put in charge of the arrangements, which included assigning visitors to hotels and camping grounds, supervising royal banquets, organizing sightseeing tours and providing guides, tents and horses. This visit provided temporary work for the local inhabitants, including many Armenians.

In Jerusalem convents and religious establishments lent Persian carpets which were laid from the top of David Street down to the Church of the Holy Sepulchre. The kaiser, dressed as a crusading knight, rode into the Jaffa Gate area through a special breach in the city walls. This breach was made to honour an ancient tradition that only a conqueror may ride through the gates of the Holy City – he came as a visitor. The kaiserin and her ladies followed in a carriage. Their entrance was greeted by a volley of gunfire from the citadel and a band played military music. From her vantage point Isquhie spotted her sisters amongst a group of uniformed Talitha Cumi girls. They were on their way to the Erlöserkirche to sing for the royal guests. Under the hawk's eyes of the Schwestern they only managed a smile and a discreet nod to their sister.

From the Jaffa Gate the procession went on foot through the Old City. After a visit to the Holy Sepulchre the kaiser and kaiserin attended the dedication of the Lutheran Church of the Redeemer, the Erlöserkirche. This church had been built on land given to Emperor Friedrich (the kaiser's father) by the Sublime Porte when he had visited Palestine as Kronprinz in 1869. On the present visit Sultan 'Abdul Hamid gave Kaiser Wilhelm a plot of land on Mount Zion. He in turn presented it to the German Catholics, who built the

76 ARMENIANS OF JERUSALEM

Dormition Abbey on the site; when completed in 1906 it was handed over to monks of the Benedictine order.

On another day the royal couple were taken round St George's Cathedral by Bishop Blyth and the clergy. A brass plate on the font with the inscription 'A Gift of Queen Victoria' – his grandmother – was pointed out with pleasure by the kaiser to his entourage. Later, at the Haram al Sharif they were shown the beauty of the mosques by the Mufti of Jerusalem, Sheikh Tahir el Husseini.

In 1908 there were festive scenes to celebrate Eid el Houriyyeh, the 'feast of freedom' to mark the Young Turks' revolution in Istanbul against the despotic Sultan 'Abdul Hamid. The reformers called for the restoration of the 1876 constitution and the holding of elections for a new parliament. Briefly, liberty and equality applied to the population in Jerusalem. The laity belonging to Christian denominations were from now on to be allowed to have a representative in their own church councils. As Ottoman subjects, Christians and Jews were to have the same rights as Muslims. However, the measures included an unpopular one – compulsory service in the army, which could only be avoided by the payment of *badal* (large sums of money). Flags and bunting bedecked the Jaffa Gate and surrounding buildings, the façade of the Armenian Convent included. Schools were closed and the celebrations, which lasted for three days, passed in an atmosphere of friendship and hope for the future.

The Feast of the Virgin Mary, Sittna Mariam, which falls on the last Sunday in August, was an event looked forward to by the Armenian community in Jerusalem. The subterranean Church of the Virgin at Gethsemane, dating from the fifth century and restored in the twelfth by Queen Melisande, daughter of King Baldwin II, is jointly owned by the Armenian and Greek Orthodox churches. A large garden with many ancient olive trees adjoins the church and is the property of the Armenian patriarchate. A week before the feast my great-aunts Heghnoug, Horop and Arousiag, accompanied by other women of the community, would scrub the massive staircase leading down to the tomb where the Virgin Mary is believed to have lain before her Assumption.

On the Friday before the feast, the garden becomes a place of entertainment with a holiday atmosphere. On Saturday morning priests, seminarians and members of the Armenian community converge on the Church of Sittna Mariam and in the afternoon *Isqun nakhadanank* (Evensong) is recited. On Sunday morning the feast ends

ISQUHIE AND HER MOTHER IN JERUSALEM 77

after the celebration of Holy Mass. Isquhie and her mother would join members of the family and walk down to picnic in Gethsemane. The garden would be packed with friends, relatives and their children, all having a good time. A variety of foods and soft drinks were on sale and swings and roundabouts provided for the young. Groups sang, others danced to the rhythm of a *durbookeh* (a locally made pottery drum sometimes brightly decorated). In their simple way this was how people enjoyed themselves.

The Greek Orthodox community celebrate the Feast of the Virgin on 8 September. A week before, a framed, jewelled ikon of the Virgin is carried by chanting priests in a dawn procession through the Old City from the Holy Sepulchre down to the church. Hundreds of people accompany the ikon, many walking barefoot to fulfil vows taken during the year. Bottles of olive oil are donated to fill the many lamps adorning the church, and lighted candles are placed down the 44 steps leading to the tomb. Gradually the church is illuminated by these hundreds of candles, each one as it were expressing the desires and hopes of the faithful. On entering the chamber containing the tomb, pilgrims rub ailing limbs and failing eyes on the stonework, such is their deep faith and hope for a cure. The ikon remains in the church until after the feast, when it is returned again in procession to the Holy Sepulchre.

When she was sixteen Isquhie joined what perhaps can be called a 'finishing school' in household management. This small establishment for just a few Armenian young ladies was run by Sitt Fulyaneh, the daughter of a prominent *kaghakatsi* family in Jerusalem. Her brother, respectfully addressed as *khawaja* Artin (mister or gentleman Artin), was head of the Austrian post office, one of several run by foreign countries – France, Italy, Russia, Germany, Britain – under franchise from the Turkish government. The girls were taught sewing, crochet, embroidery and fine needlework as well as cookery, the making of traditional cakes, jams, preserves, syrups and the pickling of olives and different kinds of vegetables. Particular attention was given to cleanliness in the preparation of food. Quantities of pomegranates, lemons, and Seville oranges were used to make distinctive syrups. Apricots, cherries, and the peel of oranges and *kabbad* (*Citrus medica*) were preserved in syrup.

Sitt Fulyaneh made no attempt to Europeanize the girls: they were shown how to use the raw materials available and to follow the customs of the country, with emphasis on the Armenian way of life. The course

78   ARMENIANS OF JERUSALEM

lasted a few months, and when it was over the girls were capable of running a household and were soon sought after for marriage.

When Isquhie left Sitt Fulyaneh's school she took up sewing, first at the Sisters of Charity and later at a Salesian convent known locally as the 'Sirizian'. Her mother sold a piece of jewellery and bought her a Pfaff sewing machine for five gold pounds. This machine lasted well into the 1950s and was in constant use when Isquhie became a professional dressmaker.

Next she joined the workroom of a *haute couture* salon run by a Russian lady, Mme Michaeloff, whose husband was a photographer with an atelier nearby. The salon, situated near the Russian Compound, was frequented by the wives of diplomats, foreigners and ladies of Jerusalem society. Mme Michaeloff, a short, plump lady who regularly wore a well-tailored suit, and whose neck was decked with ropes of large amber beads, was very kind to the seamstresses but expected a high standard of work from them. She herself cut out all the materials to a pattern and supervised the clients' fittings. Around the salon stood dress-forms in various sizes. The girls brought their own food but sometimes partook of Russian dishes sent in to them at midday by Mme Michaeloff's cook, Sonia. A large brass samovar studded with medallions of tsars gurgled away in a corner and provided a constant supply of tea. In this company Isquhie learned to speak Russian, and adopted the habit of placing a lump of sugar between her teeth before sipping tea. As the business grew Mme Michaeloff moved to larger premises in the Steet of the Prophets. Isquhie moved with her and stayed for about two years, learning the finer details of European fashions.

After the death of Sapritch Melkon in 1910 Isquhie and Mariam were alone, since Malakeh and Margaret were away in Beirut. To earn a living they took in sewing, and Mariam occasionally went out to work as a cook for some of the well-known Muslim families in Jerusalem. Her skills were particularly appreciated by the household of Feidi efendi el Alami, who were hospitable and entertained a great number of relatives and friends. Isquhie would often join her mother to help with the washing up, then they would walk home together through the city. Feidi's wife Sitt Zuleikha and his daughter Sitt Ni'amati were very fond of them both.

The el Alamis had one son, Musa, who later was to found 'Boys Town', a rehabilitation centre for Arab refugees displaced during the 1948 Arab–Israeli war. In 1949 he was given permission by the

ISQUHIE AND HER MOTHER IN JERUSALEM

Jordanian government to develop 5,000 acres of waste land in the Jericho area, which lay some five miles north of the Dead Sea. The project was a tremendous success, and by 1951 boys were being trained in dairy and chicken farming, vegetable growing, carpentry and blacksmithery. Everything produced there was of the highest quality, for sale in Jerusalem and Amman.

In 1916 epidemics of typhus and cholera raged throughout Jerusalem. Medical help was minimal and many people died. Armenians living in the vicinity of the Church of the Holy Archangels seem to have suffered particularly. Those who died of the disease were taken straight to the cemetery on Mount Zion and buried in communal graves.

Careful as she tried to be, Mariam caught typhus fever, but Isquhie escaped the infection. At first Mariam was nursed at home, visited by an Armenian doctor serving in the Turkish army. Isquhie tried to conceal her mother's illness but Mariam's condition was reported by the neighbours to Dr Pascal, who was in charge of the Armenian Convent clinic. He did not even call at the house, but sent orders that she should be removed to the Jewish hospital near the Dung Gate. The courtyard of the house was strewn with powdered lime as was the custom where outbreaks of typhus had occurred. A specially adapted horse-drawn wagon, powdered all over with lime, conveyed the patients to hospital. The horses wore bells on their collars and were draped in red to warn passers-by to keep away. Mariam was put into the wagon with other patients and driven off, leaving Isquhie in a state of distress.

Isquhie visited the hospital daily. She was not allowed to enter the ward but from a distance assured herself that her mother was still alive. Mariam recovered, but the fever left her very weak and she had to lie in bed at home and be nursed back to health.

At the time Isquhie was working three days a week in the gardener's household within the compound of the Augusta-Viktoria Stiftung on the Mount of Olives. The gardener and his wife had three children, Augustus, Frieda and Ellen, who went to the German school in Prophets' Street run by the Lutheran Propst (provost). They would ride down from the Mount of Olives to Jerusalem on a donkey led by one of the Arab staff and on his way back he would collect Isquhie at the Damascus Gate and lead her up to the Stiftung. The gardener's family were fond of her, and on hearing that her mother had been so ill suggested that a change of air would do her good, and invited her

80 ARMENIANS OF JERUSALEM

to convalesce with them for a time. Mariam and Isquhie were given a large attic room with a view stretching over the Judean hills, the Dead Sea and the mountains of Moab beyond. During their three weeks' stay they shared meals with the family and as repayment Isquhie waived her wages for sewing.

The Augusta-Viktoria Stiftung was an impressive building, the vision of the kaiserin, who on her visit in 1898 was petitioned to provide a sanatorium and resthouse for German pilgrims and missionaries. What better place could there be than the Mount of Olives with its fresh air and magnificent views? The project was approved, a large plot of land acquired, the kaiserin herself was appointed patron, and on her return to Germany she worked unceasingly to raise funds.

The buildings, named the Augusta-Viktoria Stiftung in her honour, were dedicated in April 1910 by Prinz Eitel Fritz, second son of the kaiser and kaiserin. The interior contained a fine staircase, panelled dining-room, long corridors, a considerable number of guest-rooms and cloisters, all built in German style and taste. The Stiftung included a church in Byzantine manner, named at the request of the kaiserin the Church of the Ascension. An organ built by the Sauer company of Frankfurt an der Oder had been installed in 1910. The ceiling above was decorated with a painting of the kaiser and kaiserin in medieval dress offering the buildings to heaven, supported by Sapientia and Misericordia.

The gardens were beautifully laid out with rare trees and shrubs imported from Europe, and the Stiftung was efficiently managed by Kaiserswerth Diakonissen. As it turned out, war prevented the kaiser and kaiserin from ever visiting their foundation, though they are represented by two life-size bronze statues in crusader garb in an inner courtyard.

The Stiftung became military headquarters when Turkey joined Germany in the war in 1914. It was taken over by the British in 1917 and later Lord Samuel, the first High Commissioner for Palestine, lived there temporarily and the British Mandate civil administration used it until 1927. On 11 July that year the buildings were extensively damaged in an earthquake, the worst since the terrible one of 1837, and part of the tower fell down.

When Isquhie left the gardener's lodge on the Mount of Olives, her aunt Horop found work for her with Templist families in the German Colony in Jerusalem. Later she went to work for the Fast family, who owned a big hotel on the Jaffa road close to the Jaffa Gate. There she

ISQUHIE AND HER MOTHER IN JERUSALEM 81

sewed silk shirts for German officers which were made out of *sitticroza* (raw silk) imported from Damascus. The hotel, started by the Fast brothers some years before the 1914–18 war, occupied a handsome building owned by the Armenian patriarchate. Many of the staff were German and it was well-run, popular among visitors and military personnel. The food was good and fresh vegetables grown by Templists in their gardens in the German Colony were brought in daily on a horse-drawn cart. After the defeat of the Turks and Germans an Arab family was asked to run the hotel to provide accommodation for British officers. From 1948 until 1967 the buildings stood derelict on the periphery of no-man's-land, after which this Jerusalem landmark was, alas, pulled down.

Both Isquhie and her mother, as well as many of the *kaghakatsi* women of the quarter, were involved in preparations for the hundreds of Armenian pilgrims who converged on the Convent for Christmas and Easter every year. Dormitories and rooms had to be cleaned and put in order for the influx of visitors who usually arrived ten days before the feast. To ensure a continual supply of water, a number of sealed cisterns beneath convent courtyards were opened up. Many of the pilgrims came by boat to Jaffa and then travelled on by train or carriage to Jerusalem. At the railway station they were met by a priest and a dragoman, who accompanied them to the convent where they were given lodgings. Armenian pilgrims who travelled by road broke their journeys in special hostels, *hokidoon*, maintained by local churches. *Hokidoon* were found in towns through which pilgrims were likely to pass on their way to Jerusalem: in Aleppo, Damascus, Latakia, Beirut, Jaffa, Gaza, Ramleh and finally in the convent of St James itself.

The pilgrims brought a variety of foods with them: olives, *basturma*, pickles, ropes of dried grapes, figs and other fruit, cheese and olive oil. Some brought their own bedding. Many gifts were given to the cathedral; copper plates, bowls, vases and candlesticks dated and inscribed to commemorate a pilgrimage to Jerusalem. These *yishadags*, souvenirs of a visit, also included vestments and church linen beautifully embroidered in gold thread. *Darbas* (a voluntary payment) was made by the pilgrims for their stay. The convent was transformed into a hive of activity, and when there was no more room available *kaghakatsi* families took the overflow into their own homes.

The pilgrims participated in all the religious ceremonies both in the cathedral and at the Church of the Holy Sepulchre. On Palm Sunday

82   ARMENIANS OF JERUSALEM

afternoon the patriarch leaves the convent in solemn procession for the Holy Sepulchre, where a service is held at the Stone of Unction and later in the *vernadoon*, the Armenian gallery. This is followed by the ceremony of *Terempatz* in the Cathedral of Saint James, which symbolizes Christ's entry into Jerusalem. Thoughout Lent each ikon in the cathedral and in the Church of the Holy Archangels is veiled by a curtain. At this ceremony the names of pilgrims and members of the *kaghakatsi* who have made vows and donated money to the church are called out by a priest, and they each unveil the ikon allocated to them. Every year great-aunt Arousiag took part in the ceremony at Hrishtagabed, praying that her poor eyesight would not deteriorate further.

The Cathedral of Saint James would again be filled for the ceremony of the Washing of the Feet on Maundy Thursday, when the patriarch symbolically washes the feet of twelve of his priests. During this service the Anglican bishops have over the years been invited to read the Gospel in English. On Good Friday afternoon the Burial Service takes place with deep solemnity. In the afternoon of Easter Day the patriarch blesses the four corners of the earth in a colourful ceremony – Antastan. This is held out of doors in a courtyard adjacent to the cathedral, filled with pilgrims and members of the community.

One of the most beautiful and deeply moving services, *Merilotz* (service of remembrance), follows on Easter Monday morning in the cathedral. The service is long, and the chanting includes the repetition of *Der voghormia* (Lord have mercy) which touches the emotions of the congregation. The convent bell tolls and a procession is formed, led by the choir and followed by incense bearers and deacons carrying banners. Bishops and priests, all in colourful embroidered copes and robes, carry ancient relics, the bones of the hands of Armenian saints encased in gold and silver, foremost among them the hand of Krikor Luisavorich (Saint Gregory the Illuminator). Next comes the patriarch walking under a brocade canopy carried by four young deacons. At intervals he blesses the worshippers using a jewelled cross covered with a fine muslin veil. The service ended, the patriarch leaves in procession to the throne room in the patriarchate where he receives pilgrims and members of the community. Courtesy calls are also exchanged at Christmas and Easter between the heads of the religious communities of Jerusalem.

Soon after Easter most of the pilgrims would leave for home. The

ISQUHIE AND HER MOTHER IN JERUSALEM 83

women of the community once again banded together to clean the cathedral and the empty rooms. Carpets were removed, put in the sun and beaten; linen washed and floors cleaned. Getting rid of candle-wax was an arduous task. In return the women were given goats' cheese, cucumbers and cooked macaroni to take home. After Christmas, when they had finished their cleaning, the women were allowed to collect *keshkeg* – a thick broth made from burghul and pounded meat which had been cooked in cauldrons in the convent kitchen.

During the 1914–18 war the people of Jerusalem and the rest of Palestine endured great hardship. In 1915 a plague of locusts denuded vegetable crops and trees of their leaves. The inhabitants were paid a small fee by the Turkish authorities to collect the eggs of these destructive insects. By 1917 there was terrible famine, and a halt to all work caused 90 per cent unemployment. It is estimated that 20,000 people died of starvation and disease. A blockade of the sea-coast by the British navy contributed to this distress. The children suffered most from undernourishment; later 98 per cent were found to have trachoma and other eye diseases.

After Jerusalem fell to the British forces, as announced by General Allenby in his speech of 11 December 1917 the city was put under martial law. This was extended to the whole country after the armistice of 31 October 1918 and was to last for two more years. OETA (Occupied Enemy Territory Administration) took control. One of their first tasks was to distribute food stocks which were now arriving by rail from Egypt as well as by sea. A new organization, the Syrian and Palestine Relief Fund, was formed by Bishop Rennie MacInnes and started work in all parts of Palestine. In April 1917 the organization opened a hospital and dispensary at Khan Yunis near the Egyptian border and Dr Paterson of Hebron was put in charge of the work. Later dispensaries were organized in Jerusalem and Bethlehem where the need was especially great. Tons of grain, bales of clothing and cases of medicine were dispatched from Europe via Jaffa.

On 22 December 1917 Colonel Ronald Storrs was appointed military governor of Jerusalem and warmly welcomed by the inhabitants. Not long after, he formed the Pro-Jerusalem Society to encourage the preservation of ancient buildings, in particular the two mosques, Qubbet el Sakhra and Masjid el Aqsa, in the Haram el Sharif compound. Many of the beautiful glazed tiles adorning these

84 ARMENIANS OF JERUSALEM

magnificent buildings had over the years suffered weather-damage and needed to be replaced.

Tavid Ohannessian, an Armenian potter from Kütahya who had endured great hardship escaping with his family from Turkey to Aleppo and thence to Jerusalem, was put in charge of the repairs by Colonel Storrs. First he asked Tavid to travel back to Kütahya (the artistic centre of Armenian pottery since the seventeenth century and before), to bring skilled potters as well as the necessary materials to make new tiles. Tavid returned, bringing with him Nishan Balian and Migerditch Karakashian with ten other workers. Together they put into use an ancient disused kiln near the Haram el Sharif. Later they transferred to premises in the Via Dolorosa which they named 'The Dome of the Rock Tiles Workshop'. In 1922 the original project was abandoned, the potters separated and Balian and Karakashian started the Palestine Pottery on the Nablus road in a building jointly owned by the Anglican bishop in Jerusalem and the Valero family. There they produced many fine vases, bowls and plates with designs of birds, tulips, carnations, prunus, traditionally used in Kütahya and Iznik (Nicaea). Tavid Ohannessian stayed in the old workshop and applied these ancient patterns to large designs for the façades of public and private buildings, in Cairo as well as in Jerusalem: the Rockefeller Museum, St Andrew's Church of Scotland, Government House, the American Colony and the Nashashibi house in Sheikh Jarrah are some examples.

Early in 1918 Isquhie was asked to head the sewing room at Schneller's, the Syrian Protestant Orphanage in Jerusalem. This institution had been founded in 1860 by Johan Ludwig Schneller and was commonly referred to by the local population as 'Schneynar'. The work had been directed by the Evangelische Verein für das Syrische Waisenhaus am Jerusalem. The buildings were now taken over by the American Red Cross and called ARCSO Hall – American Red Cross Syrian Orphanage Hall. The Waisenhaus could accommodate between four and five hundred orphaned boys and girls, many of whom came from other parts of the province of Syria. They were taught trades – carpentry, blacksmithery, printing, tailoring, pottery, dairy farming and market gardening. The finest artisans in the country were graduates of this orphanage and had little difficulty in finding work.

Schneller's ran trade schools for blind children, where the boys were taught wicker and cane work, basket and brush making, and

ISQUHIE AND HER MOTHER IN JERUSALEM 85

their finished products were sold all over the country. The orphanage also included a teacher-training school and a seminary training preachers for Protestant missions. The religious aspect of the work was maintained; bible classes were held daily as were morning and evening prayers.

Isquhie was in charge of nine workers and ten apprentices in the sewing room. Her aunt Horop sometimes came in on a daily basis to help instruct the girls. The women were in charge of the Waisenhaus linen, and were responsible for cutting out and sewing uniforms for the orphans out of material provided by the American Red Cross. Everyone worked hard but Isquhie enjoyed it and made many friends. She lived in, and was paid three gold pounds a month plus full board for her services. At about this time Isquhie had two proposals of marriage. A member of Schneller's staff asked for her hand, as did a teacher from Bishop Gobat School, but she refused them both. However it was while working at Schneller's that she met the man whom she was to marry.

In 1920 the Waisenhaus was handed back to Schneller's and the German lady who had previously been in charge of the sewing room resumed her work. Isquhie was asked to leave, but did not mind because she had much to do in preparation for her marriage to Ibrahim Audi.

Ibrahim Audi, an Arab from a well-known Ramallah family, often visited his cousin who also worked in the sewing room. He was a Quaker and had spent some time in the United States before returning home to Palestine intending to work in tourism. They became engaged, but Isquhie's mother did not approve: to marry someone who was not Armenian was still not easily accepted by the *kaghakatsi* community. However, objections from the family did nothing to change Ibrahim's and Isquhie's minds and the couple were married in the Church of the Holy Archangels on 21 January 1921. Desoutch Matheos Kaikedjian officiated and Isquhie's cousin, Aram Krikorian, was sponsor. A small reception for friends and relatives was held in the Old City house, after which the bride and groom left for Ramallah, Ibrahim's home town.

9 THE ROSES

My father, Harold Victor Rose, was born in Birmingham on 27 June 1897, the year of Queen Victoria's Diamond Jubilee, and given the name Victor to commemorate the occasion. His father, John Henry, born in Stratford-upon-Avon on 27 April 1866, was the eldest son of Joseph Charles Rose and Hannah Maria (née Roberts) who had been married in the Independent Chapel on 3 May 1865. They made their home at 3 Shakespeare Street, Old Stratford. Joseph Charles Rose was a farrier by profession, as was his father Thomas before him.

Harold's mother, Emma Elizabeth Swift, was a Londoner, born on 21 May 1865 in Little Newport Street, Soho. Her father, Samuel Thomas Swift, was a widower when he married her mother, Elizabeth Buffham, on 25 March 1864. On their marriage certificate their ages were concealed and given only as 'full'. Thomas Swift was an electro-gilder by profession, his father George Swift a buttonmaker, while Elizabeth's father, William Buffham, was a coachmaker. A few years after their marriage the Swifts and their young family moved to Birmingham. The city had become a centre for small industries and there were good prospects for electro-gilders, jewellers and silver-smiths. The family settled in Clarendon Street, Aston Manor, close to the centre of their trade.

My grandparents, John Henry Rose aged 26 and Emma Elizabeth Swift aged 27, were married in the Congregational Chapel, Park Road, Aston, Birmingham, on 18 March 1893. Emma's father, Samuel Thomas, had died a few years before. John Henry Rose, who worked as an insurance agent, was a tall well-built man, while Emma in contrast was a tiny woman. They had five children, three sons and two daughters. The eldest son, Harold, was to become my father; his

THE ROSES

brothers were Leslie and Henry (who died young); his two sisters were Dorothy (called Dolly) and Hilda.

The children were all musical and played various instruments, three of them becoming professional musicians. Harold played the piano, organ and flute, but his life-long interest was in organ music and in the mechanics of the instrument. Leslie played the cello, Hilda the violin, and Dolly was an accomplished pianist. They joined orchestras giving concerts in and around Birmingham. Their mother, Emma, sang beautifully, and at home the family often made their own music in the evenings. Their father's part in the music-making was never mentioned. He was a man of quick temper given to uncontrollable rages; once, when provoked by the children at teatime, he upset the table bringing everything down with a huge crash. A worse fit of temper prompted him to cut Hilda's violin strings just before she was going out to play in a concert. Emma, on the other hand, was tolerant and good natured, always trying to protect the family during these outbursts. The children had a good education, and Harold went through grammar school. From an early age he was interested in mechanics and engineering, had an inventive mind and was clever with his hands. He lived up to the reputation of the inhabitants of Birmingham known for their industrious ingenuity.

When war broke out in 1914 Harold was at first too young to join up, but he had a fervent desire to serve his country and managed to enlist in the Royal Army Service Corps. His mother, Emma, who was deeply attached to him, was very sad to see him go to the war. She went with him to London at the end of his last leave to show him the sights and to see him off.

Harold was dispatched to France and then to Belgium, where he was engaged in transporting munitions to the front line. He came close to death at Ypres, sheltering with two companions in a trench when a shell fell very close by. His two friends were killed but Harold had a lucky escape and was only wounded in the toe, an injury that was to cause him trouble for the rest of his life. From Belgium he was moved to Italy for a while, and later was sent to Egypt to join the Egypt Expeditionary Force led by General Allenby. It was now 1917. Unfortunately all official records of Harold's military service were destroyed with many others by enemy action in 1940, and he never spoke of his experiences. His parents, especially his mother, were very disappointed when their son was posted further east and feared that they would never see him again. This proved to be the case, as he did

88   ARMENIANS OF JERUSALEM

not return to England during their lifetime. Harold stayed for a while
in Egypt and then moved north to Palestine with the advancing British
forces.

Jaffa fell to the British on 16 November 1917, and Jerusalem on 9
December. Palestine was under military rule for two and a half years
until the newly formed British Mandate authorities took over in June
1920 and introduced civilian government. While still in the army
Harold, now based in Jaffa, was sent to the government hospital to
supervise the repair of machinery. It was there in 1919 that he met
the matron, Margaret Melkonian – who was to become my mother.
They were attracted to each other and soon decided to get married.
In Margaret Harold had found a clever and educated partner. He was
eight years younger than she but had been matured by his experiences
in the war. It was a daring step for both of them to take.

On receiving news of the engagement Harold's family in Birmingham were not at all pleased. His parents were very alarmed that their
son was going to marry a foreigner – and who were the Armenians?
They had never heard of them. Disapproving letters, with which he
was bombarded, had little effect and he did not waver. In those days
it was not the done thing in colonial society for an Englishman to
marry a foreigner. There were of course foreigners and foreigners: to
marry a French girl was smart, to marry a Greek was just acceptable;
bottom of the list were people who came from the Arab world. Even
though Margaret was an Armenian, she was a *kaghakatsi* who had
been born in Jerusalem and had lived there for most of her life. There
was general disapproval among Harold's compatriots in Jaffa – added
to which certain English missionaries, of whom there were many
around, cruelly told him that he had now dug his own grave and must
lie in it.

There was also opposition to the marriage from the Armenian side.
Margaret was told to think of the Arabic proverb: *Ziwan baladak wala
amh il ghareeb* the chaff of your own town rather than foreign corn.
Marriage outside the Armenian community was not customary and
the idea was frowned upon. Her Armenian friends and relatives had
their doubts about Harold: he was a soldier and in all probability
would soon leave her. In spite of all the contrary advice given, Harold
and Margaret announced their engagement and he presented her with
a ring of opals. However, her family had laid down certain conditions:
first, Harold was to provide papers from Birmingham to vouch that he
was unmarried and of good repute. These he easily obtained. Second,

THE ROSES

the marriage was to take place in the Armenian church according to the Orthodox rite, to satisfy Margaret's relatives that it was legal and binding. Mariam and Isquhie gave the couple their full support and a small engagement party was held in the Old City house. Relatives and friends came to wish them *mabruk* (congratulations) and were served with coffee and liqueurs. Margaret resigned her post at the hospital and returned home to prepare for her marriage. Harold, still in the army, stayed in Jaffa but made regular weekend visits to Jerusalem.

On 15 June 1920 they were married in the Armenian parish church of the Holy Archangels. Margaret's wedding dress of white satin was made by her sister Isquhie. She wore a veil with orange-blossom pinned in to it and held a bouquet of sweet-scented white jasmine. Helped by Isquhie, she dressed in the upstairs room of their neighbours the Simounians, while relatives and friends gathered in the courtyard of the house below. The procession through the cobbled streets to the church was led by two *kawas* provided by the Armenian convent. Then followed the bride with her uncles, mother, aunts, sister and many friends and relatives. On the way the crowd were sprinkled with rosewater from *umm umms* (small ornamented silver flasks with a spout), and as was customary were showered with rose petals.

Harold was already waiting in the church with his best man, Ibrahim Audi, who had recently become engaged to Isquhie. The marriage was conducted by *vartabet* Mesrop Nishanian, a priest and friend of the family who in 1939 was to be appointed Armenian patriarch, an office which he held until his death in 1944. The church was packed and it was a novelty for the community to witness one of the first marriages of an Armenian to an Englishman. The service was conducted in Armenian, although, prompted by an Armenian friend, Harold made his marriage vows in English. As is the custom the newly married couple returned in procession to the house by a different route – it was considered bad luck to retrace the way by which the bride had walked to the church. Once back at the house a small wedding reception was held. There were no European guests present. Young girls clapped, danced and sang in the courtyard. Lemonade and *ghreibeh* were offered to the guests, followed by sugared almonds and glasses of Chartreuse, a green liqueur which had been purchased at Christaki's, a Greek shop by the Jaffa Gate.

The reception over, Harold and Margaret left for Jaffa, where later on they had a civil wedding at the governor's office. They had rented

ARMENIANS OF JERUSALEM

part of a house owned by the Abu Khadra family, where they occupied the second floor overlooking a *bayyara* (orange grove). This was irrigated from a large square pool well-stocked with goldfish and fed by water pumped up from wells below. At night the silence was often broken by the howling of jackals in search of grapes and other fruit in the garden. Groves of citrus trees, including the famous Jaffa orange, extended as far as the eye could see and in spring the sweet scent of the blossom saturated the air for miles around.

On 30 June 1920 Sir Herbert Samuel, the first British High Commissioner for Palestine, arrived at Jaffa port to lead the civil administration of the country. A big *fantaziyeh* was put on for the occasion and Margaret and Harold joined hundreds of others at the landing stage, which was decorated with greenery, flags and balloons. Sir Herbert, dressed in white and wearing a peaked helmet, was met by Colonel Storrs and brought ashore from the *Centaur* in a decorated launch.

Palestine now had a civilian government, and the military administration of OETA was wound up. Harold was released from the army and taken on by the public works department in Jaffa. Times were very hard indeed, there was recession, living was expensive, and Harold's pay was poor. Margaret had saved a little money of her own, which was of help, and they were able to buy furniture and a small car. The car was of great use for their frequent visits to Jerusalem. On 21 August 1921 a little girl was born and named Margaret.

Harold's parents were delighted at this news, and overcame their misgivings. Emma wrote regularly to her daughter-in-law and showed great interest in her grandchildren as they arrived, often sending parcels of clothing from Birmingham for them. Harold asked for his flute and books to be sent out, which arrived together with his cap, which he had left hanging on the kitchen door before he went to the war.

10 THE MOVE TO JERUSALEM

In 1922 Harold was transferred to Jerusalem and appointed foreman at the public works department. The workshops of the PWD were on the Street of the Prophets in sequestrated German property. The offices, headquarters and stores were housed nearby in large Russian-owned buildings, the Moscobiyyeh, put up in the latter part of the nineteenth century as a hospice to accommodate the thousands of Russian pilgrims who flocked to the Holy Land.

Amenities for the pilgrims included medical care, lantern-slide lectures, food and transport. However many preferred to go by foot where they could, rather than ride and desecrate the places over which Our Lord had walked. The pilgrims were generally old; a young face amongst them was rare. With them they brought precious gifts, most of which were given to the Church of the Holy Sepulchre. Russian influence spread in the country and well-organized schools were established in villages such as Beit Jala near Bethlehem. Arab children were taught by Russian teachers, and in the next generation some were named Olga, Xenia, Volodya or Rurik. Pilgrimage ceased in 1914 and the Moscobiyyeh was taken over by the British authorities in 1917.

Harold and Margaret rented a small house in Joret el 'Annab above the Bourqet el Sultan, a few minutes' walk south of the Jaffa Gate. It was owned by an Armenian family, Dar Jiryes Vartan, and was just off the main Jerusalem to Hebron highway along which Margaret used to travel to Dr Paterson's hospital during her early nursing days. The house was primitive but conveniently near to the Old City, and Margaret's mother was able to walk down every day to help with the housework and the baby.

Facing it to the east rose the city walls and Mount Zion. To the

92 ARMENIANS OF JERUSALEM

south the valley of Hinnom ran its course down to Silwan (Siloam), passing the Potter's Field and the Convent of St Onesiphorus on the right. Locally the lower part of the valley was known as Joret el Fatayess or 'pit of the smelly carcasses', as rubbish and dead animals were just dumped there and allowed to rot in the open air. To the west a cluster of houses formed the Mishkenot Sha'ananim (tranquil dwellings) known locally as 'the Montefiore', completed in 1880 and the first Jewish settlement to be built outside the city walls.

Soon Harold was allocated accommodation within the PWD workshop compound in the Street of the Prophets. This German-style house, which had been expropriated after the war from a Mr Wieland, was surrounded by a small walled garden planted with pine trees. Next door the German Lutherans owned property which included a school and the residence of their provost. This compound was now also entirely occupied by British Mandate officials.

I was born in Wieland house on 17 April 1924, my aunt Malakeh acting as midwife. As was traditional, my Armenian relatives took great pleasure in the birth of a boy. There was discussion about the name I was to be given; my English grandparents had written to say that they would like me to be called Samuel after my great-uncle, who had a reputation for kindness and generosity. My parents had the last word, however, and on 25 July 1925 I was christened John Harold by the Reverend E. Webb at St Paul's Church in Jerusalem. This small Anglican church was situated just off the Street of the Prophets in St Paul's Road and had been built by the Church Missionary Society in 1874 for the use of the Arab Anglican congregation.

I had two godparents, my aunt Isquhie and a Mr Davies. Mr Davies gave me a silver christening cup which I still possess but I never heard from him again. My aunt Isquhie was a help and support during childhood and throughout my life. My Armenian grandmother gave me six pure silver teaspoons which she had specially ordered for me at Melkon's, a renowned silversmith in the Old City. She had them engraved with the letter 'R'.

We stayed for such a short time in Wieland house that I cannot remember anything about it and I was never taken there again. For reasons unknown to me the house kept a strong hold on my imagination, and whenever I passed it my eyes were drawn to the trees, arched windows, red-tiled roof and chimney pots.

Our next move was to a house in the Greek Colony in the Emek Rephaim, the valley of giants of the Old Testament (2 Samuel 5:18).

THE MOVE TO JERUSALEM
93

This was to be our home for over twenty years until the end of the British Mandate in May 1948.

Before 1860 there were very few buildings outside the Old City of Jerusalem; the countryside and the desert reached out to the very gates and walls. However, from that time on, private individuals and various European organizations were given permission by the Turkish authorities to buy land and build outside the city walls. One of the first areas to be developed was along the Street of the Prophets to the north-west of the Damascus Gate.

In 1868 a group of German Templists under the direction of Christoph Hoffman emigrated from Württemberg to settle in various parts of Palestine. Their aim was to establish the ideal Christian community in the Holy Land. They had taken their name from Ephesians 2:21, 'In whom all the building fitly framed together groweth unto an holy temple in the Lord'.

In 1870, with permission from the Turkish authorities, a large piece of land was secured in the Emek Rephaim about a mile from the Old City, and in 1873 the cornerstone of the first house was laid. It still stands, and engraved on the lintel of the main door is the word Ebeniezer – 'Hitherto hath the Lord helped us' (1 Samuel 7:12). Another, built in 1878, had the words 'Arise, shine, for thy light is come and the glory of the Lord is risen upon thee' (Isaiah 60:1). From then on the Jerusalem colony became the religious centre of the other Templist colonies in Palestine.

The German colony gradually expanded; a small church and a school were among the first buildings erected at the northern end of their land. A plot was put aside for a cemetery and records show that it was already in use by 1878. Most of the population of the colony were agriculturalists, artisans and shopkeepers. Among other trades they started a carpentry, blacksmithery, bakery, patisserie, and hair-dressers. Their skills were shared with the local inhabitants who, after a period of apprenticeship, were able to set up on their own.

These houses were charmingly built, surrounded by well-kept gardens in which grew a variety of flowers, vegetables and fruit trees. The whole area was planted with Aleppo pines, pepper and cypress trees, not only inside the walled gardens but along the main road, casting welcome shade in the heat of summer. The founders called their new settlement Rephaim, but to all Jerusalemites it was known as the German Colony. At first it was surrounded by fields and olive groves that extended as far as the Bethlehem hills, but, encouraged by

94   ARMENIANS OF JERUSALEM

the success of the German venture, other new suburbs were soon to rise all over that area.

At the turn of the century another suburb was being constructed, this time by Greeks. The moving force was Archimandrite Efthimios of the Greek Orthodox patriarchate. He had been brought to Jerusalem in 1855 as a boy of twelve by his grandmother, from a village beside the Dardanelles. He entered the seminary, was ordained deacon in 1863 and joined the school of theology at the Convent of the Holy Cross. In 1880 he was ordained priest and, after fifteen years of devoted service as deputy, was promoted to the important office of Superior of the Church of the Holy Sepulchre, a post he held until his death in 1917.

Archimandrite Efthimios made good use of funds collected from pilgrims, and energetically built and expanded Greek property within and without the city walls. Many Greek-owned late-nineteenth-century buildings one sees in Jerusalem today were the result of his vision. Among them was a line of shops (demolished after the 1967 war) adjacent to the city walls outside the Jaffa Gate, and the Imperial and Grand New hotels inside the gate. In the Muristan quarter of the Old City he built St John's Hospice for pilgrims with the surrounding shops. A small street not far from the Church of the Holy Sepulchre is named Suq Aftemious in his honour.

There had always been many Greeks living in Palestine. Artisans and traders had emigrated from the Greek mainland and islands and had settled in Jerusalem. Workmen had come in 1810 to carry out repairs at the Church of the Holy Sepulchre after it had been badly damaged by fire. These people stayed on and formed part of a lay community for the Greek Orthodox Church.

In 1902 Archimandrite Efthimios decided to create a residential colony for Greek families in the new city. He bought land just south of the German Colony and built a hall and four outhouses, to serve as a club and recreation ground for Greeks who wished to spend a day in the country. The rest of the land around the club was divided into small plots, and members of the Greek community were invited to draw lots for them on condition that they built houses at their own expense. Many accepted the offer and the Greek Colony was quickly established and became Jerusalem's southernmost suburb. In the vicinity Archimandrite Efthimios built a large two-storey house as a country residence for himself and other clergy. About half a mile away to the east an identical building was put up by Meletious, Bishop of

THE MOVE TO JERUSALEM

Kerak, where he too spent part of the summer. Both these impressive houses were built in Turkish style with verandas, carved stonework and red-tiled roofs.

Further south, fields stretched to the Arab village of Beit Safafa. On the skyline lay the Greek convent of Mar Elias. To the east the main railway line linking Jerusalem to the coast ran through the new Arab suburb of Baqa'a. To the west a new quarter, the Katamon, was being built on a ridge of hills around the Greek monastery of St Simeon. This was to become one of the most fashionable Arab suburbs of new Jerusalem where modern building techniques were introduced, resulting in beautifully-planned imposing villas.

By law all houses in Jerusalem had to be built of stone. Limestone was quarried in the hills around the country and brought on camel-back to the building sites, where it was cut and dressed by groups of stonemasons. As children we would watch them sheltering from the hot sun under makeshift awnings of hessian, hammers rhythmically tapping their chisels to shape the stones. By the end of the day their faces were so covered with powdered dust that only their eyes were visible.

Houses were free-standing, one or two storeys high, surrounded by walled gardens. As there was no municipal water supply, the population relied on cisterns. Every house stood over its own cistern, sometimes two. One of these, filled with clean rainwater from the roof, was reserved for household use. The other, fed with ground surface water, was used for the garden. Periodically the municipality sent round an inspector whose duty it was to pour a small mug of paraffin into the cisterns to prevent mosquitoes from breeding. We would follow the inspector and peer into our cistern when he opened it, but took fright when he banged the lid down and locked it, causing thunderous sounds to echo from the depths below.

There was great emphasis on the saving of water, a habit that became ingrained in us even after the British government introduced an efficient supply to the city. Soon most houses were connected to the municipal supply, cisterns fell into disuse and new ones were no longer excavated – rainwater was simply allowed to run to waste.

The interior of the Greek Colony houses was very simple and basic, usually with a large central *liwan* or hall, off which opened good-sized rooms with high ceilings and large arched windows. For security the windows had iron bars and wooden or metal shutters. Many of the ceilings were domed and the walls were very thick. A corridor led to a

96 ARMENIANS OF JERUSALEM

kitchen, pantry and a lavatory. Few houses had modern bathrooms and one had to manage as best one could in a large copper dish. Later on, life was made much easier by the introduction of bathtubs, showers, and wood-fired geysers.

In the kitchen of our house a small hand pump connected the clean-water cistern to a tank on the roof. We took turns to pump the water up and when the overflow gushed out sparrows and other birds would hover around to drink or bathe. A vaulted cellar of two rooms ran under that part of the house not taken up with cisterns. At first my parents had to use oil lamps as we had no electricity but this was soon seen to and a telephone was also installed. A telephone at home was a status symbol in those days. There was no need for us to be connected to the municipal water system – right up to 1948 when we left the house, we depended on our cisterns.

A Greek lady, Maria, owned the property. She had emigrated to the Transvaal with her husband, appointing Archimandrite Thaddaeus of the Greek Orthodox convent to be her *wakeel* or agent. Archimandrite Thaddaeus was a tall jovial man, whom we got to know well through exchanging visits. The word 'archimandrite' was too much of a mouthful for the local inhabitants: they affectionately called him 'Chamandreet'.

11 CHILDREN AT HOME

From an early age we were stimulated by our environment, by open-air country life and by the people around us. We loved them and they loved us; we absorbed many of their deep qualities, their friendship, their hospitality and generosity. Our contact with them enriched our childhood and we learned the Arabic language with no effort. In time I spoke Jerusalem Arabic fluently, albeit with a slight English intonation which seemed to attract amused attention. We were not prevented by our parents from mixing freely with all – Arabs, Jews, Greeks, Armenians, Assyrians, Ethiopians. In time we could recognize them from their features and our ears were well attuned to their different languages and dialects. It was a great privilege to belong to so beautiful and exotic a blend of cultures.

We were deeply attached to our house in the Greek Colony and spent very happy days there. It had a certain charm and simplicity about it – decorated wooden ceilings, spacious rooms, and two verandas, one with an open view towards the south and west. The front entrance was up a flight of steps and across the veranda on the north side. Below it grew a pepper tree (*Schinus molle*), which resembled a weeping willow except that it produced clusters of pink berries every year. The garden, which was not very large, was surrounded by stone walls. When my parents moved in, it was a wilderness. An earth road ran past the front gate – very dusty in the summer and a quagmire in winter. The residents of the colony approached the municipality time and time again to have it tarred but to no avail. At the end of the mandate in 1948 it was still in the same condition.

My mother would have preferred to move to a modern house in a different locality but my father refused. He loved our old-fashioned

98 ARMENIANS OF JERUSALEM

house and had no desire to make a change. Our childhood there was happy and secure. Arab families lived across the road; we were on neighbourly terms with them and always played with their children.

When we were young we were spoilt by our parents and Armenian relatives, not with material things but with loving affection. It was customary for women visitors to demonstrate their love by a hard pinch of our cheeks, accompanied by a purr of admiration. For all their good intentions we found this custom painful and tried to avoid it.

On the east side of our garden a Greek couple had let the top floor of their house to Frau Dietz, a German widow, who lived with her daughter and granddaughter. They kept a large black dog called Pook. Early one morning we awoke to a deafening bang. Pook had got out without his collar and muzzle and was shot dead. There had been an outbreak of rabies at the time and he was mistaken for a stray. This caused great grief and poor Pook was ceremoniously buried in Frau Ditz's back garden. After Frau Dietz had left for Germany the wife of the owner, who had a lingering illness, was told by superstitious friends that she would only recover if Pook's remains were removed. The bones were indeed dug up and disposed of but the lady eventually died.

Our other neighbour, a Greek widow called Annoo, had rented out her house and lived with her mentally handicapped daughter, Khrooshee, in a hut built in the garden of her property. Annoo, or Umm Khrooshee as she was known to all, grew many kinds of herbs and also kept pigeons, rabbits and chickens. On the dividing fence between our gardens twined a vigorous passion creeper which in summer was a blaze of bluish flowers dripping with nectar, much visited by butterflies and bees. High above other trees in her garden towered a very tall and old eucalyptus (a *quina*, or quinine tree) with a large trunk of smooth peeling white bark. Annoo made a bitter brew out of boiled bark and leaves and recommended it for bad colds. Gentle winds blowing through the tree sounded like the sea, or so we imagined; in contrast winter storms would snap many brittle branches and bring them to the ground with a terrific crash.

There were no houses to the west, only fields and hills stretching away to the new suburb of Katamon. Beneath our garden wall on that side another earth track led to the village of Beit Safafa. Alongside it ran a shallow gully which eventually joined the wadi running south to Battir. In winter after heavy rains this stream-bed gushed with water for a few days, breaking its banks and flooding the fields around. The

CHILDREN AT HOME

pleasant murmur of running water could be heard throughout the house, especially in the stillness of the night.

When my elder sister Margaret was about six years old she was taken seriously ill. It was discovered that she had a mastoid infection and had to undergo surgery. There was no penicillin in those days and her condition was critical. She was operated on by Doctor Roux at the French hospital of St Louis opposite the New Gate. She recovered, but my mother recalled the anguish they went through when the wound had to be drained. Margaret was a delicate child and later on developed scarlet fever and had to be isolated. I myself was seldom ill but the one complaint which blighted me from a young age was migraine. My parents told me that it was first noticed on a drive to Jericho when as a baby I was taken ill.

At the age of four I had a bad fall and broke my right leg. We were playing parachutes on a windy afternoon in the garden, using a large black umbrella which we had borrowed without permission from the hall. All I can remember of the incident is that there was a crash followed by screams and intense pain. Dr Kalebian was called, my leg was put into a wooden splint and I was told not to move. No walking about: I had to remain in bed until it healed. I was cut off from all that I enjoyed out of doors.

As children we secretly believed that when we had accidents or fell ill my mother seemed severe and had little sympathy, always blaming us for negligence. However she did her best, applying her own professional knowledge and resorting to doctors only when absolutely necessary.

We had a medicine cupboard in the bathroom in which my mother kept various salts, packets of dried herbs, ointments, quinine and aspirin. A powder widely used for practically every ailment was 'solfato' – what it contained was a mystery, at least to us children. Cuts and bruises were daubed with black ichthyol ointment, which we later learned was distilled from bituminous rocks containing the remains of fossil fishes! This would be followed after a few days by white zinc ointment to complete the healing. Gauze and bandages were used for binding. When we had a stubborn boil a hot bread poultice was applied, drawing loud screams. The medicine we dreaded most was neat castor oil, which had a terrible taste and smell and inevitably made us sick. To avoid this our noses were pinched tight while the spoon of oil was pushed down our throats. A bottle of Sloan's Liniment was always on hand for back-aches and strained

100   ARMENIANS OF JERUSALEM

muscles. In Arabic everybody called it *Abu Schawareb* (father of the moustache) in reference to the picture of a man with handlebar whiskers on the label. Once used you could smell it for a mile.

For influenza and persistent coughs we were cupped, an ancient remedy widely used in the Middle East. Most households had about a dozen small glass cups known as *kassat hawa* (air cups). We would have to lie face downwards while my mother lit bits of screwed up paper which she placed in each cup. Just before the flame died down the cup was clamped on to our backs and held there by suction. The vacuum created by the flame was supposed to draw out all the infected air from our lungs. As a cure for mild chest colds we were given *baboonij* (camomile tea). For stomach aches a brew of *yansoun* (anise seed) was supposed to be good as were tisanes of Jerusalem sage or mint.

Most herbs used as cures were collected from the wild during the spring and were then placed on large straw trays and put out in the sun to dry. Prepared herbs were also available in the Suq el Atarin, the covered spice market in the Old City. Herbal cures were believed in, and frequently used by the local population.

On 5 May 1929 another child was born to the family – a girl named Gertrude Dorothy. She became our parents' pet as she was five years my junior.

Both our parents were strict: we were disciplined and expected to be well-behaved. My father kept his British ways. He rarely ate Arabic food and I for myself never heard him speak a word of Arabic. We were, however, told that he understood the language and could speak it but was too shy to do so. I later learned that the reason why many Europeans were reluctant to speak Arabic freely was because mistakes often drew amused laughter. The reason for amusement was error in pronunciation: small differences could lead to unexpected meanings, sometimes obscene or irrelevant.

At home the food problem was overcome and we children had the best of both worlds. My mother was a very good cook and insisted on doing all the cooking herself. For English dishes she always referred to her copy of *Mrs Beeton's Household Management*. My father loved his roast beef and Yorkshire pudding, lemon sole and other English food, including a variety of puddings and custards. The only Arabic dish he enjoyed was *mahshi malfouf* (cabbage leaves stuffed with meat and rice).

Fresh fruit was cheap and obtainable at all times of the year and

CHILDREN AT HOME

101

puddings were seldom served. Instead, a variety of sweetmeats such as *knafeh* and *namoura* were ordered at special shops in the *suq* and delivered to the house. However, to cater for Europeans, hotels around the Middle East introduced *crème caramel* onto the menu. For a time it was the only foreign dessert that was served and was soon to become popular in many households. To overcome the lack of fancy moulds it was commonly baked in an empty coffee or margarine tin and then turned out into a glass dish.

During the summer two Armenian sisters would come and look after us for a few hours in the afternoon. My mother used to sit in a basket-chair on the north veranda, usually repairing socks, sewing, or entertaining visitors to tea while we played in the garden below. Throughout our childhood we were always sure to find her at home when we came back from school.

We had help in the house. Dikranouhie, a young *kaghakatsi* woman, was our first maid. She lived in the Armenian Quarter, and came to us every morning: we became attached to her and cried our eyes out when she left to be married. She was followed by Na'ameh, a young Arab Muslim widow from Beit Safafa who had one son 'Issa. Na'ameh stayed with us for many years and became part of the family. We loved her dearly. She was tall and handsome with fair hair and greenish-blue eyes. As a devout Muslim, Na'ameh said prayers during the day, and for this was given the seclusion of the sitting room where the floor was covered with Persian carpets. She only came in the mornings, cleaned the house and went home after washing up the lunch dishes.

Na'ameh wore a traditional Beit Safafa embroidered dress right down to her ankles. She covered her head with long white veil concealing a beautifully embroidered cap kept in place by a soft cord under her chin. When very small I would run after her and try to pull the veil off her head. One day to deter me she told me about heaven and hell – of which I had not heard before; she warned me that naughty boys would be burned in a huge fire. I believed her, was terrified and from then on stopped teasing her.

When her son 'Issa started work, he insisted, much to our regret, that Na'ameh should retire. After she left us they built a small house on a plot of land they owned on the outskirts of Beit Safafa, below the Jewish settlement of Mekor Chaim. We often visited them there and I sometimes took a few of my pigeons in a hamper, letting them loose to fly the mile home to the Greek Colony. During the 1948 war Na'ameh and 'Issa had to abandon their property and flee to their

102 ARMENIANS OF JERUSALEM

village, Beit Safafa. The house into which they had ploughed all their earnings was subsequently blown up by the Jewish defence forces.

Laundry was done on Mondays by Umm Jameel, who came from the village of Beit Iksa. This small village is situated a few miles north-west of Jerusalem near Nebi Samwil, where the Prophet Samuel is supposedly buried. She would arrive very early in the morning and her first duty was to light a wood fire under a huge cauldron. All the linen was boiled and then washed by hand in large copper *lagans* or dishes. Cubes of Colman's blue were used while rinsing sheets and pillowcases which were then starched. In the summer Umm Jameel laundered out of doors; in the winter she moved under cover into a corrugated-iron shed in the garden. My mother and Na'ameh would tie up the washing lines and hang out all the linen which dried very quickly, especially in the summer heat. Poor Umm Jameel, she looked so tired by the end of the day and her hands were red and swollen. She then rubbed them with coarse salt to drain the skin of excess water, and to our amazement they looked normal once again. The going wage for a washerwoman was twenty piastres a day, plus breakfast and lunch. For breakfast she was given tea, bread, olives and cheese; for lunch usually *mujaddara* (a dish of lentils and rice). The following day my great-aunt Horop came in to do the ironing. She used a charcoal iron until we aspired to an electric one.

All cooking was done on a three-chimney Perfection stove which had a small removable oven. A glass container filled with paraffin gurgled away as it fed the wicks. Results were excellent even though the oven had no gauge or regulator, and by experience my mother was able to control the flame and the temperature. Paraffin was delivered to the house by a large horse-drawn tanker which came round once a week, the driver calling out *Kaz! Kaz!*.

My mother showed a keen interest in gardening. On the veranda she grew a variety of lovely ferns, begonias, impatiens and hydrangeas. In the garden below we had roses, fuchsias, jasmine and other flowering plants. At weekends Hajj Arabi would come and potter around the garden. Hajj Arabi was a widower and lived with his two unruly sons in a small house in Haret el Mugharbi, just off Bab el Silsileh (Gate of the Chain) in the Old City. We were frightened of him at first, as he had lost one eye and looked unfamiliar and fierce. We soon discovered that he was dignified, gentle and amusing, and we always looked forward to his coming.

The Hajj had his own method of gardening. He would scatter

CHILDREN AT HOME

parsley seeds on a prepared bed and then proceed to dig them in lightly with a *fass* or two-pronged pick, a most useful implement widely used in Palestine. I was then allowed to water the seeds, after which the bed was covered with hessian until germination. He held various theories of his own about plants: during the winter months when newly planted shrubs lay dormant, he would tell me that they were dreaming of their roots before coming into leaf. After seeds had germinated he would say: 'The earth does not hide anything' – *subhan Allah* (to God the glory).

In the autumn we planted lettuce on raised beds, covered with wire frames as a protection against sparrows. My mother never bought lettuce from the market in case it had been grown in the village of Silwan in the Kidron valley. Jerusalem's main sewage system passed through the village and in summer the water was used to irrigate surrounding vegetable gardens. It was widely believed, chiefly by Europeans, that all greens from that area, especially lettuce, could spread typhoid fever.

By the time I was five years old I was already showing a deep interest in gardening and flowers. This interest was inborn, grew and remains with me wherever I go. I learned much from the Hajj while he was at work in the garden. He was particularly good with herbs and vegetables, successfully grew stocks and sweat peas, which he amusingly referred to as 'Swiss peas'. My mother often took us to visit the Hajj in his Old City house and he always offered us delicious sweet mint tea served in small glass tumblers. When his sons came of age and moved away, the Hajj, after many years of living as a widower remarried and we were asked over to meet his new bride.

My parents were very fond of dogs and cats, and there was hardly a bird or fowl that we did not keep in the back garden of the Greek Colony house. Our first dogs were a pair of salukis given to my father while he was on an inspection tour at Ma'an in the east Jordan desert. We soon realized that these highly strung, sensitive, slender animals were not intended for town life so they were returned to the desert where they belonged. The salukis were replaced by a rather large sheepdog called Bonzo, a loveable creature, far too friendly and useless as a watchdog. He had a companion in Tibbles, our grey tom-cat. Tibbles used to disappear for long periods during which we thought he had perished, but he always surprised us by turning up again in sleek condition. He lived for fifteen years.

In the garden we kept chickens, geese, turkeys, ducks, pigeons,

104 ARMENIANS OF JERUSALEM

rabbits, a pair of guinea fowl and for a short time a baby gazelle. Indoors we had canaries and a green parrot with pink on its wings and a lemon-coloured tail. I was fascinated by them all and used to spend hours on end in the run feeding, cleaning out, collecting eggs, and just sitting and watching. If I was wanted by my parents I was inevitably to be found in the chicken run.

On two occasions our chickens were stolen during the night. Bonzo made no attempt to alert us and we found the pens empty next morning. We started all over again but after a few months the chickens were taken once more. This time the birds had all been killed and to our horror their heads were left lying in the pen. Undeterred we introduced new stock yet again. Soon afterwards Bonzo met the same fate as Pook. He slipped out without his collar and was shot dead. We decided not to keep another dog.

Shortly after our move to the Greek Colony my father had started on one of his life-long interests, the building of a pipe organ at home. He devoted all his spare time to it, working on the project for twenty-five years. The cellar below the house was converted into a workshop. In addition to wooden pipes he made all the other intricate parts himself. Lead was melted down, moulded into sheets, planed to the right thickness and also rolled into pipes. He was very skilled and had great patience. I would often sit and watch him work.

The organ, which was housed in its own room on the ground floor, eventually had two manuals as well as a pedal board. An electric blower in a shed in the garden provided air for the bellows. My father would work on the instrument every day after coming home from the PWD. As a result he took no part in the whirl of social life which went on in Jerusalem and after a while was dropped from invitation lists, but that did not matter to him. As I grew up he would ask me to play the organ for him in the evening so that he could listen to it from a distance. He also played constantly himself, preferring above all the works of J. S. Bach. His perfect pitch and sensitive ear enabled him to tune the instrument with me as his assistant.

Another of my father's interests was restoring antique clocks and watches, many of which were thought to be beyond repair. For this he bought the necessary tools and worktable and would spend hours peering through his loupe, exercising skill and thought.

My father loved his home; he was a quiet man who did not talk much about his work at the public works department. However, in the years following the earthquake of 11 July 1927, when he was involved in the repairs at the Church of the Holy Sepulchre, we could hear him talking about the difficulties his team of men encountered when installing the huge iron girders which were to secure the walls. These girders, which saved the building, were only gradually removed after 1963 when the religious communities in charge of the church started on their joint scheme of restoration.

12 LIFE IN THE GREEK COLONY

After the British took over Palestine life continued at a slow and gentle pace for a while, but the introduction of western ideas was soon to bring about change. The war was over and there were new openings in government departments, education, business and trade, all contributing to development and prosperity.

Wages remained low but day-to-day living was cheap and there was an abundance of local produce from the countryside. Fruit and vegetables were often sold at the door by village women, who would bring their produce in round, flat baskets cleverly balanced on their heads. The Greek and German Colonies, the Baqa'a and Katamon were served by the Arab villages to the south – Beit Safafa, Malha, Walajeh, Battir and Sur Bahir. Tomatoes, cucumbers, aubergines, broad beans (*fool* in Arabic) as well as a large variety of fruit – apricots, sugar apples, quince, grapes and figs – were brought to the door. It was customary to bargain with the women and after some argument they usually brought the price down. Another source of fruit and vegetables was the covered bazaar at the lower end of David Street in the Old City. My mother often did her shopping there. On Friday mornings she would rise early and go off to the fish shop just inside the Jaffa Gate. Fresh fish arrived by rail from Jaffa on that day and included sultan Ibrahim and bouri (red and grey mullet), and sometimes imported sole.

We never had to buy eggs as we had our own hens, but we often bought live *seesan*, young cockerels or pullets for the table. They were offered for sale at the door, costing about twelve piastres for four birds regardless of their weight. My mother saw to it that they were isolated from the hen run for a while in case they carried disease. For about a

LIFE IN THE GREEK COLONY

week they were well fed to fatten them up, during which time I would become attached to them and implore her to spare their lives.

Mr Spinney, an Englishman, had opened a chain of stores in the larger towns of Palestine. Most of his goods were imported from England and were of high quality. He had two stores in Jerusalem, a large one in Mamillah Road and the other in the German Colony. His store in Mamillah included an outfitting department where we bought most of our clothes. Both stores had meat departments, which were well patronized by expatriates as they were run on European lines.

There were many Arab butchers inside the Old City, but to westerners they seemed primitive. The sight of carcasses hanging in rows appalled them, there were no 'cuts' and it was usual to buy a leg of mutton or lamb or a piece of beef. Men always went shopping for meat and Arab women were discouraged from doing so. Translated into Arabic a leg of lamb is a *fakhdeh*, which strictly speaking means 'thigh'. It was beneath a woman's dignity to mention such a word as 'thigh' in front of a butcher; besides which there was fear that it could lead to undesirable conversation. With the passage of time this rule no longer applies.

Fresh milk was delivered to the house each day sent by Migerditch, a *kaghakatsi* who kept a few cows in the Old City not far from the Dung Gate. Mohammad, a young Muslim from the village of Bethany, brought the churns round on the back of a white mule early in the morning. At the garden gate he would give a loud whistle, my mother would tell him how much we needed and he would measure it out by weight in *rotls*. The milk had to be boiled as it was neither pasteurized nor homogenized. Mohammad always managed to come, even in very bad weather and during the frequent violent disturbances that occurred in Jerusalem. Bread was also delivered daily in a horse-drawn box carriage from Frank's bakery in the German Colony.

Winters in Jerusalem were very cold and extended from November to March. The worst weather often occurred between the Greek Orthodox Christmas on 6 January and the Armenian Orthodox Christmas on 19 January, when it usually turned wet and sometimes snowed. For heating the house we resorted to Perfection paraffin stoves. We loved it when the electricity failed and the stove provided light, flickering pretty patterns on the walls and ceilings of the room, giving us a sense of security. We also had a blue-tiled German wood stove which my father lit up in the hall when he came back from work. In it we burned chunks of olive wood which exuded a pleasant smell.

108 ARMENIANS OF JERUSALEM

Wood was easily available and cheap; it was delivered on the backs of camels. These bad-tempered animals disobediently pranced around and made the most frightening growling sounds while being coaxed to kneel by their owners. In stubborn fashion they would bare their teeth and refuse to obey, which made unloading difficult. Watching, we stood well away fearing that in their fury they would suddenly kick or bite us.

Soon after the first rains the parched countryside is gradually transformed into a lush green meadow which early in the new year changes into a patchwork quilt of wild flowers. We had only to walk a short distance from the house to find the most lovely wild flowers growing in abundance among the rocks – sweetly scented winter crocus (*Crocus hyemalis*), scarlet anemones (*Anemone coronaria*) and pink cyclamen (*Cyclamen persicum*). Our special haunt, which we visited each spring, was a mound of stones which we named 'Cyclamen hill'. Through every crevice these lovely flowers found space to bloom, forming a haze of pink above their dark-green marbled leaves.

It is hardly possible to list the varieties of wild flowers that grew in the area: as winter developed into spring and summer there was a quick succession of plants and change of colour and scene. Spectacular were the fields carpeted with deep pink *Silene aegyptiaca* broken by yellow patches of *Senecio vernalis* and interspersed with inky pools of speedwell (*Veronica syriacus*). Among the wheat grew purple gladioli (*Gladiolus segetum*), along with yellow *Chrysanthemum coronarium*.

We learned the colloquial Arabic names for these flowers, which were usually associated with animals, the gazelle featuring often. A cyclamen flower was known as *qarn el ghazal* (gazelle's horn) or sometimes as *ghalyoun sidi* (my grandfather's pipe), or *sabounet el ra'i* (shepherd's soap). The corms of cyclamen were in fact used in ancient times for the washing of clothes. *Silene aegyptiaca* was referred to as *qutain el ghazal* (the gazelle's dried fig) for the sticky calyx of the plant resembled a miniature dried fig. Gladioli, which usually grew in wheat fields, were described as *danab el warwar* or foxes' tails from the way they bobbed back and forth in the wind. To the local inhabitants flowers had to have a strong scent; beauty alone was not enough. Wild flowers were seldom picked unless they happened to be a source of food.

At night we would be lulled into sleep by the lethargic song of myriads of dreamy crickets, only to be woken at times by the distant wail of jackals or the shriek of an owl. At the first glimmer of light from the east, in summer as early as four in the morning, large groups

LIFE IN THE GREEK COLONY 109

of sparrows that had spent the night in the pines would greet the day. A single bird would break into song, others would gradually join in to build up a deafening chorus. The chatter would go on for some time, then amazingly at one stroke the sparrows would all fall silent. The chorus would be taken up by the raucous cry of hooded crows calling from one treetop to the other and the persistent shrilling of cicadas heralding a hot day. We scanned the trunks of trees to find the insects' hiding places, but they always eluded us. No matter how hot the day, a cool breeze would blow in from the west at about five in the afternoon and the temperature would drop.

After the autumn rains the fields around the house were ploughed. No machines were used, just a ploughshare usually drawn by a pair of oxen or a horse. Wheat, barley, chickpeas or lentils were planted, to be harvested by hand in May and June. Villagers would help each other, moving from field to field. There was much merry-making, chatting, singing and flute-playing during that time. Before returning home after a week's work in the fields around the Greek Colony house we would often hear the villagers sing with delight:

> Ya azziz eini, wa bidi arraweh baladi
> Baladi, ya baladi, wa bidi arraweh baladi
> Thou beloved of my eye, I am going back to my village,
> my village, Oh my village, I am going back to my village.

The harvest completed, shepherds brought in their sheep to eat the stubble. Some fields were ploughed in the spring and planted with vegetables such as *lubieh* (a black-eyed bean), okra, tomatoes, gherkins and cousa (a form of courgette much used in the east). These crops were not watered, relying entirely on the heavy dew which was frequent during summer nights. The flavour of summer vegetables was tasty and distinctive, far superior to the produce of present-day irrigated fields. The *fellaheen* (village farmers) built temporary hessian shelters to stay in overnight. After dark they lit fires to cook on and to keep away wild animals.

The summer over, the villagers would move away to their olive groves. The ministry of agriculture set a date for *jdad el zeitoun* (the olive-picking season) to begin. Family and friends, as well as hired labourers, take part in this annual working holiday. It is the young who clamber up trees by means of tall wooden ladders, where they either pluck the fruit by hand or thrash it off the branches with a long

110 ARMENIANS OF JERUSALEM

cane. Sheeting is spread on the ground to catch the falling fruit, which is then collected and packed into sacks.

In the crisp autumn air the valleys echo with sounds of merriment. Days are getting shorter and nights damp and cool. Nocturnal sounds shatter the silence, the laughter of a hyena, the bark of a fox, the hooting of an owl. Under the trees groups of pink colchicum, *siraj el ghul* (wolf's oil-lamps) light up the dark-brown earth. Silhouetted on the verges of terraced fields, long white spikes of squills, *bassal el far* (mouse's onions), stand pointing to the sky. The leaves of both these plants will follow after the first rains. Climbing up stone rubble walls, untidy thickets of spiny *smilax* display bunches of red berries among leathery heart-shaped leaves. Wild pistachio (*butum)*, plum, fig and grape vine show hints of autumn colouring. Coveys of rock partridges lurk under the bushes and take flight as soon as disturbed.

After the olives are gathered, the trees are pruned and the ground around them ploughed. This accomplished, the sacks are transported on donkeys or mules back to the villages. There the olives are spread out on roofs and terraces to catch the sun for further ripening in preparation for the extraction of oil.

Since biblical times there have been oil and wine presses in the country. Many of these, hewn from solid rock, have been uncovered at archaeological sites. The *massra'a* (press) of today has been mechanized, but is still conveniently located to serve towns and villages within an olive-growing district. Payment to the owners of the press is made in kind, in proportion to the quantity of olive oil extracted.

During our childhood many vendors and travelling craftsmen came round to the house offering their services, and my mother made use of them. Our kitchen knives and garden implements were sharpened by a fierce and handsome Afghan who called twice a year. His equipment included a grindstone attached by a leather strap to a large wooden wheel which he manipulated with his foot. We would watch him work under the trees in the garden, standing well away from the sparks that flew around. Many of the Afghans who had settled in Jerusalem were knife-grinders. They worked on pavements around a disused fountain in the Muristan near to the Church of the Holy Sepulchre, sharpening blades for the inhabitants of the city.

Our shoes were repaired by a roving shoemaker who came to the house bringing a portable last and his tools with him. He would work under the trees in the garden, and told us stories while we watched.

LIFE IN THE GREEK COLONY 111

Later on a shoe-repair shop was opened in the German Colony by an Armenian, Yeremiah by name. He had been trained at Schneller's orphanage and had a reputation for good work. However we much preferred our roving friend as Yeremiah always looked solemn and a smile never crossed his face.

We slept on cotton mattresses which had to be fluffed up every year by a *mnajed*, a cotton-beater from the cotton *suq*, Suq el Qattatin near the Haram el Sharif. He worked on the veranda using an implement which looked like a long one-stringed harp made of lightweight wood. A thick wire cord, attached to both ends, was thrust into the pile of cotton and beaten lightly with a large wooden pestle. The rhythmic action created musical sounds, while lumps of cotton were flung all over the place, separating and becoming soft again. The *mnajed* would then collect all the cotton and sew and button it up into the mattress case which had in the meantime been washed. Cotton-filled mattresses, quilts and pillows were commonly used all over the Middle East and were believed to be cool in a hot climate. With the introduction of interior-sprung and foam-rubber mattresses the *mnajed* lost most of his work.

Every autumn we were visited by a *sangari* who inspected the tin gutters around the roof, soldered any holes, removed pine needles and birds' nests and swept the gutters in readiness for the rains. The pipes to the cisterns were only connected in January after the roof had been well washed by a number of downpours.

In the afternoons vendors came round with various delicacies which they advertised with a loud cry. These foods were placed on large rectangular wooden trays carried on the head, where for comfort's sake a small cloth-padded ring was worn. Large copper trays that had been tin-plated were used for sweetmeats smothered in syrup. A tripod was also carried around on which to rest the tray while selling.

We were tempted to buy toffee-apples, green almonds and a variety of sticky cakes, some of them date-filled. The most common cake was *ka'ek*, circles of crusty bread thickly covered with sesame seeds. On the tray were a choice of accompaniments – oven-baked eggs, *fallafel* (fried chickpea rissoles) or *za'atar*. Green almonds came into season around April and were usually placed over and around a lump of ice to bring out the flavour and make them deliciously cold. My mother did not allow us to eat them as she feared stomach upsets.

An icecream man calling out '*Booza, booza*' sold a variety of water ices on hot days. One of his specialities was a delicious milk-ice

112   ARMENIANS OF JERUSALEM

flavoured with *mistka* (gum arabic) and sprinkled with pistachio nuts. Cold drinks were brought round and usually sold at street corners or in the main thoroughfares. These were refreshing, extracted from liquorice (*soos*), tamarind or carob. The vendor commonly wore baggy trousers, an embroidered waistcoat and a tarboosh. The juice was contained in a large polished urn of copper or brass with a spout. The urn was strapped to his back at such an angle that he only needed to bend slightly forward to fill a glass. In one hand he held two small brass bowls which he clapped together to attract attention.

A great favourite with everybody, *hamleh*, was sold at the beginning of summer and consisted of a tied bunch of lightly roasted chickpea plants laden with little pouches, each containing a pea. The roasted peas, which were delicious, were picked off individually and eaten then and there in the street. One seldom sees *hamleh* bunches any more; the pouches are now removed beforehand, roasted and sold in small brown paper bags.

We did not have an electric refrigerator at home; instead we used a large icebox. Blocks of ice from a factory in the Katamon were delivered daily in a grey-painted horse-drawn covered cart. To make the ice last longer my mother wrapped it in a hessian sack. We would often go for walks to the ice factory which was owned by a Greek family, the Shtakleffs. Simple pleasures: we stood and watched the water trickling through layers of wooden-slatted troughs filled with dried *natsh* (*Poterium spinosum*), a thorny plant that grew wild in the hills. The *natsh* aerated the water to speed up the freezing process, while many birds hovered around the troughs waiting to bathe and quench their thirst.

Street entertainment for children was provided in various ways. The most exciting was the *sanduq el ajam* or Persian peepshow. The owner would go round from street to street with a large semicircular blue wooden box on his back which he put down on a stand, and for a fee we were allowed to sit on a bench and peep inside. As we watched, he intoned his story and wound the highly coloured pictures in the box across our field of vision. We could not understand a word of his rough guttural language but it did not really matter as it was fascinating just to watch the story unfold. On top of the box sat two live fantail pigeons with wings clipped and tails dyed pink and green. When frightened they would try to fly away but always crashed helplessly to the ground. At other times we joined groups of children in the street to watch a dancing bear. It was brought round on a chain attached to

LIFE IN THE GREEK COLONY 113

a huge ring in its nose, and performed to the sound of a tambourine. Sometimes monkeys and chimpanzees would also entertain us with their tricks.

One event which my mother forbade us to have anything to do with was fortune-telling. A gipsy woman known as a *basara* came round calling: '*Basara, basara, ibtiftah el bakhet!*' (Fortune teller, fortune teller, will reveal your luck!) We understood that by looking into a tray of sand and playing about with shells she was able to foretell the future. She was kept well away from the garden gate and we were not allowed to have any contact with her, although we secretly longed to.

One often wonders how these people made a living, as they usually had large families to fend for and they earned very little. What counted to them was that they should be *mastoureen* (maintaining dignity) in the eyes of friends and relatives. Amassing riches was out of the question: one of their sayings was *bidna in'eesh* (all we want is to be able to survive). Unfortunately even this dignity was to be denied to them, as thousands had to abandon their homes and villages in the face of the wars which were to plague their country. They were driven out to become refugees in 1948 and again in 1967 with no possibility of return.

Our daily contacts made life exciting and interesting and at the time we thought things would continue for ever in this pleasant manner. As very small children we were oblivious of the political unrest in the country. We only became aware of it when there was serious trouble in Hebron in 1929 and my father was appointed special constable and sent on reserve duty there. During that time he kept a large rifle in the house, which frightened us children. The only thing we understood was that something serious and terrible was happening in the country. Even though I was only five at the time, from listening to my parents' conversation I gathered that my mother was always anxious lest my father should come to harm. Everybody discussed the political situation, so much so that it had a lasting effect on us from our early years. I could never understand why people should be so cruel to each other. Soon I was to discover that I had been born into an age of violence, and from then on all my life in Palestine was beset by danger, riots and war. Unfortunately I grew up in surroundings where it was common to hear the sound of explosions and rifle fire and to learn of daily killings.

In various discussions the name Balfour was becoming a household

114 ARMENIANS OF JERUSALEM

word, and there was much talk about *wa'ed* Balfour – the Balfour Declaration of 2 November 1917. This stated:

> His Majesty's Government view with favour the establishment in Palestine of a National Home for the Jewish people, and will use their best endeavours to facilitate the achievement of this object, it being clearly understood that nothing shall be done which may prejudice the civil and religious rights of existing non-Jewish communities in Palestine, or the rights and political status enjoyed by Jews in any other country.

To the villagers as well as the townsfolk the word Balfour conjured up fear that one day in the future they would lose their land and be displaced by the Jews. Dissent and protest by the Arabs against the Balfour Declaration had started as early as 1919 but to no avail. An amusing story that went around at the time was that a government official heard a villager induce his donkey to walk faster by a hit on the back with the words '*Yalla! ya Balfour*!' (Get a move on, Balfour) – an insult as a donkey was considered to be a dull and stupid animal.

13 CHILDREN AT SCHOOL

During the First World War education in Palestine was disrupted and most foreign schools were closed for four years. Only the Germans, as allies of Turkey, had been permitted to carry on with their educational work. When the British took over, it was intended that schooling should be available for all.

After the capture of Jerusalem in December 1917 the British military authorities ordered all German nationals to leave the country. The Diakonissen at Talitha Cumi (my mother's old school) had to abandon their work and buildings, leaving behind about a hundred Palestinian girls, many with no homes to go to. The school was taken over by the Syria and Palestine Relief Fund. Miss Mabel Warburton, who had been headmistress of the British Syrian Girls' School in Beirut and had worked in the Near East since 1903, was put in charge of the girls' welfare. She had served in Egypt and the Sudan during the 1914 war and was fluent in Arabic.

In 1919 the Relief Fund came to an end, but at the direct request of General Allenby the Talitha buildings were commandeered for a further five years. By now the number of pupils had risen to 200, of whom 100 were orphaned. To continue their education, Miss Warburton, sponsored by the Jerusalem and the East Mission and other missionary societies, founded the British High School for Girls in 1920. No rent was to be paid for the use of the Talitha buildings for five years but Miss Warburton immediately set to work to ensure the future of the school by raising funds for land and new buildings, to be ready when Talitha had to be relinquished. Forty thousand pounds was raised, a company formed and a large plot of land secured in west Jerusalem close to the Ratisbonne monastery, in what was to become the Jewish suburb of Rehavia.

116 ARMENIANS OF JERUSALEM

Only one of the new school buildings was completed when the Diakonissen returned from exile on 1 July 1925. Miss Warburton, however, opened her school for the autumn term in the new premises in Rehavia. The name of the institution was changed to The Jerusalem Girls' College. It grew to be one of the best educational establishments for young ladies in the city, the only college in the Arabic-speaking Near East to provide education for girls on British lines up to university standard.

The majority of the pupils were Arab Palestinian girls, both Muslim and Christian, joined by a few Jews, Armenians, Greeks and Assyrians. The girls were given a good secondary education and acquired a perfect knowledge of the English language; on graduating many found positions in government offices. Miss Warburton retired in 1926 and was succeeded by Miss Jameson. In 1928 Miss Winifred Coate was appointed principal, but after ten years moved to the Bishop's School at Ain Anoub in the Lebanon. She was succeeded by Miss Ruth Barlow.

The college operated normally until February 1947, when riots and disturbances made it unsafe for Arab girls to attend school in a Jewish suburb. By government order it was closed and the buildings used to house Jewish refugees evicted from elsewhere. Classes were temporarily moved to St George's Close with an overflow at the American Colony hostel. In January 1948 an exchange of premises was agreed between the Jerusalem Girls' College and the Evelina de Rothschild School (run by Miss Annie Landau, famous for her beautiful garden). It was in the Arab quarter of Musrara now unsafe for Jewish students. This arrangement did not last; the situation worsened and many of the college's teachers were evacuated. One of them, Miss Marston, who had loyally stayed behind, was shot dead by a sniper on Easter Day 1948 while on her way to the Evelina. It was now impossible for the college to continue; closure came soon after in April 1948. A noble missionary endeavour in the field of education for girls in Palestine had come to an abrupt end after 23 years.

In 1929, when I was five, I joined my elder sister, Margaret, at the preparatory school founded the previous year under the aegis of the Jerusalem Girls' College. This was known as the British section, it was co-educational and only English and American children were admitted. The school occupied a two-storey building within the compound of the Girls' College grounds. We had a separate entrance and playground and were not allowed to mix with the pupils of the

CHILDREN AT SCHOOL

117

college, who were divided from us by a tennis court and netball field. The whole came under the direction of Miss Coate, who had her office in the college building. She was an able administrator, a strict disciplinarian who commanded respect from staff and pupils alike.

Children were admitted between the ages of five and twelve for girls, ten for boys. Miss M. M. Bayley was in charge of the British section, assisted by Miss Bennett who took the kindergarten. They were both experienced teachers with higher certificates from the National Froebel Union. Miss Daisy Cross, who had formerly been an assistant housemistress at Cheltenham Ladies' College, was in charge of the household. Miss Bayley and Miss Cross were very strict, and my sister and I imagined that they were even more so with us. We were not in awe of our other teachers and found them sympathetic.

Children in the kindergarten attended from 8.30 to 12.00; the older ones remained for lunch and had classes in the afternoon. At lunchtime under supervision we took turns to lay the table. The food was good, a large plate of semolina with a floating dollop of golden syrup was served as pudding every day.

The day started with prayers and the singing of a hymn. The school curriculum included English, Latin, French, history and geography, mathematics, singing and dancing, as well as games, drill, knitting and handiwork. Eurythmics was taught by a lady who came in once a week; she was tall and athletic and wore her hair in what looked to us like two plaited earphones. Mlle Robert taught us French and Miss Elinor Moore came over from the Girls' College to teach history.

In our singing lessons we were taught new hymns and traditional English songs. The singing would occasionally get out of control and wind down to a dead halt. Our teacher, Miss Richardson, would then ask me to sing a certain line of music on my own, much to my embarrassment. I never understood why I was picked out. Many years later when I mentioned it to Miss Coate she told me that it was very unusual for so young a child to be able to carry a tune and I was the only one in the class who could do so.

We were encouraged to work in the garden and were given a small plot each in a sheltered spot in which to plant annual seeds. At the end of term a prize was given to the child who grew the best flowers. One day in 1931 there was great excitement: we were told to look up into the sky to see the *Graf Zeppelin* fly over Jerusalem. To us young children it was indeed a frightening sight.

In class we were closely supervised and bad habits were firmly

118 ARMENIANS OF JERUSALEM

checked. Paul, one of our classmates, used to chew the end of his pencils. After repeated warnings a nasty mixture of mustard and bitter aloes was placed on adhesive tape and wrapped around each one as a deterrent. At first he bravely claimed to like the taste but his habit was soon broken.

In the afternoons we had handicraft lessons and made canvas needlecases, or knitted scarves in rainbow wool with colours that ran into each other producing fascinating patterns. A small group was taught to play on percussion instruments, tambourines, cymbals and triangles. On the first of May we danced to music around a tall maypole, each excited child singing and clutching a different coloured ribbon. Thus were spent our very early formative years, under teachers whose Froebel training introduced us to rhythm, harmony and the arts.

There was, however, another side to our school life, for my sister and I still felt that Miss Bayley and Miss Cross did not really approve of us. We were sure that this was because we were half Armenian, and that they took a dislike to us due to our foreign connection. I was often picked upon for unruly behaviour and was obviously an annoyance to them, although other teachers did not react in the same way. I was frequently sent by Miss Bayley to be scolded by Miss Coate in her office across the compound. As a result I lived in terror of Miss Coate, who would make me wait for what seemed an age outside her office. In the hall stood large glass cases containing fossils, flints, ancient iron implements and a preserved sunfish. I would pass the time enthralled by all these antiquities, forgetting what was awaiting me. Then into the office, warnings, stern words and threats of dismissal if my behaviour did not improve, and I was to be reported to my parents.

As young children we had many activities outside school. We were regularly sent to Sunday School held in the Templist meeting-house in the German Colony. The classes were taken by some of our teachers, assisted by ladies who came from St George's Cathedral – Mrs Campbell MacInnes among them, remembered with great affection. After we had settled down we were marched round the church to music – *The Merry Peasant* or March from *Scipio* – strummed on an untuned piano by one of the teachers. We were then broken up into small groups and instructed in Old and New Testament stories.

For Christmas a few children were chosen to put on a tableau of the Nativity. I inevitably took the part of a shepherd, my costume that

CHILDREN AT SCHOOL

of an Arab Palestinian villager. The angels wore white organza dresses and had golden wings made of cardboard. Some of the children were so young that they were lifted bodily on and off the stage by teachers who stood behind the curtains. It always amused us when a pair of hands appeared and a small frightened angel disappeared from the scene.

We had long holidays during the year – nearly three weeks at Christmas and Easter and three months during the summer. In the summer holidays we spent much of the time with my grandmother and aunt Isquhie in Ramallah. When at home, for me it was back to chickens and gardening and other exciting hobbies. Other English children were members of the junior section of the Jerusalem Sports Club and spent their summer afternoons there. The club was out of bounds to non-Britons.

We sometimes took a shortcut across the club football field. One day while doing so my sister Gertie and a friend (whose mother was Greek) were stopped by a forceful English lady exercising her horse. 'Do you not know that only English girls are allowed here?' she bellowed. They told her they *were* English and continued defiantly on their way. This is only one example of the patronizing attitudes which prevailed in a colonial society.

We often played at the homes of other English children. For a time we were regularly invited to spend the afternoon and play in the garden with a young girl called Gillian, an only child whose parents lived up the road from our house in what had been Bishop Efthimios's summer residence. The arrangement came to a sudden end when her grandmother reported me to my mother for being rude: all I had said was that we were tired of playing with Gillian every day of the week and wanted a change. On another occasion I accidentally pushed a friend of mine, William, into the mud in the lane outside our house. His mother came over and said I had been very rough and was never to play with him again. My mother refused to be humiliated by these reports and always defended me.

There were some children's parties to which we were not invited. However, one we always went to was that given by the then High Commissioner for Palestine, Sir Arthur Wauchope, which took place in the ball-room at Government House every Christmas. All British children up to the age of twelve received invitations. A magnificent tea was provided, with coloured jellies in baskets made from scooped-out

120 ARMENIANS OF JERUSALEM

oranges, and biscuits covered in brown icing with figures of animals picked out in white.

Afterwards there was a hush when Father Christmas appeared down the chimney of a large fireplace overhung with a decorated conical stone hood which stood at one end of the room. Many of the younger children were frightened and would burst into tears, only to be consoled by the presents he distributed from his large sack. Sir Arthur was very kind and made sure we all had a good time.

My days were full of interest and there was always something going on. I was busy – walking into the fields around the house to look for flowers, catching butterflies, spending hours fascinated with tadpoles and toads in pools of water which had accumulated during the winter months, flying kites in the autumn winds and of course gardening. At weekends my father would often drive us out into the country in his Wolseley, my mother beside him and us children windblown in the dickey.

We were given five piastres a week pocket money and no more. This we usually spent on chocolates and sweets at Nichola's corner shop near the Greek Club. Nichola was a Greek, and like Yeremiah the shoemaker seldom smiled. After years as a bachelor he surprised us all by marrying an Arab lady who worked for the Claytons next door to his shop. My father used to buy his whisky at Nichola's. When he had finished an evening's work on his hobby, building the pipe organ, he would relax in a Morris chair with a glass of whisky beside him and puff away at his pipe. Before going to bed we went up to him, said goodnight and kissed his cheek. We were brought up to address our parents in the old-fashioned way – Papa and Mama.

14 SUMMERS IN RAMALLAH

After their marriage my aunt Isquhie and her husband, Ibrahim Audi, settled in the Arab town of Ramallah, about ten miles north of Jerusalem, the town where he had been born.

Ibrahim's father, one of three enterprising Audi brothers, had owned an olive oil press which served Ramallah and the surrounding villages. In an accident he lost part of his hand. He developed gangrene and died on the very day on which his second child, a son, was born. It was his wish that if the baby were a boy he should be named after him – Ibrahim. At the time his wife was only eighteen years old. Later, encouraged by her in-laws, she married Nichola Michail of Ramallah. They had four sons and three daughters. The eldest son was named Najib and after his birth the household was called Dar Abu Najib.

The first years of Ibrahim's and Isquhie's marriage in the early 1920s was a time of recession throughout the country and work was scarce. Ibrahim was impatient and restless and decided that he should return to North America to seek work there. To raise money he sold his inheritance, and on 15 August 1923 set out for the United States. They had planned that Isquhie should follow as soon as Ibrahim was settled, but this was not to be. She never saw him again. At first he wrote and sent money and presents but soon letters became few and far between then ceased. Ibrahim was one of many who just disappeared in the vast continent of the United States. Isquhie remained a close friend of the Audi family, and after her husband's departure rented rooms in her mother-in-law's house. Dressmaking became her profession and only source of income.

In 1930 Mariam, my grandmother, left her Old City house and went to live with Isquhie in Ramallah. After their marriage in 1929

122 ARMENIANS OF JERUSALEM

Malakeh and her husband, Sahag, had moved in with her, but it was not a satisfactory arrangement. Even though she was deprived of her house, community, and above all participating in services in the cathedral of St James, she enjoyed living with Isquhie, who looked after her with love and care until her death in 1941.

When we went to Ramallah during the summer holidays, my sister Margaret and I were driven there by my father, who would stay with us for a few hours before his return to Jerusalem. After he had left my aunt and grandmother tried their best to ensure that we were happy and secure and felt at home. However as darkness fell we began to feel lonesome, and during supper we burst into tears and demanded our immediate return to the Greek Colony. Of course this was impossible and after comforting words we settled for the night. The same thing happened after our return home at the end of the holiday. We missed my aunt and my grandmother so much that we burst into tears, again during supper. We were indeed very young and sensitive.

At the time Ramallah was a charming and unspoilt town of about 5,000 inhabitants, most of whom belonged to the Greek Orthodox Church. In 1869 British and American Quakers had visited the town and over the years their influence had spread. Their educational work developed and they founded two schools, Friends' Girls' School in 1889 and Friends' Boys' School in 1901, both of which continue to this day.

The summer months were cool, making Ramallah a popular resort, a rival to those found in the mountains of Lebanon. There was only one hotel, the Grand, owned by Ibrahim's cousin Hanna Audi and run by the family. It had retained standards of elegance and a friendly old-world atmosphere. To escape the heat many families from the coastal areas would pass part of the summer there. At weekends guests came for lunch and spent the afternoon enjoying their meals and drinks in the shady grounds around the hotel. In the evenings a dance-band played foxtrots, tangos, rumbas and English waltzes from a stand, while couples glided round the floor below. Periodically a waiter would sprinkle Lux soap flakes over the tiles to make them slippery and facilitate the dancing. The view from the garden led one's eyes over hills and valleys, right down to the Mediterranean coast where lights could be seen twinkling on clear nights.

At the time Dar abu Najib, the house where we spent our summers, lay on the edge of the town. Now it is flanked by main roads and surrounded by shops. It was very old, built of stone weathered by time

SUMMERS IN RAMALLAH 123

to the colour of honey, two storeys high with a red-tiled roof. Part of the house was divided into small apartments let to summer visitors. My aunt had one large room and shared a spacious hall, on the ground floor facing south. We all slept in the large room which was fresh and airy with a vaulted ceiling, two arched windows protected by iron bars shutters which were closed at night. Outside grew a tall Comice pear tree, its leaves rustling in the slightest breeze.

The kitchen was out of doors, and a hut under a mulberry tree served as a lavatory; there were two cisterns in the garden, one filled with rainwater, the other fed from a natural spring and used only for drinking. To the south stretched acres of vineyards with not another house in sight. In the crannies of the loosely built stone boundary wall a sprawling *Ephedra* bush grew, providing a home for a colony of glow-worms which shimmered with green light as soon as night fell. We were in awe of these marvellous insects and accompanied by my aunt made regular visits to see them.

My aunt's in-laws treated us as relatives, and we affectionately called Abu Najib 'Ami Inoola (Uncle Nichola). Umm Najib wore traditional Ramallah *twab*, long gowns of black or white linen embroidered with red cross-stitch. Imported skeins of white silk thread, which had been coloured at home with vegetable dyes, were used. The threads were then wound round a sheep's bone as a spool. The *twab* had long wide triangular sleeves which were kept out of the way during work-time by knotting the points behind the neck. A heavily embroidered headdress was worn, fringed with gold or silver coins and covered with a long tasselled shawl – lightweight for summer, wool for winter.

'Ami Inoola wore a *qumbaz*, a gown of blue and white stripes made of cotton with a silken finish. Around his waist he wound a cummerbund in which he kept his gold watch. Indoors he wore a skullcap which he covered with *hatta* and *'agal* when he went out. Their youngest son Boulos, together with his charming wife Badi'a, lived with them. Badi'a, who also wore traditional Ramallah dress, was very beautiful, with the most lovely smiling blue eyes.

'Ami Inoola had worked in the Friends' Girls' School as an odd-job man and in their bakery. Every few days he would drive a horse and cart from Ramallah to Jerusalem, buy provisions, collect the mail and carry out errands for the staff. The pupils trusted him; he joked and sympathized with them to the point of covering up for their pranks, which indeed he often encouraged. When the girls stole eggs

124 ARMENIANS OF JERUSALEM

from the chicken house, they would ask him to bake them in rounds of dough and he did so without a word of reproach.

'Ami Inoola was ambitious and after some years emigrated to North America where he hoped to find better-paid work. He left his family behind, but Umm Najib did not approve of this move and bombarded him with letters pleading for his return. He finally gave in and came back to Ramallah where he started a grocery store. By then he had acquired a strong American accent, and always called me 'Jan', whereas most of my Arab friends referred to me as 'Jawn'. 'Ami Inoola lived to be 100 years old, stayed in the same house, and after the death of his wife Umm Najib was looked after by his widowed daughter-in-law, Badi'a.

As Ibrahim sent no money, my aunt relied on dressmaking to earn her living and soon built up a clientele among the residents of Ramallah. She was a perfectionist and if finished clothes were not to her satisfaction they were completely taken apart. She would often stitch away by lamplight well into the night and we would be lulled to sleep by the sound of her sewing machine. My grandmother, who never needed glasses, would help by basting seams and sewing on buttons. On request, Isquhie would go into Jerusalem to work for a short time at Khoury's, a fashionable *haute couture* salon.

On most days of the week my aunt would have to get up at 4 a.m. to prepare dough for bread. She never bought bread but made her own loaves from wholemeal brown flour which was kept in a large earthenware jar covered with a wooden lid. The dough was kneaded in a *batieh* or bowl made from a single piece of hollowed-out wood. A baker's boy would call to collect the risen loaves, put them on a flat, floured wooden tray, cover the whole with a cloth and carry the tray on his head to the local oven. He would soon bring back lovely round fresh-baked loaves. My aunt always grumbled on breadmaking days, it being a chore she could well do without.

Our milk was brought in very early by Zuhra, a woman who came from nearby Bireh. Zuhra also brought fruit, eggs, and occasionally young chickens for us. After she had finished her work in the town she would come back to do the lunch dishes. These she washed in a round copper bowl under the trees in the garden, supervised by my grandmother. First she would get rid of the fat by rubbing all the plates and pots with charcoal ash, after which she washed them with Nablus soap.

Coffee beans were bought green and roasted at home in a tube-

Above. Garabed and Heghineh Gazmararian with their three eldest sons, *c.* 1868. *Below.* Garabed and Heghineh Gazmararian with sons, daughters-in-law and two grandchildren, *c.* 1895.

Above left. Sahag and Abkar Gazmararian, grandsons of Garabed and Heghineh, students at Collège des Frères in Jaffa, 1915. *Above right*. Saprich Kevork Stepan, Melkon's son-in-law, 1888. Father of Varbed Christine. *Below left*. Soghmon efendi Krikorian, Secretary to the Armenian Patriarchate. *Below right*. Heghineh Krikorian, widow of Soghmon, 1938.

Above left. Doctor Krikor Krikorian, Medical Officer in the Turkish army, 1914. *Above right*. Doctor Krikor Krikorian, 1940. Deputy Chief Medical Officer, Palestine Government. *Below*. Hagop Krikorian, shoemaker, engaged to Haiganoush Sarafian, 1904.

Above left. Haiganoush Sarafian, the bride from Damascus, 1904. *Above right*. Hagop Krikorian, widower with four young children, 1918. *Below left*. Aunt Arousiag Krikorian, *c.* 1935. A life of hard work had formed her character. *Below right*. *Kaghakatsi* marriage, Kevork and Nazouhie Aghabegian, 1912.

Above. In the courtyard of St James's Cathedral, after the ceremony fulfilling vows for Haig Aghabegian, 1925. *Below.* After the Christening, family group with priests and kawases outside the Church of the Holy Archangels, 1918.

Above left. Dirouhie Markarian, the fiancée from Egypt, *c.* 1912. *Above right*. Sophie, Najla, Frieda, young Palestinian women, 1920. *Below*. The pipe organ built by Harold, with swell manual complete, 1930.

Above. Harold and Margaret, engaged, 1919. *Below left*. Takouhie (Malakeh) Melkon, 1929, nurse and midwife. *Below right*. Isquhie Melkon engaged to Ibrahim Audi, 1920.

Above. Doctor Paterson and staff, Hebron hospital, 1908. Malakeh and Margaret, trainee nurses in centre. *Below.* Palestinian pupils at the Jerusalem Girls' College with Miss Elinor Moore, 1925.

Above. Pupils of the English Preparatory School in the grounds of the Jerusalem Girls' College, 1932. *Below*. Teachers and pupils at St Gayantiants School, 1908.

Above. Pupils outside St George's School – Jewish, Polish, and English – 1939. *Below left* 'The Inseparables', John and Issam, 1940. *Below right*. Garabed Krikorian, noted Jerusalem photographer, *c.* 1870.

Above. Graduation at St George's School, 1942. Presentation of certificates by Sir Harold MacMichael (centre), to class containing Armenian, Jewish, British, Muslim and Christian Arab students who had worked happily side by side. *Below*. Bishop and Mrs Stewart with some of the St George's Close and Hostel staff, 1955.

Above. On Krikor's terrace. John, Isquhie and Arousiag confined to the perimeter, 1949. *Below*. Margaret, Malakeh and Isquhie in the garden in Jericho, 1970.

SUMMERS IN RAMALLAH

shaped metal container. This had a handle and we rotated it over a specially made brazier. Great care had to be taken as in an instant the beans could become scorched. Once roasted, the beans were ground by hand in a brass coffee-mill.

Cooking was done on a charcoal-fired *tabakha*, a clay brazier which could be bought in all sizes to fit any pot. In the top layer charcoal was placed over a few twigs and ignited with the help of a drop of paraffin. An opening below provided a draught and a catchment for ashes which could be easily removed. After lighting her *tabakha* my aunt would place it on the garden wall where it caught the wind and burned away, spitting sparks everywhere. Once the charcoal caught fire it created a red-hot source of heat which lasted for a long time. Dishes that required baking or roasting were sent out in round tin-plated copper trays to the local oven.

Tin-plated copper pots, *tanajer*, or *qidar* (clay fired pots) were used for cooking. Food was never kept in copper pots overnight for fear of poisoning. Periodically the pots had to be re-plated or 'whitened' by the *imbayed*, the tinsmith – a hot and dirty job. There was a special *suq* in the Old City where this was done. Many Armenians who came to Jerusalem after the Turkish massacres had been tinsmiths in their country, since the raw material for whitening copper pots was mined in the mountains of Armenia. Cooking in *tanajer* has now gone out of fashion because of the expense of maintenance; pans and pots of stainless steel or aluminium lined with Teflon have replaced them.

In season, when tomatoes were cheap, my aunt would make tomato paste to last her for the year. Pulped and sieved raw tomatoes to which salt had been added were poured into large copper trays, covered with muslin against insects and put on the roof to dry in the sun. I was often sent up there to give the mixture a stir with a wooden spoon. Every evening the trays were brought down to keep them out of the dew, and the mixture tipped into pottery bowls for the night. When it had thickened the paste was stored in glass jars and covered with a thin film of olive oil.

After a few years my aunt moved to a room in another house in Ramallah, just off the main road and opposite the Quaker Meeting-house. Here too the kitchen and lavatory were both in the garden. This two-roomed house was owned by Umm and Abu Bishara who occupied the other room. Their only son, Bishara, was away in America and they had not seen him for years. For their kitchen they used a rubble-walled outhouse with a corrugated-iron roof commonly

126 ARMENIANS OF JERUSALEM

called a *skeefeh*. The house itself, which was very old with domed ceilings, was built on a huge expanse of solid granite rock which served as its foundation and a natural terrace. Beyond the granite terrace, in a garden at a slightly higher level grew two large Casuarina trees and a mulberry. From there rough steps led down to another garden on a lower level planted with almonds and apricots and bounded by the main road.

My aunt had her own plants all along the front ridge of the garden. There she grew many roses, dahlias, jasmine and tuberoses all planted in four-gallon paraffin tins painted green. She loved flowers with a strong perfume, and would often pick a heavily scented white waxy tuberose and wear it in her blouse. Individual blooms of jasmine were picked off and formed into a cluster by inserting the needles of a pine twig into the tube of each flower. Another common climber she grew was a *halazouneh* or snail-creeper (*Phaseolus caracala*). Its bunches of mauve-white flowers, coiled like snailshells, were also sweetly scented.

Water was drawn from a deep cistern which had been excavated in the granite terrace at the back of the house. A bucket with a long rope was used and through carelessness was sometimes lost in the depths of the well. When this happened Umm Bishara came to the rescue and would manage to retrieve it with a *khatafeh* – a grappling iron to which different-shaped hooks were attached. A third small raised fruit garden extended from the cistern to the other boundary wall of the property. This one was planted with plum, apple, almond, apricot and walnut trees, and the door to it was kept locked. Unfortunately there were no glow-worms in the rubble walls around these gardens.

In a house adjoining the fruit garden Miss Siranoush Ketchejian had her home for blind Arab girls. Miss Ketchejian, who was Armenian and herself partially sighted, had been a pupil of Miss Mary Jane Lovell, an Englishwoman who had devoted her whole life to working among the blind in the Middle East. Miss Lovell, from Stickney in Lincolnshire, who had previously worked with the blind in England, went out to Lebanon in 1892 and joined the staff of a small school at Bhamdoun. Legend has it that she arrived with only two gold sovereigns in her pocket. At first she taught sighted children and studied the Arabic language until she moved on to work among the blind. She realized the lack of a Braille alphabet for the Arabic language, and painstakingly devised a system which from then on was used for many decades. Christian prayers and the twenty-third

SUMMERS IN RAMALLAH 127

Psalm were among the first transcriptions into Arabic Braille by Miss Lovell.

In 1895 she moved to Jerusalem where she pioneered work among the blind. With great determination and little outside help Miss Lovell started the first school for blind Arab girls. She refused to leave them during the 1914–18 war but the Turkish authorities did not permit her to carry on teaching. Instead she widened the girls' knowledge by reading poetry and literature to them. Her life's work was to transcribe the Holy Bible into Arabic Braille, and with the help of another of her pupils, Miss Adele Dafesh, the work was completed and published before Miss Lovell died in 1932 aged 84. She was much loved, taught and worked unceasingly, and on her tombstone in the Mount Zion cemetery are rightly inscribed the words in Arabic, *Umm el 'umyan* (Mother of the Blind).

Miss Siranoush Ketchejian, or 'Mama' as she was affectionately called, had been sent by her parents as an infant to Miss Lovell's school. Along with four other girls, one of them her elder sister, she travelled in the care of a young Armenian pilgrim to Jerusalem. They were escorted from their home in Hadjin to Adana on donkey-back, two girls in a pannier balanced by another one full of food supplies. From there they travelled by ship to Jaffa and then on to Jerusalem where they were handed over to Miss Lovell. Shortly afterwards Miss Ketchejian's family perished in their home in Hadjin during the Armenian massacres.

After Miss Lovell's death Miss Ketchejian returned to Palestine from Aleppo, where for ten years she had been teaching in a school for blind children. She wished to continue Miss Lovell's work and opened a school for blind girls in Ramallah in 1936. For this she used her own savings and relied on scant local donations. Miss Ketchejian had faith and the school gradually developed in spite of the political disturbances in the country. At first she had two pupils, as in those days parents of blind girls were reluctant to send their daughters to a Christian school. However after many visits to families in the villages around, Miss Ketchejian gradually won their confidence.

Most of the girls were Muslim, but were given a Christian education and instructed in the bible. Many had been born blind and some had additional handicaps. Although they were never obliged to convert to Christianity, on reaching adult age some did so of their own free will. Miss Ketchejian loved them all and did her best for every one of them; pupils who could do so learned to read and write in Braille and

128 ARMENIANS OF JERUSALEM

were taught regular school subjects. They were also taught to use their hands, they became expert knitters and made useful household objects in beadwork. In time many spoke perfect English, a remarkable achievement for children whose mother-tongue was Arabic and who had never heard the language before they came to the school. Singing played a large part in their daily life. Miss Ketchejian, who was very musical, trained them herself and accompanied them on a harmonium. The sound of the girls' singing could be heard as far away as my aunt's house. My friendship with Miss Ketchejian and support for her work started at this early age and was to continue throughout my life.

As she grew older my sister Margaret no longer joined me on summer visits and my other sister, Gertie, was still too young to come. For me, time in Ramallah spent with my aunt and grandmother remained the highlight of my summer holiday. The day began with breakfast out on the rock terrace in the cool of the morning. Every day I was given a very soft boiled egg which I had to suck through tiny pin-pricked holes, one at each end. In addition to Isquhie's own home-made bread neighbours often sent us *khubez taboon* (flat loaves of village bread). These were baked in a *taboon*, a clay oven, on an inside ledge covered with pebbles made hot from the wood fire beneath. The pebbles left fascinating patterns on the underside of the bread.

We ate the bread with *labaneh*, a home-made cream cheese made by my aunt, along with *za'atar*, powdered leaves of *Origanum maru*. Plants of this herb grew wild in the surrounding valleys and hills. The leaves were picked, dried, crushed, and mixed with sesame seeds and various spices. I was also given fresh fruit – figs, apricots, grapes, and sometimes sliced sugarcane.

After breakfast I would go for a walk or play with other children in the grounds of the Grand Hotel. By that time Hanna Audi had tragically died and his widow Zahiyyeh gallantly carried on the work of the hotel on her own. She had three young children, Lillian, Joseph and Aida. I used to come back for early lunch and then was required to rest until 4 p.m., during which time I was covered up with a sheet and told to keep silent. My grandmother would also have a rest while Isquhie got on with her sewing.

After teatime as it grew cooler my grandmother would take me for long walks in the country. There were three or four favourite places to walk to, one Batn el hawa (the belly of the wind) where there was always a westerly breeze. Sometimes we walked to one or other of the

SUMMERS IN RAMALLAH

two perennial springs not far outside the town – Ain Musbah or Ain el Mkarzam. I loved going to each of these, just to hear the sound of water tinkling into the pools below from rocks thick with maidenhair fern. Villagers would use the water for drinking and the rest was channelled to irrigate small vegetable gardens of aubergines, gourds and cucumbers.

On these walks my grandmother would talk to me as we went along. Something she told me many times over was that she hoped I would not forget my aunt Isquhie when I grew up. She used the words, 'Take care of her, and don't throw her away, John.' At the time I did not understand, but her thoughts remained with me and the hope that I would fulfil her request.

On our return my feet were washed and my grandmother scrubbed my ankles until I thought the skin was coming off. She kept a small loofah in a hole in the rubble wall – the granite rock was warm from the sun's rays, I stood barefoot and she splashed water over my legs. This was an evening ritual. After a light supper we went early to bed. Isquhie usually retired last, latching the door and finally blowing out the lamp. We often continued talking and laughing, until my aunt and grandmother stopped answering my questions or gave a small grunt indicating that it was enough. Sometimes Isquhie would have to sew on well into the night, in which case there was no talking – only the purring of the sewing machine.

We were awakened early by Zuhra who brought the milk at 4 a.m. This had to be boiled and then placed on the north windowsill to cool. Next came the delivery of fruit and vegetables still covered in bloom and wet with dew. Ice-cold figs were a special treat for breakfast. Sometimes we would go early to the fruit garden at the Grand Hotel to pick mulberries and figs ourselves. The mulberry tree was a *shamiyyeh*, of the Damascus variety, with dark red squishy fruit delicious when eaten cold. On other occasions, before sunrise I would walk with Umm Bishara to her *maris* or *ta'mireh*, plots of land they owned on the outskirts of the town. We went there to pick tomatoes, okra and grapes. To quench my thirst she would often cut a huge tomato in half and give it to me fresh, flavoursome and sour.

I loved these outings. Best of all were walks to the valleys around Ramallah to pick wild flowers – especially the different pastel-shaded anemones that grew in early spring, to be followed later by wild tulips. Again we would start before sunrise and take a picnic breakfast with us.

130 ARMENIANS OF JERUSALEM

There were three valleys where we could find these beautiful flowers. Wad el kalb (valley of the dog), Khalet el addas (place of wild lentils), and Wad el shomar (valley of fennel). If one was ambitious one could walk through all three in a day as they were connected, but my aunt thought that I was too young for that at the time. My favourite was Khalet el addas, at the lower end of which we were in deep shadow and away from the hubbub of town and village life. The silence was broken only by the call of rock partridges and other birds. The partridges, now paired up for the breeding season, would fly away as it were from under our feet, raising the alarm as they sailed through the air across the valley. We would sometimes see a surprised and sleepy jackal disappear into the bushes. At the lower end of Khalet el addas a spring, Ain Umm el louzeh (spring of the mother of the nut tree), gushed out of the rocks surrounded by fragile cyclamen, anemones and ranunculus. Every single anemone was a different shade, some were lighter, some darker, in hues of pink and purple as well as white and crimson.

In the valleys we passed many *ksoor* (lodges) where families spent months in the summer tending their fig and olive trees. These lodges usually consisted of two rooms and were built either of loose rubble with rounded walls, or as square towers of large cemented stones. A strong iron door kept out jackals and other wild animals. Fig trees grew along the terraces, their smooth white bark standing out among silver-leaved olive trees. These terraces, painstakingly built up through centuries, were supported by dry-stone walls over which sprawled *Clematis cirrhosa* with its scented, pale yellow, bell-like flowers. In between the stones *Cyclamen persicum* in shades of pink and white flowered in abundance. The valleys were very deep, and at the bottom of each ran a *wad* into which the water from the surrounding hills drained during the winter months. This often formed a roaring torrent which cascaded over the rocks into deep pools carved out below. In late spring shallow pools became a breeding ground for frogs and toads, the water almost blackened by thousands of tadpoles. We would pause for breakfast while my aunt lit a small fire between two large stones to heat up coffee. After a short rest a steep climb up the hill brought us from deep shade into the sunshine above. At home my grandmother had prepared lunch for us.

Another favourite excursion was to the *teen* or fig grove in Wad el kalb which belonged to Dar abu Abdallah, relatives of Badi'a. Most Ramallah families owned fig groves miles out of town in the valleys

SUMMERS IN RAMALLAH 131

around. At the end of summer relatives, usually the older ones, would take provisions and bedding and go ahead to prepare the lodges on their property for those coming later to pick, prune, plough and repair walls. Donkeys or mules were used as means of transport. During this time ripe figs were picked and spread out to dry on the roofs. In the process the figs had to be turned and gradually flattened before they were ready for storage. Dried figs were delicious eaten with walnuts, a popular dessert after meals.

We were taken by my aunt on a weekend visit to our friends in their lodge at the *teen* which entailed a very long walk. Life there was at its simplest. A few hens provided eggs for breakfast and an occasional lunch. Sometimes pancake-thin bread (*shrak*) was cooked over a heated iron toadstool – a *sajeh*. As a special treat for lunch we were given *imsakhan*, a spring chicken flattened on to dough, covered with onions, spiced with sumach, drenched with olive oil, and baked in the *taboon*. Water was fetched from a nearby spring.

During the day we would go for walks or visit neighbours in their *ksoor*. At night we slept in the cool on cotton mattresses on the roof, chatting to each other and gazing at the stars, our bliss spoilt only by marauding mosquitoes. The distant cry of a jackal or owl was almost drowned by the deafening chorus of frogs and toads in the pools below. We were always sad when time was up and we had to go back to civilization. The affectionate sharing of a simple life with our Ramallah friends and the introduction to the beauties of nature at a very early age, together with my grandmother's words, created a life-long bond between me and aunt Isquhie.

15 THE COLLEGIATE CHURCH OF ST GEORGE

My happy, carefree, daydream existence was not to last: reality came to the fore. I was now nine years old and Miss Coate advised my father that I should move to St George's Anglican Boys' School as a boarder. I received this news with absolute horror and could not understand why I should go as a boarder to a school which was only two miles away from home. However, like the proverbial ostrich I decided to bury my head in the sand and forget about the matter until the time came.

St George's School already had a long history within the Jerusalem bishopric. In 1841 an Anglo-Prussian protestant bishopric had been created at the suggestion of King Friedrich Wilhelm IV of Prussia. By act of parliament the crowns of Great Britain and Prussia were to appoint bishops alternately. This agreement was dissolved when Prussia decided to withdraw in 1881 after the death of the third bishop, Bishop Barclay. Christ Church, built in 1841 inside the Old City of Jerusalem near the Jaffa Gate, was the seat of the first bishops. Later it became the headquarters of the London Jews Society. After an interval of six years, a wholly English bishopric was revived, starting with the appointment of George Francis Popham Blyth. After serving for 21 years in Rangoon, latterly as archdeacon, he was consecrated Bishop of the Church of England in Jerusalem at Lambeth Palace on 25 March 1887. The title bishop 'in' not 'of' Jerusalem was used because the successive Greek Orthodox patriarchs are by prior right bishops *of* Jerusalem.

Bishop Blyth arrived in Jerusalem in 1887 planning to build a new church, cloisters and bishop's house to be known collectively as St George's College. Large properties in Palestine were already owned by Russia, France and Germany, and it was considered important that

THE COLLEGIATE CHURCH OF ST GEORGE   133

Britain too should create a presence. At first the bishop lived in a rented house, from which he made arrangements with the Turkish authorities for the purchase of land; he was supported financially by the Jerusalem Bishopric Fund and three English missionary societies, all with their headquarters in London. He also appealed untiringly to private donors for funds, sending innumerable letters in his own hand, very often written late into the night.

In 1893 three and a half acres of freehold land about half a mile north of the Damascus Gate, along the road leading to Nablus, were bought for £3,300. For centuries this land had been an olive grove with many trees of great age, and as few as possible were cut down to make room for building. The legal formalities to build a church were concluded with an imperial firman from Istanbul granted by Sultan Abdul Hamid II. This was dated 20 January 1894 (11th day of rejib 1311 in the Muslim calendar) and stipulated that the land was *waqf* – dedicated for ever for religious purposes. In 1903 before additional buildings were erected another imperial firman was obtained, stating that it was to be 'a religious entail, with exemption from taxation'.

The bishop was greatly helped in all his dealings with the Turkish authorities by his *kawas*, Daoud Kamal efendi, a member of a notable Muslim family. Daoud efendi had been *kawas* to Bishop Barclay and during the vacancy between 1881 and 1887 worked for the British consulate in Jerusalem. He was reappointed to the bishopric as *wakeel* (steward) at twelve pounds per annum. In 1902 Daoud efendi was recognized as official *dragoman* by the Turkish authorities and his salary was increased to 24 pounds per annum. A dragoman's position carried important official responsibilities, including authority to make agreements on behalf of his employer with the Ottoman authorities and other bodies. His knowledge of English, Arabic and Turkish made him invaluable. Daoud efendi was the bishop's right hand both for the purchase of the land and in the engagement and supervision of the stonemasons and builders during the construction work that followed.

The cathedral took four years to build and the first part was completed in 1898. Under the cloisters outside the west door a large cistern was excavated to supply water for the bishop's house. The surrounding buildings, cloisters, library and second storey of the clergy house, also built in stone in Gothic style, were completed later, modelled on a college in an ancient English university but with certain features of local Arab architecture. The main entrance to the close is

134 ARMENIANS OF JERUSALEM

a narrow cobbled passageway through a gatehouse, built for horse-drawn carriages to enter. Mounting blocks stand outside the gate with tethering rings in the wall. Over the entrance a large room served as a chapter house and was used for choir practice.

During the excavation for the foundations many interesting finds came to light: mosaic floors of Byzantine rooms, in one of which lay gold coins of Justinian; a square stone tablet in memory of a tribune of the Tenth Legion; many tombs, some of Roman soldiers of Hadrian's time; a cistern. The whole area had been a third century AD burial ground.

Bishop Blyth always insisted that the church should be known as the Collegiate Church of St George, since the Church of the Holy Sepulchre is the Cathedral of Jerusalem. However, the building was commonly referred to as 'the cathedral', in Arabic *knisset el mutran* (the bishop's church).

Many gifts had been received for the cathedral, among them a screen of Carrera marble; a 500-year-old processional cross; a fine font from Queen Victoria; from Ireland a pulpit of green marble; a litany desk with a carved figure of Moses from Archbishop Frederick Temple; and from the Bishop of Salisbury, the bishop's seat.

The collegiate church was consecrated on St Luke's day, 18 October 1898, by the Bishop of Salisbury, John Wordsworth. Prelates of the Greek, Armenian, Coptic, Assyrian, Syrian and Jacobite churches, three Lutheran pastors, consuls and acting consuls of eight nations attended. Absent were the Latins. By 1910 the building had been extended to include a transept and choir and now measured 140 feet in length. The organ, built in the nave by the London firm of Bevington & Sons in 1904 at a cost of £892, was moved to the new choir.

The extension of the cathedral was consecrated on All Saints Day, 1 November 1910, by Dr Winnington-Ingram the Bishop of London, assisted by two Irish bishops, Ossary and Meath. A free-standing tower named the Edward the Seventh Tower, modelled on that of Magdalen College, Oxford, was completed in 1912 at a cost of £1,700. In May that year building work had been hampered when the Turkish authorities took all stonemasons and their camels to work elsewhere. Bishop Blyth took pride in the fact that during the whole course of the building of St George's no fatal accident occurred.

Education was to be part of the work of the bishopric. In 1888 a girls' school founded by Miss Alice Catherine Blyth, the bishop's

THE COLLEGIATE CHURCH OF ST GEORGE 135

sister, called The Bishop's Home, had already been started in a private house. Miss Blyth was the first superintendent of what was specifically 'an industrial home for Jewesses'. In 1900 it was decided to expand and offer a general education to girls of all communities, to train as teachers for mission schools throughout Palestine. For the sum of £1,000 a plot of land opposite the main gateway to St George's Close was bought. A further £2,000 was raised to put up school buildings, and the name of the institution changed to St Mary's Home and Orphanage.

Girls between the ages of nine and seventeen were admitted, 30 boarders and 60 day pupils. They were taught English, Arabic, and French in addition to music, needlework and other subjects. Most of the teaching staff came from England and included Anglican deaconesses. On the outbreak of the 1914–18 war St Mary's Home School closed, never to reopen. The buildings were occupied by the Turkish army until 1917, when the Syria and Palestine Relief Fund used them briefly, followed by the American Red Cross.

Soon after his arrival in 1887 Bishop Blyth was approached by Arab notables from the Muslim, Greek and Latin communities of Jerusalem, who asked him to open a boys' school where English education would be available for their sons. After consultation the bishop agreed that he could do so, and St George's Boys' School was opened in 1898 on the lower floor of the Clergy House in St George's Close. There were 24 boarders under the supervision of Canon Woodhouse, and the headmaster was an Arab Anglican priest, the Rev. Jacob Khadder. The bishop intended to develop it into a choir school, where Christian boys would be selected for their voices and trained to sing at services in the cathedral. The following year the school was enlarged to include day boys and the boarders moved into a hired house, named St James's Hostel, run by Mr Shibli Jamal. Boys came from Jaffa, Nablus, Salt in east Jordan, Broussa in Syria, Rhodes, Samos and Cyprus.

In 1905 Mr K. L. Reynolds, an Englishman who had been Bishop Blyth's secretary, was appointed headmaster. By 1906 there were 83 pupils from many communities – Muslim, Greek Orthodox, Greek Catholic, Roman Catholic, Anglican, Coptic, Armenian – all studying harmoniously together. Many leading Muslim families living in Jerusalem and other parts of the country were attracted by the education given at St George's, and did not hesitate to send their sons, even though it was a Christian school. There was no direct attempt at

136　ARMENIANS OF JERUSALEM

proselytizing and interestingly enough the scripture prize was often won by a Muslim boy.

The education offered was modelled on English public school lines. Teachers were sent out from England to join the staff; there was stress on sports and physical education and pride in cricket and football teams. In addition to English, Arabic and French were taught; Turkish also, a necessity for those who would in the future seek employment in the Ottoman government. Greek was taught upon request.

In 1905 there were sufficient funds to start building the ground floor of what is today known as School House, on a plot of land owned by the bishopric and protected by imperial firman. In 1912 a second storey was added as a boarding house for between 30 and 40 boys. The school was built entirely of local stone in a massive square, with a red-tiled roof. A large piece of land adjoining the new building was secured as a football field.

While on her way by sea to England, Mrs Blyth was taken ill and died. In appreciation the students of St George's put up a brass in the cathedral cloisters which reads:

> To the glory of God and to the dear memory of Mrs Blyth and for all she did in and for the school, this brass is dedicated by the masters, old boys and boys of St George's School, Jerusalem, June 10th 1908.

In February 1914 three title deeds issued under new Ottoman laws for land and buildings were placed in Bishop Blyth's hands by Daoud Kamal efendi. He had, as instructed, arranged that the property should pass from Bishop Blyth to his successors, the official bishops in Jerusalem and the East. Daoud efendi had himself effected all the complicated negotiations for this transfer through the British consulate and the Turkish authorities.

With the outbreak of war between Britain and Germany in 1914, all Bishop Blyth's work was in danger of closure. When Turkey allied herself with Germany he was obliged to leave Palestine with the rest of his family and the British members of his staff. On 17 July 1914 he put Daoud efendi in charge of all St George's property and handed him the keys of the buildings. He also gave him a written statement:

THE COLLEGIATE CHURCH OF ST GEORGE 137

Daoud efendi Kamal is my official Dragoman and is left in charge of the bishop's house and property contained in it during my absence. He is also in general oversight of the buildings and their repair. The keys of the house will be left in his charge as they always have been.

Daoud efendi served the bishopric for 30 years, and in gratitude for good and faithful service was awarded a pension of £48 per annum. When he died in 1929 an obituary in *The Times* paid tribute to a man who had carried great responsibility with integrity, and had been 'a true and trusted friend during Bishop Blyth's episcopate'.

Bishop Blyth left Jerusalem for England on 21 July 1914 after 27 years of service. He took pride in the fact that he left no debt on any of the buildings put up during his time. On 5 November in the same year he died at the age of 82, and was buried in Hammersmith cemetery: his grave also commemorates Mrs Blyth, their only son aged 37, and two grandsons aged 23 and 19 who were all killed in the war. 'God will give you to me again with joy and gladness for ever.'

During the war the bishop's house was occupied by a Turkish general, *kütchük* Djemal pasha. The cathedral was sealed and the church plate deposited with Crédit Lyonnais bank for safety. Later the American Consul, Dr Glazebrook, claimed the packets just before they were to be confiscated by the Turks. The school was closed and the buildings used as sectional headquarters by the Turkish military. During the war, services were continued by Canon Ibrahim Baz in St Paul's church for the Arab Anglican congregation. He worked in constant danger, visiting the wounded and distressed and trying to improve conditions for British prisoners of war. He had been ordained in 1886, appointed to St Paul's in 1890, and served that church for more than 30 years.

St George's School was reopened in February 1918 under new circumstances – the British Mandate in Palestine. Mr Reynolds returned as headmaster and found many boys waiting to be enrolled. It had been decided not to reopen St Mary's Home School and the buildings were officially made over to the boys' school. From then on it became the junior school for both boarders and day boys, and to the present day this complex of buildings is referred to as St Mary's. The two school buildings were divided by the Nablus Road, which with the introduction of the motorcar became an awkward and dangerous crossing point.

138 ARMENIANS OF JERUSALEM

As a consequence of the massacres of Armenians by the Turks, a small number of Armenian refugee boys were brought into the school by Mr Reynolds. He had found them in a tented camp in Egypt during the war, took an interest in their welfare and offered to provide some of them with scholarships to St George's School. Among them was Haroutiun Boyadjian, then aged fifteen, a survivor of the heroic resistance against the Turkish attack on the mountain villages of Musa Dagh in September 1915. After graduating he was appointed sports and geography teacher, and stayed with the school for over 40 years. He was later to be of tremendous help to Bishop Stewart in defending the school and cathedral close during the 1948 Israeli–Arab war, and soon after that was appointed headmaster. It was said of him that 'his enthusiasm for St George's was unquenchable'.

Mr Reynolds retired as headmaster in 1929 after serving the school for 25 years. He had worked hard for the boys and was much loved and respected; he and his wife stayed on in Jerusalem to run a dispensary for sick animals. He was succeeded by the Rev. Cyril R. N. Blakiston, who was headmaster until 1933. This was the school I was to join in the autumn of 1933, aged nine, there to spend the next ten years.

16 SCHOOL DAYS AT ST GEORGE'S

As usual I spent part of the summer holidays with my aunt Isquhie and my grandmother in Ramallah, which was as pleasurable as ever and I conveniently forgot about boarding school. But there was no escape and the fatal day arrived, the day for leaving home. I sat on the kitchen window-ledge and gave a last look at all my pets and the garden and burst into an uncontrollable flood of tears.

I was driven to school in my father's new green Morris saloon car, and upon arrival was handed over to the housemaster, Mr Shukri Harami, who showed me to a dormitory which I was to share with five other boys of my age. When all the boarders had arrived we were sent out to the playground in the forecourt of St Mary's where the new boys, feeling out of place, eyed everyone apprehensively. A bell summoned us to assembly where after prayers, roll-call was taken, introductions made and notices given out. Then followed supper, for me every mouthful of which was interrupted by tears which I did my best to hide. Shortly afterwards we were sent to bed and ordered to be quiet.

The headmaster of St George's at the time was the Rev. J. P. Thornton-Duesbery, whose father had been the Bishop of Sodor and Man. He was young, of kindly disposition with an infectious laugh, but commanded respect. He lived in a flat above the boarding house with his mother, and sister, Jean. Miss Jean Thornton-Duesbery ran the school clinic and looked after the general health of the boys.

Our day started early as is customary in the east. Breakfast over we attended prayers, after which we were led by prefects across the road to the main playground just below school house where we were subjected to half an hour's physical training. On return we collected our books and went into class. I was placed in Primary Two where the

140   ARMENIANS OF JERUSALEM

mistress in charge was Miss Zahra Hannoush, who had joined the staff in 1928 and was to serve the school loyally for 32 years. Some of the new boys began in Primary One under Miss Nada Halaby, an attractive young teacher. Both ladies came from well-known Jerusalem families and were trained in child education. There were 25 boys in my class, and throughout the school none had more than 28. Miss Hannoush was strict and always in full control. When she asked a question we all tried to get in first by putting up our hands, saying '*biseer*, Miss' (May I, Miss?) and causing a loud noise which made her angry. For misbehaviour she would grab us by the shoulders and give a vigorous shake, but she meant us no harm.

As my English was good I was pushed up to Primary Three by the end of the first term. From then on our teachers were all men, both Arab and English. English language and literature were taught by experienced teachers who came out from Britain, and all subjects were taught in English. As most boys spoke their own language at home the rule laid down at the foundation, 'English is the spoken language of the school', was strictly enforced. If we were caught speaking Arabic or another tongue we were given 'language marks' which were deducted from credits received for class work in English. A common stumbling-block was the fact that Arabic is a very expressive language and more than often during an English conversation we were liable to burst forth with a few words of Arabic to stress a point. As conversations in the Middle East are usually emphatic and carried on in loud voices, we were often overheard. Most boys were bilingual which enabled us to enjoy puns between Arabic and English. Shakespeare became Sheikh Izbeer; the reply to 'What is the time?' when the answer should be half past nine was 'Abbas naim' (Abbas is asleep) and so forth.

Boys of all nationalities, Palestinian Arabs, Jews, Armenians, Greeks, Assyrians, Ethiopians, Poles, Persians and Britons worked peacefully side by side in class and lived happily together in the boarding house. Many of them came from well-to-do Arab Palestinian families in Jerusalem, both Muslim and Christian. A few boarders came from east Jordan and some from as far away as Iraq. The school roll-call included a variety of interesting names; among our classmates we had Archimedes, Odysseus, Antippa and Rousseau. Haile Selassie, a young member of the Ethiopian royal family exiled during the Italian occupation, also joined the school. At the time the political unrest prevailing in the country passed us by.

SCHOOL DAYS AT ST GEORGE'S 141

Classes ended in the early afternoon and it was time for games and sport. Every boy had been allocated to a 'house' which was divided into football and basketball teams. On certain days we played cricket, on a thick coconut mat as there was no grass pitch. Unfortunately I had no enthusiasm for any sport. Tennis was the only game that I enjoyed and played fairly well, and I represented my house in cross-country runs. Our two very keen sports masters, Mr Haroutiun Boyadjian and Mr Fawzi Ma'atuk, tried to encourage me to take part in team games, but I was for ever getting 'excuse chits' on the grounds of being 'out of sorts', preferring to pay the penalty – swallowing a large draught of bitter liquid quinine administered by Miss Thornton-Duesbery.

After an hour's study period in the late afternoon, Christians among the boarders were taken to the cathedral for evensong. Among other humns, we sang 'Father, hear the prayer we offer', 'Rejoice O Land in God thy might' and 'Be Thou my guardian and my guide'.

The choir school founded by Bishop Blyth in 1889 had grown and changed but boys with good voices were still chosen to sing in cathedral services on Sundays. The choir master and organist at the time was Mr H. B. Sharp, who also taught English literature in the senior school. He was an excellent musician who knew how to get the best out of a group of boys, many of them unfamiliar with the Anglican form of service. My father encouraged me to join the choir, which I did. We practised daily in the chapter house, and on Thursday evenings we had full choir practice in the cathedral when we were joined by the men (including some of our teachers) who sang tenor or bass, and also by three women who sang alto. The Book of Common Prayer was used at all the services and we were trained to sing the psalms, versicles and canticles, as well as hymns and anthems.

The boys who sang were not necessarily Anglicans; many belonged to other communities, Greek Orthodox, Armenian or Syrian. As the Anglican church did not want to be accused of taking these boys away from their own churches, permission for them to sing in the choir was always obtained from the heads of their communities.

On Sundays at matins the High Commissioner for Palestine, Sir Harold MacMichael, with his wife and two daughters, Araminta and Priscilla, sat in the front row in a cathedral filled with government officials and their wives. Many other British residents attended regularly, among whom I remember vividly the venerable archaeologist, Sir Flinders Petrie, and his wife. My father, who was one of the

142   ARMENIANS OF JERUSALEM

churchwardens and for some time a member of the church council, would always take up the collection, attending both matins and evensong each Sunday.

On Christmas Eve the bishop, clergy and choir, along with members of the congregation, were taken by bus to Bethlehem where a carol service was (and still is) held with permission from the Greek Orthodox patriarchate in the courtyard adjoining the Church of the Nativity. In those days the words 'how silently, how silently' in the hymn 'O Little Town of Bethlehem' were true to the atmosphere. Bethlehem was silent and dark – no fairy lights, no television screens, no visiting choirs, nor the thousands of curious tourists. The coming of the Christ child was greeted by all with silent reverence.

On Sunday afternoons we went for walks to the brow of the Mount of Olives or to the Convent of the Cross. Annual picnics took us to Jaffa or to the Dead Sea for the whole day, where we much enjoyed playing games and swimming. The rest of our time was spent within the school confines. However, I was not utterly cut off from my parents during term time. My father, who was in charge of the upkeep of the cathedral organ, came to St George's every afternoon. Before leaving he would wait for me at the school gate and I would spend a little time with him, very often in silence. My mother and sisters never came to visit me.

I stayed as a boarder for only two years, after which I joined the day boys. When I completed primary school I moved up to the senior department in School house, where I formed a close friendship with one of my classmates, Issam Nashashibi. The Nashashibis were one of several aristocratic Muslim families in Jerusalem and it was a member of this family, Ragheb bey el Nashashibi, who for a while served as mayor of Jerusalem after his appointment in 1920 by the military governor, Colonel Ronald Storrs. Issam, whom we nicknamed 'Nash', was as good at maths as I was at English so we were able to help each other with our homework. We were called 'the inseparables', had a secret sign language, and needless to say were an annoyance to all. Like me Issam hated any form of sport and we found the same trivial things amusing – we were kindred spirits.

I spent many happy days in the Nashashibi home in the Sheikh Jarrah quarter, and was accepted as one of the family. Memorable were the warm evenings when we sat on the veranda under a bower of scented jasmine, with a magical view of the city in the distance, often joined by Issam's two older brothers, Hisham and Nasri, and by their

SCHOOL DAYS AT ST GEORGE'S

143

father, Abu Hisham. There we laughed and chatted away in Arabic and French with Sitt Kauthar, Issam's mother. The sound of water splashing into a pool in the garden below, in which grew heavily scented old-fashioned roses enhanced these idyllic visits. From St George's Issam went on to the American University in Beirut where he graduated. A few years ago he tragically died in a car accident on the Jericho road.

Our school days were stimulating and amusing and we were fond of our Arab and English teachers, although in awe of them. Discipline was not considered a form of repression, and various methods of punishment were used. The worst was the cane. The housemaster, Mr Shukri Harami, was responsible for caning, and he was reputed to put chalk on his cane so that he could bring down the second and third strokes on exactly the same place as the first. There were other forms of punishment, a painful stroke on the hand with a ruler, or the pulling of one's ear followed by an unexpected hard slap on the face – very painful and indeed dangerous. Sometimes we were given 200 lines or more to write out at home, and another punishment was to clean the playing fields of stones for an hour or more under the blazing sun.

In general we complied with the rules of the school and did not dare arrive late for class or absent ourselves for trivial reasons. Very often the whole class would be punished for the sake of one or two badly behaved boys and made to stay behind after lessons on a Friday afternoon, or worst of all to come back on Saturday, our free day.

Late on a Friday, after detention, I would walk home past the ultra-orthodox Jewish quarter of Me'ah She'arim, where I was sometimes asked into a house to adjust the flame of the *petillia* or cooking stove on which the Sabbath meal was being prepared. As a gentile I could do this: the Law prevented religious Jews from handling a light or flame on the Sabbath. Some households had devised an ingenious method of switching off an electric light without touching the switch. A piece of string connected the switch to the winder of an alarm clock and at the appointed time, off went the alarm, the winder would rotate, shorten the string and bring the light switch down.

Our senior English teacher, Mr L. D. Cook, who was also the deputy headmaster, had been on the staff since 1926. He was very tall, thin, serious and forbidding, and tolerated no nonsense. He taught us grammar, putting us through the throes of parsing and analysis which most of us found complicated.

Mr Sharp, the organist, took us for English literature. In our last

144   ARMENIANS OF JERUSALEM

year in preparation for the Oxford and Cambridge School Certificate we studied *Macbeth*, and were each given parts to learn and act.

Mr Munir Bayyud, our maths master, came from the Lebanon. He was very strict and did not suffer fools gladly. Under him we learned arithmetic, algebra, geometry and trigonometry. One of his methods was to send us in turn to the blackboard to solve an equation or mathematical problem in front of the whole class. This was a terrifying experience for many, who on failing were told in an icy voice, 'Take your place, the stage has cooled off' – breaking the rules he forcefully commanded in Arabic, '*Barad el masrah*.' He would then point to a clever and favourite pupil of his, an Armenian, Sarkis Broussellian, and ask him 'to show us how'. Much to our annoyance Sarkis never failed to solve the problem. When demonstrating intricate mathematics on the board, Mr Bayyud would accuse those who did not understand of treating the blackboard like cinema credits, 'reading half, just noticing part, and forgetting about the rest'. At other times he referred to a dull boy as 'a stone'.

Arabic classes were taken by Professor Khalil Beidas and *ustaz* Khoury. Both were disciplinarians who instilled a deep love of Arabic literature in those pupils who came up to their standards of scholarship. I was not taught by them, but with other non-Arab boys had lessons with Mr Dagher. We also studied French with Monsieur Sam Loya and Mr Emile Ayyash.

Our school year passed quickly, ending with a service in the cathedral where we sang the usual parting hymns, 'God be with us till we meet again' and 'Lord, dismiss us with thy blessing'. Then came the anxiety of waiting for reports, grades, place in class and the question of promotion. We looked forward to our long summer holiday, but it was often marred by the increasing political difficulties in the country, and by violent disturbances.

17 INTERESTS OUT OF SCHOOL

In our summer holiday ways of occupying our time had to be found. The Young Men's Christian Association with its many activities filled the gap. The Jerusalem YMCA buildings were the most beautiful owned by that organization anywhere in the world. The cornerstone had been laid on 23 July 1928 by Lord Plumer, the second High Commissioner for Palestine.

On 18 April 1933 Field Marshal Viscount Allenby returned to Jerusalem to open the buildings. The main door was unlocked by Mr Humphrey Bowman, director of education. Psalms were read, the 91st in English, 122nd in Arabic and 23rd in Hebrew. The Anglican bishop, Rennie MacInnes, led prayers for the peace of Jerusalem and the benediction was given by the *locum tenens* of the Greek Orthodox patriarchate. An organ recital followed in the auditorium, after which melodies were played on the carillon in the tower.

In his inaugural address Lord Allenby called the YMCA 'a spot whose atmosphere is peace; where political and religious jealousies can be forgotten, and international unity be fostered and developed'. If only these wonderful aspirations could have been fulfilled; instead the country was to be torn by strife which continues to the present day.

As soon as I was old enough I was enrolled as a member of the boys' department. At that time 95 per cent of the members were Arab Palestinians. We took part in many activities, athletics, tennis, squash, handicrafts and evening classes, and used the up-to-date gymnasium and large swimming pool.

Day outings on mule-back to sites of interest were organized. We visited Tekoa (II Samuel 14:2) and the caves of Adullam (I Samuel 22:1) and on the way back climbed the Herodium. At the caves of

146 ARMENIANS OF JERUSALEM

Adullam boys who wished to enter were attached to a rope and had to crawl on their stomachs from chamber to chamber. I did not go in myself as rumour had it that a Greek priest had entered, was lost and never seen again and only the rope was found. Other day trips took us to Nebi Samwil (the tomb of the prophet Samuel), to Emmaus, and to the Wadi Qelt, the gorge of the brook Cherith. On our return from these trips we found on dismounting that we could hardly walk.

Summer camps were also organized, which usually lasted for a month. I went to one on the shores of the Mediterranean near the ancient city of Asqalon. We left Jerusalem by train for Majdal, a small Arab town north of Gaza. At this picturesque place, with pencil-sharp minarets and luxuriant gardens planted with date-palms and citrus, we alighted and picnicked under a huge *jummayz* (Egyptian sycamore tree) covered with edible fig-like fruit. A tented camp was ready for us on the beach near the ruins of Asqalon, the antique city destroyed by Bibars in AD 1270. The camp was well-organized and we were kept busy with visits to archaeological sites alternating with swimming in the usually rough sea. All along the coast flowered *Pancratium maritimum*, the sea lily of the Mediterranean, filling the evening air with its sweet scent.

One Easter holiday our geography teacher, Mr Denis Baly, led a group of senior boys on a week's visit to Transjordan. Our unforgettable eight-day trip started with a night at our sister school, the Bishop's School in Amman, where we were joined by one of their teachers, Mr Christopher King.

Early next morning we headed south for Madaba, with a stop at Jiza to see the Roman reservoirs. At Madaba we were shown wonderful sixth-century mosaics, the most famous of which is the map of Jerusalem forming part of the floor in the Greek Orthodox church. The priest removed the wooden covers for us and threw a bucket of water over the mosaic to bring out the colours. Other mosaic floors had been incorporated into privately owned houses, and for a small fee we were allowed in to see them. One of the most fascinating depicted Salome dancing for the head of John the Baptist. It was a sad visit, as the mosaic formed part of the floor of a bedroom in which lay a dying man surrounded by his family. We then visited Mount Nebo where Moses viewed the 'promised land' (Deut. 34:1). From there, in the distant haze beyond the Dead Sea and the greenery of Jericho, we could discern the towers of the Augusta-Viktoria Stiftung and the Russian church on the skyline of the Mount of Olives.

INTERESTS OUT OF SCHOOL 147

We drove on, zigzagging through the Wadi Mujib, to the town of Karak with its imposing crusader castle. Our aim was to reach Tafila before nightfall, and we had to cross the Wadi el Hissa with its rugged, breathtaking scenery. We spent one night in the government school at Tafila and left next morning for Shaubak on our way to Petra. It was spring, the countryside was green, patterned with vivid patches of wild flowers. Groups of storks, *abu sa'ad*, resting on their flight back to Europe foraged for frogs and insects amongst the lush greenery. Along the roadside and in the fields grew clumps of the black iris of East Jordan, plum-coloured Egyptian henbane, and the delicate spikes of *Fritillaria libanotica*. Some groups of black iris were so large that from a distance we mistook them for bedouin women in their black dresses bending to work in the wheat fields.

A first visit to Petra is always the best; my second and third visits did not make the same impact. On arrival at Wadi Musa we were greeted by bedouin, who offered to lead us through the Siq on their horses. Some of our group accepted but most of us preferred to wander in on foot. We soon reached the entrance to the Siq, a spectacular natural cut joining the outside world to Petra. There we were at the bottom of this huge ravine, the sky miles above, with massive cliff walls in places leaning so close that only a tiny streak of daylight came through. The floor of the ravine was covered with inches of loose pebbles, and only the crunch of our footsteps broke the eerie silence. Suddenly from the shadows we saw light ahead. We had come upon that masterpiece, the Khazneh (treasury), standing in a shaft of sunshine framed by cliffs. We were silenced by the indescribable presence and beauty of this building carved in the cliff of rose-pink sandstone. We lingered as long as we could, then made our way into the ancient Nabataean city of Petra, which opened up before us like an enormous bowl.

The rest of that day was spent exploring the amphitheatre, caves and tombs hewn into cliff faces, and the remains of Roman Petra. In the dry river bed grew masses of oleanders with their pink clusters of flowers. An exciting moment for us was seeing the Sinai rosefinch for the first time, flitting from one bush to another. Eventually we installed ourselves in the caves where we were to spend the night.

We spent three days at Petra, during which we visited the High Place, the Monastery and finally Ras el Sleissal where a panorama of the Wadi Araba unfolded before our eyes. Reluctantly we left for Aqaba on the Red Sea, stopping on the way at Ras el Neqab with its

148 ARMENIANS OF JERUSALEM

moonscape view towards the Wadi Rumm hidden in the distance. Aqaba was a tiny hamlet in those days, with a few mud houses surrounded by palm trees. We slept on the beach and enjoyed swimming in the warm waters of the Red Sea.

The return journey was less exciting. One night was spent in the government school at Ma'an, capital of southern Transjordan. Next day we paid another short visit to the crusader castle at Karak before returning to Amman. Throughout the trip we were lectured to by Mr Baly on the geographical and historical aspects of our surroundings.

For part of the Easter holidays I often went to Jericho to spend a few days with my aunt Malakeh, travelling by bus, a journey of three quarters of an hour down the winding road to the Jordan valley. During the feast of Nebi Musa the bus would divert to the Muslim shrine believed to be the tomb of Moses. The elegant domed buildings were built by the Sultan Bibars during the thirteenth century to house the hundreds of pilgrims who took part in the celebrations.

The feast of Nebi Musa, which takes place during Christian Holy Week, lasts for seven days and ends on Maundy Thursday of the Orthodox churches. Muslim pilgrims meet at various points in Jerusalem. Those coming from Nablus and the north of the country would gather outside St George's School in their hundreds, their leaders on horseback brandishing swords, others carrying banners. Police would be out in force to control the crowds.

After a service at the Haram el Sharif in Jerusalem the procession, now counted in thousands, moved on foot and horseback with much pomp and noise to the shrine. The grounds around the buildings, for the rest of the year a wind-blown desert, were now a scene of activity with decorated tents of various colours, amusements for children, the sale of fruit, nuts and soft drinks, kebabs cooked over charcoal fires. While waiting for the bus to go on to Jericho I mingled with the crowds, who were always friendly and hospitable.

As the political situation in Palestine worsened, the Nebi Musa pilgrimage was banned by the British government.

Aunt Malakeh owned a small house surrounded by four dunums (an acre) of land which she had planted with citrus, grapes, pawpaw, custard apples and dates. At the back of the house grew a large flame-tree which in early summer was covered with scarlet flowers. Near it a *fitna* (frangipani) wafted its strong fragrance through the house. Over the front veranda jasmine and vines covered a pergola. The house itself was simple, built of *libin* in Jericho style, with an outside wooden

INTERESTS OUT OF SCHOOL 149

staircase which took us up to the flat roof and a small square room called by my aunt the *tayara* (kite). On hot nights we slept up there, protected by wire-mesh doors and windows against biting insects. It was exciting and wonderful to absorb the moonlit view of Jericho with the mountains of Moab gleaming in the distance, the Milky Way above. Very early in the morning we were awakened by the whistling of bulbuls, the persistent calls of hoopoes and other birds in the trees, followed by the *adhan* wafting over the orange-groves from the minarets in Jericho town. The call to prayer always evoked deep thoughts in me, temporarily pushing cares and triviality aside.

Aunt Malakeh's nearest neighbour was a Coptic priest, Abuna Philipos, who looked after a chapel and a few rooms reputedly built on the site of the house of Zacchaeus in which there were a number of tombs beneath the floor. In his garden were ancient mosaics, cisterns and pools for fish, around them lying many antiquities – fallen pillars, carved capitals, storage jars and pots. Abuna Philipos was tall and elderly; despite the heat he always wore clerical robes and the Coptic priest's headgear. While Malakeh's gardener, Ali Flayyeh, tended his goats in the late afternoon, Abuna would sit with him on the grass at the verge of the *wad* where they would chat for hours on end. Their silhouetted figures seemed outside time, the essence of companionship freed from the rush and cares of the world.

Hundreds of Coptic pilgrims, mainly from Egypt, would come to the house of Zacchaeus on the feast of St John the Baptist after visiting the *shrih'a*, the place of baptism on the river Jordan. They were welcomed by Abuna, who led them in prayers and New Testament readings, after which they were each given a loaf of bread, cheese and fruit. Aunt Malakeh was always called in to help serve the influx of visitors.

Aunt Malakeh's house stood on *kitf el wad* (the shoulder of the wadi) in an area known as *arad el asab* (land of bamboo). Her garden ended on a cliff overlooking the Wad el Qelt, which gushed with water for a few weeks after heavy rains. On fine days the banks below the garden became a picnic ground for the people of Jericho and visitors from Jerusalem and other towns. The surrounding fields were thick with wild flowers, dominated by huge patches of golden *Chrysanthemum coronarium*.

As well as a passion for flowers and gardening, I inherited a deep love for music. I was deeply attracted to the piano, and drawn to a lesser degree to the organ. I started piano lessons at an early age with

150 ARMENIANS OF JERUSALEM

a young American missionary, Miss Peel, whom I remember as amiable and plump, with masses of brown hair piled on her head. She was a good teacher and there was stress on finger exercises, scales, and studies by Clementi and Czerny.

All the activities in which I participated, at school and in the YMCA, had taken me out of the wholly British environment which I had been thrust into as a small child. However my short time at the all-British preparatory school had had a lasting impact on me, and had given me a dual character. I really belonged to two worlds, the European and that of the Middle East. This put me in a difficult position as I was not quite sure which culture to identify with, but I did not regret this state of affairs as it made my life much more interesting. I enjoyed the company of the local people and felt entirely at ease in their presence, made possible by my fluent knowledge of Arabic. I was often asked whether I actually thought in English or in Arabic, a question which I could not answer. Although the British were constantly blamed for the troubles in the country I did not feel that any blame was focused on me personally. My two sisters developed differently. They were more British than I was; they mixed with the expatriate community of Jerusalem and spoke little Arabic.

Through years of schooling at St George's I naturally had many Arab friends, but as a result was cold-shouldered by some English acquaintances. My parents did not object to the course I was pursuing, but they kept an eye on me and tried to make sure that I was mixing with the right company. To me the right company was not necessarily what my parents thought it to be, but I was determined to go my own way.

My sister Margaret and I, followed later by my sister Gertie, often took part in the English children's hour broadcast on the PBS (Palestine Broadcasting Service). Ralph Poston, alias 'Uncle Ralph' and Mrs Weisenberg ('Aunt Judy'), with Richard Humphries, produced the programmes. We were given parts to read in various plays adapted for radio. Mrs Karl Salomon, wife of the well-known conductor, gave singing classes and trained us for musical programmes.

The broadcasting studios were located in the old Palace Hotel, a large moorish-style building owned by the Waqf (Supreme Muslim Council). The Palace Hotel had closed. In the opinion of many it was doomed to failure because of its locality, built on a plot of land opposite the vast Muslim cemetery of Mamillah. Visitors from Arab

INTERESTS OUT OF SCHOOL 151

countries did not fancy looking out of their bedroom windows only to see rows of tombs.

Before it was taken over by the PBS the building had been used for various Arab exhibitions and conferences. In the autumn of 1933 one such *ma'rad* (exhibition) displayed arts and crafts from neighbouring Arab countries to demonstrate solidarity among Arabs both Muslim and Christian. The exhibition was opened by the mayor of Jerusalem and lasted for a month.

Brocades, silks and lengths of materials from Damascus, Cairo and Baghdad were on show, together with a large selection of copper and brass artefacts. Pastry cooks came from Beirut and Damascus and produced delicious sweetmeats, such as *baklaweh*, *knafeh*, *katayif* and *bourma*, all known to Europeans as 'sticky cakes'. Water-ices were on sale, flavoured with a variety of fruits, pistachios and gum arabic, as well as ice-creams. From Syria came *qamr el din* – sheets of dried apricot paste from which is made a dessert flavoured with rose-water, a speciality during the month of Ramadan. Among the display of bottles of pure rose- and orange-blossom-water stood a selection of hand-painted round wooden boxes. These contained a variety of glazed fruits – apricots, pears, plums, sugar apples and whole walnuts. The people of Damascus specialized in the preserving of fruit, which is grown all over Syria. In the centre of each box there was the pièce de résistance, a crown made of sugared pistachios. Also on sale were inlaid mother-of-pearl boxes, silk-lined, filled with chocolates and containing a silver-plated spoon.

A whole room was given over to a selection of soaps made in the towns of Nablus and Jaffa. Olive oil is the chief ingredient of this soap, which in those days was made in all shapes and sizes, some in the form of a ball with a blue or brown marbled design. The soap was perfumed, though not excessively. Furniture made in Jaffa, as well as olive-wood and mother-of-pearl souvenirs from Jerusalem and Bethlehem were also on show. For entertainment there were players of Arabic music and troops of acrobats. Turkish coffee was served all the time. The exhibition was a great success, a sign of happy co-operation between Arab states and it was hoped that many more would follow.

In the same year, 1933, His Eminence the Grand Mufti of Jerusalem, Hajj Amin el Husseini, put forward to the British authorities proposals for an Arab university. Plans were drawn up by an architect from Cairo. There was to be a school of religious knowledge and instruction in the compound of the Haram el Sharif, medical and

152 ARMENIANS OF JERUSALEM

law schools in the old Palace Hotel buildings, and an agricultural school on the Mount of Olives. The Mufti travelled far and wide to raise funds, but the project ran into political and financial difficulties and never got off the ground. This caused bitterness among the Arab population, as permission had long since been granted for a Hebrew university on Mount Scopus.

Christmas brought pantomimes, tableaux and other entertainments held in the YMCA auditorium. My sister Gertie often took part and we always went to see her act. The Jerusalem Dramatic Society put on plays ranging from Shakespeare to Wilde, also musicals, particularly Gilbert and Sullivan. The actors were almost all amateurs, but two stood out, Mr and Mrs Aylmer Harris, who one year gave a brilliant performance as Macbeth and Lady Macbeth. They were an interesting, artistic couple who lived in a small Greek house by the railway line, formerly a cafe known as 'Kahwet el khanazeer', the coffeehouse of the pigs. On their veranda a large grey parrot never failed to fascinate me. It squawked to attract my attention when I was on my way to visit my great-aunts and great-uncle Hagop in the Baqa'a.

At about the age of fifteen we boys shed our short trousers for long ones and considered ourselves to be men. New excitements were in store, new friends made and girls included in our company. However there were many restrictions as young girls were very much under the control of their parents and were not allowed out without permission. If a man visited a girl at her home an aunt or parent would be present throughout.

Seldom did an Arab girl pick her own husband. Elopement before marriage and separation after were both rare, but did occasionally happen causing tremendous scandal. Marriage between people of different denominations occurred, generally against the wishes of parents. Many Arab women married Britons; some Christian Arabs married Muslims or Jews.

During my youth we were already breaking away from traditional norms, and both sexes were beginning to mix in an atmosphere of moderate freedom. However close friendship or excessive passion had to be carefully expressed and kept as secret as possible – making it all the more exciting. It was the day for rendezvous in down-town cafes, private parties and moonlit picnics by the Dead Sea. *Thés dansants* became a popular pastime, indoors or at open-air cafes where couples danced to the romantic music of a foxtrot, quickstep, English waltz,

INTERESTS OUT OF SCHOOL 153

tango and rumba. Life was sweet, full of short-lived love affairs and crushes which inevitably turned out to be one-sided but provided experience for the next time.

After a few years our circle at the Palestine Broadcasting Service was wrecked by tragedy. 'Aunt Judy' was killed while on duty in her office by a bomb which had been placed in the drawer of her desk. We were devastated, profoundly affected by this outrage. This crucial period of our lives was marred by unrest and constant disturbances throughout the country which intensified until the outbreak of the Second World War.

When the British had taken over Palestine, and published the Balfour Declaration of 1917 promising a homeland to the Jews, the Arab population expressed their displeasure by rioting, strikes and disturbances. Even though they were in the majority, they felt threatened. During the 1930s disturbances increased until the Arab Rebellion was at its height from 1936 to 1939, then followed a lull for the years of the Second World War. Both before and after the war widespread acts of murder and sabotage were carried out by armed gangs, communications were disorganized, telephone wires cut, trains derailed and roads blocked. British soldiers, airmen and police, as well as many Arab and Jewish civilians, fell victim to the violence. No one felt safe.

Early in the dispute local Arab leaders tried hard to bring their fears and grievances to the attention of the mandatory authorities, but they were not listened to. An attempt had been made to form a legislative council with proportional representation, but this was strongly opposed by the Jews and dropped by the British government. Had this democratic course been followed much misery and harm might have been avoided.

At the time there were five political parties among the Arabs in Palestine. On 21 April 1936 they called for a general strike, and on 25 April their leaders united to form the Arab Higher Committee under the chairmanship of Hajj Amin el Husseini. The strike brought commercial and economic activity in the Palestinian sector to a halt for six months. All shops in the Arab part of Jerusalem, as well as in towns and villages throughout the country, closed down and there was general unrest and civil disobedience. Public transport came to a standstill. To frustrate the drivers of private cars, thumb-tacks were strewn on the roads. This was the work of women who strolled the

154   ARMENIANS OF JERUSALEM

streets in the cool of the evening wearing their long skirts, under which they were able to carry out their mission unobserved.

To quell the disturbances the British used force instead of dialogue and understanding. Curfews were imposed on the Arab inhabitants. The freedom fighters naturally had the support of fellow Palestinians in towns and villages all over the country and in consequence they were subjected to collective punishment; many people were imprisoned, houses dynamited and property destroyed. There was harassment, with serious breaches of elementary justice. Men were rounded up and treated brutally. Those wearing tarbooshes had them knocked off their heads; when they stooped to retrieve them they were kicked and beaten. Villagers lived in fear of the British army. Houses were searched, oil jars large and small were smashed; paraffin poured over stores of olives, rice, lentils and flour, rendering them inedible. Furniture, sewing machines and radios were damaged or destroyed.

On 1 May 1936 our school, St George's, together with others in Jerusalem, had to close before the end of term due to continual picketing and harassment. Pleas and protests to people in authority within the country and abroad continued. On 6 June 3,000 Arab Anglican laymen signed a petition to the Archbishop of Canterbury protesting against British policy, affirming that their aspirations were one with the Muslim community in Palestine. On 30 June Arab senior government officials signed a joint memorandum to the high commissioner supporting the national demands formulated by the Arab Higher Committee. The Arab Women's Committee also appealed to the women of England, explaining their case. These and many other petitions fell on deaf ears.

On 29 July a Royal Commission of Enquiry headed by Lord Peel was set up to investigate the causes of the unrest. The commissioners did not reach Jerusalem until 11 November. Hajj Amin el Husseini, chairman of the Arab Higher Committee, saw no reason to co-operate as it seemed obvious that the British did not intend to change their policies or to heed Arab demands. However, before the commissioners arrived, the Kings of Saudi Arabia and Iraq with the Emir of Transjordan managed to persuade the Arab Higher Committee to call off the strike, so this massive protest ended inconclusively. There was a pause in the rebellion while the Peel Commission toured the country. They published their report on 7 July 1937, recommending the partition of Palestine into two states, one Jewish and one Arab. If necessary there was to be 'forcible transfer of the Palestine population

INTERESTS OUT OF SCHOOL 155

out of the Jewish state'. This plan was rejected by the Arab Higher Committee and the rebellion intensified with unprecedented violence.

In October 1937, after the murder of the Nazareth district commissioner, the Arab Higher Committee was declared illegal. It was dissolved and four of its members exiled to the Seychelles where many more were to join them later. These remote islands in the Indian Ocean were used by the British authorities to remove from Palestine those with nationalist and political ideals. The exiles were released from captivity in December 1938 but were not allowed to return to Palestine, although they could go to an Arab country of their choice. Deportation for political reasons, practised to this day, was and is a very harsh punishment now condemned by the United Nations. Many of the Seychelles exiles suffered permanent damage to their health due to separation from their families, harsh conditions and the debilitating climate. The chairman, Hajj Amin el Husseini, and other members of the committee managed to evade arrest and escaped to neighbouring Arab countries.

In October 1938 after a night of bombing and shooting the Old City of Jerusalem was taken over by Arab resistance fighters. The city gates had been shut and the British forces were trying to regain entry. After almost a week the siege came to an end on 19 October; many Arab prisoners were taken and severe restrictions imposed.

The underlying aim of the mandatory authorities was, as promised, to give the Jews a homeland in Palestine. This they would achieve by patient and subtle means. Nothing was to stand in the way of their plan. The consequences for the Arab population were dismissed. It is true that many commissions of enquiry were held in order to solve the problem, but inevitably if one of the parties to the dispute agreed to the findings the other did not.

18   THE SECOND WORLD WAR

During the Second World War Palestine did not suffer hardship and deprivation comparable with that in other countries. Local rioting practically came to an end, and as a result of an unofficial truce a fragile peace prevailed. What was now termed the 'Palestine problem' had been temporarily driven underground where it simmered, only to reappear once the war was over.

It was necessary to impose a number of restrictions. Blackout was enforced, a food-control authority set up and coupons issued for certain foods and items of clothing. Dehydrated potato and egg powder, as well as soya bean flour and powdered milk were put on the market. Attempts made to educate the population in the use and nutritious value of these foods were of no avail and they continued to be regarded with suspicion. A thriving black market developed and at a price everything was available. It is a well-known fact that in the Middle East *nizam* (order) and the temperament of the people just do not fit, so the controls were only partially effective.

A consequence of the war was full employment. Army institutions provided work, both clerical and domestic, in offices, canteens, clubs, the Naafi, military camps and hostels. Jerusalem was full of soldiers from all over the world, prominent among them men from Australia and New Zealand. Romance blossomed between local girls and officers, men of other ranks and members of the Palestine Police Force, often leading to marriage. As expected this was frowned upon by the upper class of British society who tried to frustrate such unions. When their efforts failed the Englishman in question would jeopardize his career.

As soon as war was announced all German nationals who lived in colonies in various parts of the country were taken into custody. Those

THE SECOND WORLD WAR

who did not leave for Germany were sent to their coastal colonies of Sarona and Wilhelma, which were converted into POW camps. Their former houses came under the control of a new department, the Custodian of Enemy Property. The British government also interned a number of Arabs who had had a German education, were married to German wives, or were considered to be sympathizers with Germany. Upon their release at the end of the war many of the Templists preferred to leave the country, some to Germany, others to Australia, rather than face the dangers of living in a Jewish state which already seemed a possibility. The Templist community established in Palestine in 1868 saw all their efforts disintegrate after a period of eighty years.

For myself, the war years brought deaths in the family, my graduation from school and entry into work. In 1939 my great-uncle Hagop died during the night, of heart failure following pneumonia, aged 67. I was saddened by this news as I was fond of him and he in turn was amused by me. As was the custom, a poster announcing his death and the time of the funeral was pinned up on the door of the Armenian Convent. In Palestine the dead are buried on the same day or at most on the next day after death and there is no cremation.

This was to be my first experience of a family funeral. We were taken to the house by my mother, children not being banned on such occasions. There my uncle lay in an open coffin, dressed in a suit, covered in flowers and flanked with lighted candles to guide his way to the next world. We were greeted with tears by his three old sisters – my great-aunts Heghnoug, Horop and Arousiag, who had been seated for hours around the coffin. Soon after, an Armenian priest arrived and recited prayers for the dead which brought on more grief and tears. The coffin was then closed and transported in procession to the Church of the Holy Archangels. Many attended and the service was beautifully sung by a bishop, priests and seminarians. The most moving part is the chanting of '*Der voghormia*' (Lord have mercy). We then proceeded to the ancient cemetery of Pergeech, where on arrival the coffin was placed on a raised tomb and reopened. This tomb, which stood under a mulberry tree, served as an altar at all funeral services. More prayers were recited (at this point it is believed that the soul finally leaves the earthly body). The coffin was then transferred to the grave in the family plot; more prayers, the scattering of blessed soil by Aram, his eldest son, the final leave-taking and the descent into the earth next to his wife, who had died in 1918. All those present

158 ARMENIANS OF JERUSALEM

then proceeded to the parish club where coffee was served and condolences received by the family.

It is customary for close relatives to return to the graveside with a priest and his attendant early in the morning on the two days following the funeral. Prayers are recited and the grave censed. Memorial services for the dead are held at the church on the seventh and fortieth days after the funeral, then again after a period of half a year and a year.

Pergeech has been a burial place for the Armenian community in Jerusalem for nearly three and a half centuries. Before then Armenians were buried in a plot of land near Akeldama, the Potters' field of Matthew 27:7, which also served as a burial ground for members of other Christian communities and for foreign pilgrims. Armenian patriarchs, however, were buried in the courtyard outside the Cathedral of St James. Among them, just inside the entrance, lies Patriarch Abraham II, who died in AD 1192 during the reign of Salah el Din in Jerusalem. Pergeech is situated on Mount Zion south of the city walls. An ancient building in the cemetery is believed to be on the site of the house of Caiaphas. It flanks a small cloistered courtyard, which serves as a resting place for the Armenian patriarchs and bishops buried there since 1645. Large oval marble tombs stand witness to the life and work of men who led the Armenian church and community in Jerusalem over the centuries, often during difficult times. Embedded in the surrounding cloister walls are glazed pottery tiles, some decorated with geometric designs in yellow and black, others with floral motifs in green and blue. In the courtyard tiles decorate a small altar, and an inscription in Armenian reads:

David Ohannessian of Kütahya who in 1919 founded the art of pottery in Jerusalem, produced these tiles here, in his workshop, in order to embellish the altar in memory of his parents and all deceased of his family. In the year 1928 in the tenure of Patriarch Elisha Turian.

An old vine draped a pergola, casting shadows on the tombs of bishops, sacristans and priests buried under inscribed slabs in the centre of the courtyard below. On the slabs are carved mitres and croziers for bishops, linked keys for sacristans, signifying the position held by the deceased in life.

During my childhood I was frequently taken to Pergeech with

THE SECOND WORLD WAR

Malakeh, Sahag and my young cousin Morris. We would visit the priest in charge, Hair Khoren, a tall man with clear blue eyes and a greying beard. He lived in rooms above the cloister and, as a good friend of my uncle Sahag, was always pleased to receive us. It might seem strange to think that we looked forward to an outing to the cemetery. Hair Khoren and my uncle would have drinks and play a game of *tawla* (backgammon) while we ran about exploring tombstones and other ancient monuments.

It is not the custom to inscribe biblical texts on Armenian tombstones. Only the name with dates of birth and death are recorded, and the word *hanqisd* (rest in peace). On early tombstones one finds a variety of craftsmen's tools carved into the stone slabs. Some examples are keys for a locksmith, scissors for a tailor, hammer and chisel for a stone mason, indicating the profession of the deceased. This custom has now been abandoned. In the old days all inscriptions were carved in Armenian script. Today one finds that English has been introduced in order to enable those Armenians living abroad, who might have lost their native tongue, to trace the graves of their forebears while on visits to Jerusalem.

Kaghakatsi families had private plots reserved for them in the cemetery, and no outsider was allowed interment in the area. My mother's family had two such plots – one for the Gazmararians and the other for the Krikorians.

Between the wars of 1948 and 1967 the cemetery fell into an area of no-man's-land, was mined and inaccessible. It divided the Jordanian army on the city walls from the Israeli army in the Dormition Abbey. In spite of that, looters were able to break into the courtyard from a narrow street below the Dormition Abbey. They picked off most of the tiles, badly damaging the ones that were left. Attempts were made to break open the tombs of the patriarchs in the belief that valuables had been buried in them, causing further considerable damage. A small side chapel on the site of the house of Caiaphas was completely ransacked.

In May 1942 my grandmother died at Isquhie's house in Ramallah, aged 86. She was buried in Pergeech in the family plot next to my grandfather, who had died in 1910. Little did we know that a much bigger blow was in store for us. Early in the following year, 1943, my elder sister, Margaret, now 21 years old, had a recurrence of the ear trouble she had suffered as a child. She was put under the care of a specialist, Dr Salzburger, who advised that she should undergo an

160   ARMENIANS OF JERUSALEM

operation for mastoid. Unfortunately she developed meningitis after the operation, never regained consciousness, and died within a few days. Had penicillin been available the tragedy might have been averted. She was buried in the Anglican cemetery on Mount Zion, her funeral attended by hundreds of friends and relatives.

In 1943 my class at St George's School graduated. We all passed our final exams and were awarded school leaving certificates. In addition we had studied for one of three Department of Education higher examinations, any of which would admit us to a university. I chose the Oxford and Cambridge school certificate and passed in seven subjects with credits in French and English.

Our St George's School leaving certificates were presented to us by Sir Harold MacMichael, the High Commissioner for Palestine, on 22 June 1943. The headmaster, Mr O. O. Postgate, presided, with Mr Sharp, our English literature teacher. Canon Bridgeman represented the bishop, who was away in England. Parents and friends were invited to the ceremony, which was followed by tea and photographs. We were now free to make our various ways and pursue the careers of our choice. There was a sadness on leaving school, our teachers of so many years and fellow-pupils. Of the eighteen graduates that day two were English, one German, one Armenian, two Jews, four Muslim and eight Christian Arabs.

Most of my student colleagues went on to university to become chemists, engineers, lawyers or doctors. Many went to the American University in Beirut, others to Cairo and some to Damascus. A few students had already arranged to go to the United States. Attracted by the new world I thought of doing this myself, but soon discovered that even though I was a British subject I was on the Palestine quota and would have to wait for many years. Deep down I wanted to be a musician or to pursue horticulture, but both were considered by my parents to be unremunerative. They suggested that I take up auditing and accountancy as a profession. I found it surprising that of all people my father, who was so musical, should take such a view. In fact I soon realized that I had no great ambition and the best thing I could do was to look for work.

Friends told me that I should apply to the Army Base Command Pay Office in Jerusalem, where I would get a reasonable salary. I did so, and was accepted as an accounts clerk. The offices were not far from home in Triangle Building on Julian's Way. I joined a staff of Jews, Arabs and others, and we worked on accounts and pay packets

THE SECOND WORLD WAR
161

under the supervision of English army sergeants and corporals. There was a friendly atmosphere in the office but I found the work boring, and hated accounts though I could do them with ease. It was there that I had my first taste of smoking; Woodbine and Victory cigarettes were issued to all the staff. After a few months at Triangle Building we were moved to new premises in Schneller's Orphanage, in north-west Jerusalem, which had been taken over by the army. The move out of town made me hate my job all the more and I decided that a change was imperative.

I put in for a job at Messrs Russell & Company, a reputable firm of auditors where I could work and study at the same time. I was taken on as a junior clerk at a salary of 18 Palestine pounds per month. I had already gained some experience at Base Command Pay and in the meantime had passed touch-typing exams at the YMCA night school. Junior staff at Russell's were encouraged to study book-keeping and accountancy, and the firm paid for the courses. The offices were in Julian's Way, opposite the building where I had worked before.

The staff was mostly made up of Jews with about three Arabs and myself. Partners and directors in the firm were Mr A. N. Young and Mr J. Scott-Smith. Mr Shimon Schurr occupied the position of chief clerk. One of his assistants was Mr Wadie' Gumri, the son of an Arab Anglican priest. Two secretaries, Miss Aviva Lipsky and Miss Rachel Mackowsky, did the immaculate typing of letters, final accounts and balance sheets. For almost a year juniors like myself were given the job of casting or adding up. No calculating machines were allowed and we each had to initial the work we had done with green ink. As we progressed we were given more responsibility. Some clients sent their books to the office for an audit, to others we had to go out, in each case keeping strict record of the number of hours spent on a particular job.

Our clients included businesses, army institutions, hotels, hostels, charities, schools and religious establishments. Among them were the Agudat Israel, the Keren Keymeth le Israel, the Greek Orthodox patriarchate, Russian Ecclesiastical Mission, the Naafi, Jerusalem Sports Club, St George's School and Close, the King David Hotel, the American Colony Hostel (as it was then) and also their souvenir store at Jaffa Gate.

Visits to clients provided variety and an opportunity to meet many interesting and influential people in all sections of the community. The Anglican bishop in Jerusalem (Bishop Stewart) had no accountant

162 ARMENIANS OF JERUSALEM

at that time and I was sent to his office every month to do the book-keeping. We also worked at the King David Hotel, where we sat in an enclosed terrace overlooking the gardens with a view of the old city walls in the distance. Their accounts were beautifully kept, hand-written in French by the chief accountant, Mr Fakkides, and his team. An Egyptian waiter in fez, *gallabīya* and red cummerbund would serve us with tea out of polished hotel silverware.

There was very little to do after work, although I was well occupied with my various hobbies. A choice of about five cinemas put on a variety of films: Garbo in *Ninotchka*, *Alexander's Ragtime Band* and *Gone with the Wind* were some of many that came our way. Sunday afternoons were spent visiting friends and relatives.

In the suburbs of Beit Hakarem and Talpiot open-air cafes provided a popular pastime – *thés dansants*. Many also flocked to the summer resort of Ramallah to enjoy the cool air and amenities provided by the Grand Hotel. Numerous cafes in west Jerusalem, such as the Alaska, the Attara, the Cafe Europe and Cafe Vienna, were always well patronized by Jews, Arabs and others. A favourite haunt, the Viennese Tearoom, was conveniently situated on the ground floor of Triangle Building. It was owned and run by a charming Viennese couple assisted by the wife's old mother. It was indeed a corner of civilization and culture, a favourite and safe place for respectable rendezvous, frequented by people of society. The standard was high, everything of the best – the coffee, ices, cakes, and above all meringues with cream.

Day trips to the coast were very popular, as were moonlight trips to the Dead Sea. A visit to the Mujib in east Jordan, a spectacular gorge through which the river Arnon flows, was often organized by office employees. After spending a night on the shores of the Dead Sea, where one was continually buzzed by gnats and mosquitoes, a motor launch arrived at dawn to pick up the group. It then lazily made for the eastern shore, stopping briefly at hot sulphur springs. The scenery seemed to change by the minute: in the distance to the east the mountains of Moab and to the west the Judean hills shimmered in various shades of brown, purple and blue, enhanced by the hot, crystal-clear air. On arrival at the gorge a short walk brought us to a waterfall cascading into a series of pools below. Swimming and a picnic lunch followed, then it was time to make the return boat trip and the journey back to Jerusalem.

There were two popular tennis clubs in Jerusalem where the young could meet. One of them, the Jerusalem Sports Club, catered mostly

THE SECOND WORLD WAR

for the British and foreign community and applicants had to be vetted before joining. On the other hand at the YMCA the courts were open to members of all communities. When I joined I was enlisted as a junior and played tennis every afternoon during the summer. Club members, both Jewish and Arab, mixed amicably and freely together, and it was there that we made many friends. In my last year as a junior I won the singles championship and was awarded a silver cup by Sir Arthur Wauchope, the High Commissioner for Palestine.

This happy interlude in our social life was short-lived. The political situation was deteriorating fast and it affected Arab–Jewish relations on a personal level. The amicable pairing up of Jewish and Arab tennis players was thwarted by threatening letters, bringing to an end an impending tournament and leading to the final disbanding of the YMCA tennis club.

I constantly visited my Armenian relatives, and paid weekly visits to my great-aunt Heghnoug in the old city. I provided her with flowers from my garden for the Armenian cathedral and the parish church of the Holy Archangels, where she was in charge of decorating the altars. Every Friday in the late afternoon I could be seen going through the Jaffa Gate carrying a bunch of flowers. This was by no means a chore, as I was very fond of her and she was indeed an interesting person. Aunt Heghnoug lived in the old family house where my great-grandparents Anna and Krikor had lived. Around the courtyard a raised bed still nourished a variety of scented plants and the wall was draped with a yellow-blossomed *banksiae* rose.

She always prepared tempting food for me and after a gossip, usually about other members of the family, instructed me in the history of the Armenian martyrs and saints. Her favourite story was that of Krikor Luisavoreech, Gregory the Illuminator, who was condemned by King Tridates to be imprisoned in a pit, which resulted in the king's transformation into a wild boar until he repented and accepted Christianity.

Pet cats suspiciously watched canaries in large wire cages, and tortoises walked about freely in Aunt Heghnoug's courtyard. Among her many visitors were people who were poor, both materially and in mind, and had few relatives or none at all. They were made most welcome, given food and talked to on the level of their understanding. Two such regular visitors come to mind: Vehanoush, who arrived with carton boxes and straw piled on her head, practically covering her eyes; and another Armenian woman called Shafeeqa, who went about

164 ARMENIANS OF JERUSALEM

wearing a *gallabiya* with a cummerbund round her waist. She had come from Aleppo, escaping the Turkish massacres, but the experience had left her bewildered. I was intrigued and fascinated by these two harmless women and the normal and kind way my aunt treated them. Shafeeqa finally died alone in her room, cared for by members of the Armenian Benevolent Union. Vehanoush broke the curfew during the war of 1948, presumably not knowing it was on, and was shot dead, thus ending her sad and troubled life.

In the 1950s my great-aunt became too old and blind to look after herself and against her wishes she was moved to Beirut to live with her nephews and nieces. Krikor sent his sister Nazouhie to Jerusalem to arrange the move and to dispose of the old family house. Nazouhie wound up that lovely dream place, gave away the plants and pets, and took her aunt away to Beirut. There she died at the grand old age of 108.

To Heghnoug, Beirut was an unhappy place of exile even though she was among her dearest relatives. When Armenian friends who still lived in Jerusalem visited her, she would implore them upon their return to light candles for her at the Kilkhateer, the shrine in St James's Cathedral, and to pray for her speedy death. I myself was never to see her again after the city was divided in 1948.

The old house was transferred to another Armenian family, who modernized it. The beautiful rose-coloured stone walls were concreted over against the damp. The courtyard was roofed in with plastic corrugated sheeting and the old stone floor, once a playground for the tortoises, was torn up and replaced with modern cement tiles. It had been unchanged for centuries and now was robbed of its ancient character.

19 YEARS OF VIOLENCE

As soon as the Second World War was over, the political situation in Palestine, as feared, went from bad to worse. It was obvious that there would be bloodshed and the gloomy Egyptian saying *il dam lal khulkhal* (there will be blood up to the ankles) was used in daily conversation.

The aim of both parties in the conflict, Arabs and Jews, was not only to bring a speedy end to British rule but also to take over the country. Both claimed the land as their own and feared that the British authorities would not grant the independence apparently promised in secret agreements to each side. Violence escalated and had to be accepted as part of daily life.

The Arab freedom fighters had various local commanders who did their best to instil discipline into the inexperienced men under their control. Of many, two were outstanding – Fawzi el Qawukji, a Lebanese who was likened to Garibaldi, and Abd el Qadir el Husseini, son of Musa Kazim pasha el Husseini. Musa Kazim pasha had been appointed mayor of Jerusalem shortly after the British occupied Palestine, but was removed from office in April 1920 for his opposition to the government's pro-Zionist policies. Abd el Qadir was a brave fighter and a respected leader. After he was killed on 9 April 1948 in the battle to recapture Kastel on the Jerusalem–Jaffa highway, many thought that Arab resistance would decline. Treachery, feuding and above all spying did much harm to the Arab cause of freedom from foreign rule.

The people of Palestine had never experienced independence. There was no proper leadership, as many nationalists had been imprisoned or sent into exile, and the majority of the population were poor and uneducated. A further effect of foreign rule was that the people had begun to cleave to western culture, preferring comforts

166 ARMENIANS OF JERUSALEM

and money to *watan* (homeland) and the immense sacrifice that went with the struggle to attain it.

In the meantime, having suffered a terrible holocaust at the hands of the Nazis, the Jews won world-wide support for the creation of their national home. The Arabs of Palestine could not understand how they became the scapegoat for these awful deeds in Europe in which they had played no part. The Jews, afraid that their homeland might be in doubt now that Arab opposition had grown, set up two underground movements the Irgun Zvai Leumi (Jewish National Military Organization) led by Mr Menachem Begin who later became Prime Minister of Israel; and the Stern Gang, a group of Irgun dissidents led by Avraham Stern. These two Jewish groups were ruthless and well-organized. They carried out bombings, killings and assassinations with meticulous planning and precision, and attacked the British and the Arabs, both of whom they considered to be a danger to their ultimate goal of a Jewish state in Palestine. The murder of young British policemen, soldiers and others by both Arabs and Jews became frequent occurrences and is attested to by the rows of graves in cemeteries all over the country.

By 1946 conditions were so bad that the Jewish and Arab inhabitants kept to their respective areas of the city. City Arabs identified themselves, to enable them to walk freely in their own quarters, by wearing fur kalpaks, Christian women large crosses, others large headscarves. Those from surrounding villages were easily recognizable in their traditional costumes. Even these means of identification were not enough to ensure safety. Bombs were placed by Jews in Arab *suqs*, incurring tremendous civilian casualties, usually in reprisal for similar deeds committed against Jewish inhabitants. Buses were ambushed or shot at and explosives placed under cinema seats, in cafes and other places of entertainment, in markets and public places.

To avoid sniping along a section of the route overlooked by the Jewish settlement of Montefiore, armour-plated buses were introduced between the southern Arab suburbs and the Old City. It was an experience to travel in one of those capsule buses with no ventilation and a driver whose only view of the outside world was through two tiny slits at the fore. Shots would be aimed at it, luckily bouncing off as the bus accelerated to top speed to reach safety within the Jaffa Gate. We became used to living precariously.

I had many friends in Jerusalem whom in spite of all the troubles I continued to visit, among them the Markarian family living in a street

YEARS OF VIOLENCE 167

off Princess Mary Avenue next to the fashionable Hesse's restaurant. Nubar, the younger son, had graduated at St George's School with me. His widowed mother, an engaging and good-looking woman of personality, came from Egypt and had married a *kaghakatsi* who had been an official in the Austrian post office in Jerusalem. In spite of the danger I would spend my evenings with them, leaving between nine and ten o'clock and often walking home to the Greek Colony through deserted streets.

Most of the land and buildings close to the Markarians' house was owned by Armenians, either privately or by the patriarchate, and a small Armenian suburb had grown up close to the Old City. The Armenian convent used their land to build shops, flats and office blocks all along what was known as Princess Mary Avenue (now Shlomzion HaMalka) and its environs. Rents received were used for the running expenses of the Armenian cathedral and convent. On the keystones of arched doorways of shops and over entrances to these buildings are embossed the Armenian patriarchate's monogram: 'Surp Hagop' (St James). As a gift to the British Mandate government a plot of land in the vicinity was donated by the Armenian patriarchate, on which to build the general post office.

On one of my evening visits to the Markarians' a loud explosion rocked the house, bringing down the chandelier and plunging us into darkness. I left for home immediately, challenged many times on the way by the military. Next day we were told that part of the CID building on the corner of Jaffa Road had been blown up by the Irgun, and ten Basuto soldiers who were guarding it had perished under the rubble.

Worse was to follow. On the morning of 22 July 1946 while I was at work in the office of Russell & Company a tremendous explosion was heard all over the city. We rushed down to the street to be told that the wing of the King David Hotel which housed the government secretariat had been blown up. Members of the Irgun underground had managed to smuggle milk-churns full of explosives into the basement below. Over 90 people had been killed, Arabs, Jews, British, Armenians and others who all met their death under a huge mound of rubble. Many of them were our friends and the shock and grief which gripped the city was unbelievable. Much has been written about this horrific incident in which so many innocent lives were lost. The office telephone at Russell & Company was busy with calls from inquiring relatives. We could not continue our work that day and were sent

168 ARMENIANS OF JERUSALEM

home early. My parents were very pleased to see that I had come back safely as they had been unable to make contact with me at the office. My father had a narrow escape: he had left the King David building, where he had been attending to some mechanical problem, only a few minutes before the explosion.

We were thrown into a state of confusion, anxiety and suspense and craved for information on the fate of our many friends. Soon the names of those missing were released and listed among them was Eugenie Markarian, the 29-year-old sister of Nubar, Eddie and Sophie. I had spoken to her while she was on her way to work that very morning. She was one of many young secretaries killed. A day and night emergency telephone service set up at the Jerusalem YMCA provided first-hand information to relatives and friends and was inundated with calls. Many rumours circulated. At first it was thought that a few people might be trapped alive under huge slabs of concrete. Bulldozers roared through the day and by torchlight at night, the noise rumbling through the hot July air as far as the Greek Colony. The whole city reeked of death and it was days before the last body was recovered. We attended funerals daily. Numerous graves in a section of the Anglican cemetery on Mount Zion still bear witness to this cruel incident.

On 5 August 1946 a memorial service for the 90 people who met their death while on duty at the secretariat was held at St George's Cathedral regardless of their creed. It was a moving event and the church was packed with friends and relatives. So far as I am aware no punishment was ever imposed on the perpetrators and no curfew followed. The bombing of the King David cast a black cloud of foreboding over the whole of Jerusalem and the atrocity is continually mentioned to this day.

In January 1947 the situation became so grave that the mandatory authorities decided it was prudent to evacuate all British women, children, and non-essential persons. As I was working in a private firm I came under the last category. My father was to stay behind, but my mother, my sister Gertie and myself were to join the evacuation scheme named Operation Polly. Notices signed by the Chief Secretary, Sir Henry Gurney, were issued on 31 January 1947 stating that we were to be ready to leave within 48 hours as our continued presence 'would hamper the police and military in their task of maintaining law and order'.

I did not know how to take this news. Thoughts of my departure

YEARS OF VIOLENCE 169

for boarding school came to mind resurrecting the horror of leaving our Greek Colony home, and above all Jerusalem which I loved. I feared that I might never see it again. On the other hand it was going to be my first visit to England to meet my father's family and to visit the country which the people of Palestine were brought up to believe was the greatest, most honest, impeccable, efficient, fair and reliable of all nations in the world. The phrase *kilmeh ingleez* (English word of honour) was in common use in daily conversation to vouch for the authenticity of a piece of gossip or news. In their simplicity the Arabs of Palestine were full of admiration for the British, even though they were aware that they had been badly let down over the years.

During 30 years of mandate rule the Palestinian Arab mind and way of thinking was never properly understood by the authorities. It was assumed that in time the Arabs would adapt to western culture and break away from their old traditions. Many, especially those who had been educated at mission or foreign schools, did so. They had a genius for learning languages and quickly took on western habits at home and in daily life. It is still a matter for debate as to whether this was the right course to follow, since those who made the change alienated themselves from the land and the rest of the population. Punctuality, however, so important in the west, continued to be treated casually with infuriating results. A British lady, exasperated by a long wait for an appointment, was told, 'Don't be upset. Eternity matters more than time.'

Our evacuation was to start on 4 February 1947. We were instructed to meet at assembly points in Jerusalem. Buses took us to Sarafand, a military camp in the coastal plain, part of which had been converted to house civilians. Two days later we were flown to Cairo in RAF Halifaxes. We sat on rows of wooden benches especially installed for passengers. My mother and Gertie left on a flight before me and weathered the journey well. In contrast I had a very bad attack of sickness as the plane bumped its way over Sinai and the Bitter Lakes. On landing we were put into trucks, driven to Ma'adi Camp and shown into a dormitory where I collapsed with gratitude on to my camp bed.

Ma'adi Camp, a British army establishment, was situated a few miles outside Cairo close to one of the most fashionable suburbs inhabited mainly by foreigners and the very rich. The army had been about to close the camp and move into the Canal Zone, but made every effort to put it back into working order for our arrival. It had

170 ARMENIANS OF JERUSALEM

been divided into three areas, each with an office, dining room, comfortable lounge, post office, Naafi shop, children's playroom, and cinema where a different film was shown each day. There were over 900 evacuees from all walks of life to be catered for. Our wants were provided for and the food was adequate and well-cooked. We were looked after by young German POWs, who were most efficient and courteous. The two men in charge of our section, Albert and Wolfgang, were extremely helpful though at first cautious and withdrawn.

With us in the camp we also had a good friend, Sopheeg, whose *kaghakatsi* parents the Kaplanians had for years been neighbours of my grandmother in the Armenian Quarter. Her husband, Jim Toon, was English, and she was evacuated from Haifa with her three small children. Sopheeg was full of humour and able to make light of all difficulties; she raised our spirits and kept us sane.

Needless to say social barriers followed us from Palestine to Ma'adi Camp. Snobbish women who considered themselves better-off and upper-class congregated to talk in loud-pitched, posh accents. They had little to do with foreign wives or their children, who in their eyes were natives.

It soon became clear that there was to be a long wait before passages to England would be available. During our stay the High Commissioner for Palestine, General Sir Alan Cunningham, came to see conditions for himself. Discontent grew, mostly among families with young children, because there was little for them to do and they were bored. This group was given priority for repatriation and the first 162 evacuees left on the SS *Ascania* on 20 February. We ourselves were to travel with the main body of 479 evacuees on 3 March on the SS *Empress of Scotland*.

As we had a whole month to wait we were granted day passes to go into Cairo, provided we reported back to camp at night. A bus took us to Ma'adi station where we joined the train which after a short journey arrived at Cairo's Bab el Luq. I took advantage of this liberty to leave camp and visit many historical sites. The picturesque atmosphere at Bab el Luq always fascinated me. It was crowded and noisy with village folk, their livestock, fruit, vegetables and other wares. Women in local dress steered their way through a mass of humanity with wicker baskets of live Muscovy ducks, geese, chickens or pigeons on their heads, children at their heels. Men in *gallabiyas* transported sacks and boxes full of vegetables and fruit, all aiming for the city market

YEARS OF VIOLENCE 171

and a good price for their produce. The accompanying loud babble of Egyptian Arabic fell like music on my ears. I could understand most of it, even though an unaccustomed hard 'g' is in common use, giving Egyptian Arabic the allegria for which it is noted.

I was greatly attracted to the atmosphere and life in Cairo, and would have loved to have found work as an excuse to stay there. My mother, however, was displeased at the thought and told me that I was in the grip of emotion. She pointed out the many temptations that could lure a young man of my nature, to which she thought I might be easily susceptible. Usually I rebelled against her suggestions but this time I took notice of what she said and dropped the idea, even though Cairo exerted a tremendous magnetic hold on me.

I enjoyed every minute of my stay and the historic, friendly and easy-going feeling prevailing in the city enthralled me. Of course much was lacking in hygiene and orderly living, but it is not for tourists and visitors to keep on criticizing as they commonly do. The eastern way of life is different from the western, a fact that has to be accepted sympathetically.

I divided my time between the Pyramids, the Sphinx, museums, *suqs*, Gizeh with its zoo and Tea Island, and Groppi's with its banyan trees, delicious pastries, marrons glacés, cassata and ice creams. Trips in feluccas on the Nile, the waters of which provide a living for millions of people, revealed magnificent views at every turn. In the distance the Citadel rises above the whirl of city life below. Minarets reach up into an evening sky softened by a haze of different colours. At dusk to the sound of various birds, ducks and ibis vying for their nocturnal perches is added a chorus of frogs. The noise rises to an unbelievable volume and wafts over the water and through the still air as far as Ma'adi Camp.

In the meantime a letter arrived from my father, telling us that he had taken leave and would be sailing direct for England on a cargo boat from Haifa. He had made arrangements for our house in the Greek Colony to be cared for by my aunt Malakeh, who would move in there with her husband and son Morris.

This was to be my father's first visit to England since he had left to go to the war in 1915. His parents had already died, his father, John Henry, in September 1941 at the age of 75 and his mother, Emma Elizabeth, aged 78, in September 1943. His brother, Leslie, and two sisters, Dolly and Hilda, with their families still lived in Birmingham as did many other of his relatives.

172   ARMENIANS OF JERUSALEM

On the day of our departure from Egypt we were taken by bus to Abbassia station and then by special train to Port Said where we embarked on the 20,000-ton liner, *The Empress of Scotland*. Late on 3 March we slipped out of port leaving the 'palmiers d'égypte' and the statue of Ferdinand de Lesseps to melt away in the distance. There were no stops on the way and we docked at Liverpool after eight days. The sea was generally calm and no land came in sight until we passed Tangiers and then Gibraltar. At night we sometimes saw the lights of boats fishing for sardines just off the North African coast. All went well until we entered the Bay of Biscay and the liner started to pitch and roll. Seasickness forced me to remain in my shared cabin for a few days without food. My poor mother was so ill that in a moment of weakness she announced that it would be best that we should both be thrown overboard.

20 ENGLAND IN 1947 AND THE RETURN TO JERUSALEM

It was early in March 1947 when we docked at Liverpool. Crowds had gathered on the quay and among them we were delighted to spot my father. It was not the ideal time to arrive in England, as the country was just emerging from the coldest winter in living memory. Nevertheless, to us the train journey was new and interesting. Snow still covered the ground and from the carriage windows we were reminded of scenes on Christmas cards sent to us over the years in Jerusalem.

Evacuees who had no relatives or friends to go to were directed to ministry of health hostels until they were able to move on to more permanent quarters. We were fortunate as my father had arranged for us to stay with his elder sister, Dolly, who lived in Leominster Road, Sparkhill, Birmingham.

Aunt Dolly was a handsome woman, fair, with blue eyes, intelligent and musical but rather shy. She had never seen us before and was perhaps apprehensive of our foreign upbringing. Two things I had in common with her were music and gardening and from her I learned much about English flowers, many of which I had not seen before. As my aunt was out working for most of the day we had the run of the house and my mother cooked for us. Aunt Dolly's marriage to Mr Banks had come to an end and her two sons, Douglas and Philip, had already married and left home.

As soon as I got my bearings I started to go into town by bus. There I passed most of the time window-shopping in Corporation Street and New Street, overwhelmed by the large department stores, the like of which I had never seen. I would often take coffee or tea in the Kardomah Cafe where I tried to recapture the atmosphere of the Viennese Tearoom in Jerusalem. A totally new and modern way of life

174 ARMENIANS OF JERUSALEM

was unfolding before my eyes. Most of all I enjoyed the teeming market in the Bull Ring with the hustle and bustle of its stalls offering a variety of goods. Compared to Jerusalem everything seemed on such a large scale, particularly the huge crowds of people – a sea of faces totally unfamiliar to me. After an interesting but solitary day I would catch a bus home in Station Street. There I greatly enjoyed watching the huge shire horses with plaited tails and heavy fetlocks, pulling their loads along the street. The rhythmic clopping of their hooves and jangle of their brasses always fascinated me.

In the afternoons we often visited my aunt Hilda, her husband, Jack, and small son, James, in Shirley just outside Birmingham. We felt at home with them and had much in common. They were professional musicians and my aunt would often invite us to concerts, where she was first violin and leader of the orchestra and Jack played the cello. To acquaint us with the country they would take us for drives in their car, and we sometimes stopped to collect firewood. Later they took me with them on a delightful visit to north Wales.

My father's only brother, Leslie, also a cellist, lived with his wife, Evelyn, and daughter, Beryl, in the suburb of Acock's Green where we often paid them visits. We were constantly invited out to tea to meet more of my father's relatives. He had two uncles, Samuel and William Swift, his mother's brothers. Samuel had made a successful career in the building trade. As a young man his sister, Emma, my grandmother, had lent him the money to start his own business and he later returned her kindness by paying her a small pension for life.

One afternoon on a visit to my great-uncle Sam and his wife, aunt Florrie, in their lovely house in Moseley, he made what seemed to us a strange comment. In the course of conversation he suddenly announced that we reminded him of what he imagined the biblical Hebrews in the Old Testament to have been like – this because of our dark hair and eyes and the eastern tinge about us. We were amused, did not resent his comments, and managed conveniently to divert the conversation to admiration of the white cockatoo in his sitting-room.

My great-uncle Will and his wife, Ada, lived in Handsworth. They had one child, Grace, who was already married, also to a musician. Uncle Will was a jeweller by profession and with pride would show us some of his work. Aunt Ada had been crippled in a serious accident but still managed to run her own household. She always provided a delicious tea, which sometimes included crumpets or pikelets, food hitherto unknown to us. During the war they had volunteered to

ENGLAND IN 1947 AND THE RETURN TO JERUSALEM 175

rescue pets abandoned by their owners in bombed-out houses. Frightened and injured animals were searched for, sometimes at night, and brought home by uncle Will at great risk. With food rationing, feeding these animals was an added difficulty, but they had managed and gladly used their house as a haven and hospital for animals. By the time of our visit only one very jumpy dog, Toosy, remained from those days and had become the family pet.

I went for walks with uncle Will who conversed with me in his gentle voice. He would take me to his allotment on the railway embankment, where among his vegetables grew the finest pastel-shaded hollyhocks that I have ever seen. All our relatives did their very best for us in a difficult time, when Britain had not even begun to get over the hardship of war.

Soon after our arrival my aunt Dolly embarked on a second marriage, which meant that we had to leave her house. Before this happened my father left us to return to his work in Palestine but we alas were not allowed to accompany him. It was arranged that we should move next door to the house of a neighbour, Mrs Evason, a widow who had a son, Raymond, and daughter, Joyce. Raymond was a keen Scout and there was great excitement when he was chosen to go to a jamboree in France. Mrs Evason was most kind to us; we enjoyed our stay with the family and became good friends.

I only travelled down to London twice, intending to see old friends from Jerusalem. On one visit I spent a couple of nights in Dagenham where Sopheeg and her family were settling in. They told me that they had decided not to return to Palestine. London never failed to interest me and travelling on the underground to visit historic sites was an exhilarating experience.

My former headmaster at St George's School, the Rev. J. P. Thornton-Duesbury, now principal of St Peter's Hall in Oxford, invited me there for the day. I gladly accepted and after lunch he kindly showed me the town and many beautiful college buildings.

The very cold winter was succeeded by one of the hottest summers known for many years. The countryside, wooded, green and beautiful, was a great attraction to me as it was such a contrast to the dry landscape we were accustomed to in Palestine. I used a bicycle to visit my aunt Hilda in Shirley and would also ride for miles to surrounding villages and nearby woods. There I sat, listening to birdsong and admiring the sheets of scented bluebells and lily of the valley growing wild under the trees.

176 ARMENIANS OF JERUSALEM

It soon became apparent that we were to remain in England indefinitely and after about a month I decided to look for temporary work until our return to Jerusalem. This proved difficult as I had never been employed in England before, and the fact that I came from abroad led people to think that I was a new immigrant or a foreigner. I wrote countless letters in answer to advertisements but the replies if any were negative. As a last resort I was advised to contact an employment agency who could only offer me a job as an accounts clerk in the Nechells gas works at Saltley, which was not really my scene but I had no choice. At Nechells I was interviewed by the chief clerk and taken on.

It took me more than an hour each morning, with two changes of bus, to reach Saltley. Once through the gate of the works the final walk to the office took us past huge gas-holders, heaps of coal, smoking chimneys and puddles of black water. Over all hung a permanent smell of gas. It was a far cry from the clean air and blue skies that I was used to in Jerusalem. All employees had a clocking-in card and I had to be at the office half an hour earlier than anyone else, as on arrival I had to calculate gas pressures and then telephone the figures through to the main office. During the week we made up pay packets for the workers. Although I hated my job I made new friends there and it was my first encounter with informality between working colleagues. I found it difficult to call people by their first names, especially if, like the chief clerk, they were older than I or in a senior position. This degree of familiarity between working colleagues was still unheard-of in Jerusalem. I also had to learn that in England it was not done to call on friends and acquaintances without prior notice. By contrast, in Jerusalem one is welcome to drop in unannounced at any time of day.

Weeks slipped into months and we were waiting anxiously for permission to return to Jerusalem. It never occurred to me that I might like to stay on and make England my home. The only place where I knew I wanted to be was in Jerusalem. Although my situation was different I now understood the suffering of Arab notables banished by the mandate authorities to the Seychelles for their political views.

After I had been working at Nechells for nearly six months, we (my mother, my sister Gertie and I) at last received permission from the Colonial Office to return to Palestine to rejoin my father. After 30 September 1947 we were allowed to apply for places on the waiting-

ENGLAND IN 1947 AND THE RETURN TO JERUSALEM 177

list for passages. Priority was to be given to those living in ministry of health hostels. Children under seven years old were not permitted to return. A few friends of ours who had been evacuated with us, and with whom we maintained contact, decided not to go back to Palestine as they had already become well settled in England. As for me I could not contain my joy and wanted only to return as soon as possible.

We were to travel on *The Empress of Australia* sailing from Liverpool on 15 October 1947. I relinquished my post at the gas works with no regrets. The staff wished me well, although they could not understand why I had chosen to return to such a troubled land. Shopping occupied us in the few remaining days, but it was still difficult to buy clothes, which were rationed and could only be had with coupons. Plants had no such restrictions. I packed seeds of runner beans, English tomatoes and sweet peas in my suitcase. I also carried a strawberry-red hydrangea and half a dozen chrysanthemum plants as cabin baggage, dismissing any fear of rules regarding the import of plants and seeds.

My mother and Gertie were equally glad to be going back to Jerusalem. We had made no permanent home in England as we always knew that our enforced stay would be temporary. It was good to be acquainted with my father's relatives who had hitherto only been names to us. Life in England was attractive and different but six months was much too long to be away from home. The pull of the east had not weakened and we longed to take up again our familiar life in Jerusalem.

We travelled by train to Liverpool where I arrived with a horrendous migraine. I retired to my cabin, which I shared with tourists who were on their way to Malta. When I recovered an elderly Englishman who shared my cabin revealed that he had thought that I was a 'Wog' because he found me lying on my bunk. If I were truly English I would have been up and around in the fresh air. Taken aback, I told him that he was rude, imperialistic and intolerant towards foreigners. From then on he became a congenial travelling companion.

Characteristically, the sea was rough in the Bay of Biscay and again the ordeal of seasickness had to be endured. Our only stop on the way to Port Said was at Valetta harbour where I bade farewell to my cabin companion. There, and again at Port Said, we were besieged by men in small boats laden with souvenirs. Haggling and bargaining went on in loud voices between the deck and the depths below. This was a certain sign that we were heading East.

178   ARMENIANS OF JERUSALEM

I met many interesting people on the ship, among them a French couple who were returning to their home in Cairo after a short holiday in England. When the Egyptian coastline came into view there was great excitement, 'Gaston, tu vois les palmiers d'égypte,' exclaimed Arlette with great delight. I knew exactly what they felt. It also delighted my heart to see the coastline with palm trees on the horizon framed in a haze of pink and blue evening light. We disembarked and had to go through customs before leaving for Kantara East where we were to pick up the midnight train to Lydda. My plants had survived the sea journey well. However they were noticed by the Egyptian customs' official who ordered me to destroy them on the spot. Pretending to do so I opened a tin trunk of my mother's and packed the lot in, hoping for the best.

Our wait for the Kantara train to start seemed endless; no one was able to tell us the official time of departure. Facilities were extremely primitive and the heat and noise only added to our discomfort. We finally left hours late, passing through el Arish, Rafah, and arriving at Gaza at dawn. There we stopped and breakfasted on fresh figs, prickly pears, bread and cheese with mint tea to drink. We travelled on to Lydda, where my father had sent a car to drive us straight to the Greek Colony house where we arrived dusty and exhausted. My plants had survived their chequered journey and were duly planted, the chrysanthemums in time to flower in the autumn.

We found that during our absence Jerusalem had been divided into four security zones, A, B, C and D. These wire cages covered about a third of the municipal area of the city. Zone A enclosed the German and Greek Colonies, the railway station and part of the Bethlehem road. Zone B was in the centre of the city and included King George Avenue, the King David Hotel, the YMCA and Julian's Way. Zone C was known as the Jerusalem fortress as it contained police head-quarters, the Russian Compound area, the post office and prisons. Zone D, the smallest, enclosed the area around Schneller's Orphan-age, which was in the hands of the British army. Zones A and C had three entrance gates each, while Zone B had four, all of which were manned by the army. After careful scrutiny of applications, passes were issued only to those who lived in the zone or had business there. British subjects were given passes for all zones, whereas the movement of the local inhabitants was restricted. For convenience many government offices such as town planning, commerce and industry, price

ENGLAND IN 1947 AND THE RETURN TO JERUSALEM 179

control, moved into one zone. The Old City of Jerusalem was not included.

The scheme came into full operation at noon on Thursday 13 February 1947 and was rigidly enforced. British subjects remaining in Jerusalem had to live inside the zones, some in pensions or hotels. This scheme caused much inconvenience but was no solution to the violence which continued unabated. Soon after my return in October I took up my former employment at Messrs Russell & Company and tried to lead a normal life once again.

Towards the end of 1947 the situation deteriorated further. Recommendations given by various royal commissions were not acceptable to the parties in dispute and violent disturbances continued. The United Nations voted on 29 November to partition Palestine between Jews and Arabs. The Arabs did not accept the plan and 29 November was proclaimed and remains to this day a day of protest by Palestinians living in Israel and the Arab world.

On 8 December Britain recommended to the United Nations that the Palestine mandate should be terminated on 14 May 1948. The local Arab population greeted this decision with shock and dismay and many thought that the announcement was a trick. Time and time again I was told, 'Don't believe it, they will go out of the door and return through the window.' Others said, 'They must go, the British promised us our independence.' As in all crises there was no firm news. Some thought this, others said that, all looking for signs to prove that the British were indeed leaving. Their departure would be much regretted by many, who feared that their lives would become insecure and their employment and businesses end. In spite of all the political difficulties encountered during the 30 years of mandatory rule, it is amazing how kindly the Arab population spoke then of the British, whom they admired and trusted. Unfortunately this flattering view no longer prevails.

With the end of the mandate approaching, British policy towards Palestine remained unclear. The Jewish underground stepped up their campaign of terror against the authorities, whom they felt to be more hostile now that restrictive immigration laws were implemented. Thousands of Jews who had escaped the holocaust and managed to come by boat under very hard and uncomfortable conditions were turned back and put into camps on the island of Cyprus. These incidents made the British, and for that matter anything English, hateful to the Jews. The British Foreign Secretary, Ernest Bevin, was

180 ARMENIANS OF JERUSALEM

very unpopular and was burned in effigy by fanatical Jewish crowds. The Arabs also remained suspicious of both British and Jewish intentions and pursued their own objective of Arab rule for the whole of Palestine. After all, they had been the inhabitants of the land for over 2,000 years and were still in the majority. Gradually it was becoming evident to all that the mandate was indeed to be given up – the deadline of 14 May 1948 was persistently announced through government information offices, in the press and on the wireless. Yet this was still hard to believe.

21 THE DISPERSAL

The year 1948 ushered in a period of uncertainty, with a large part of the Arab population of Palestine on the move in search of a place of safety. With the end of the mandate instability and violence were predicted, but it was assumed that they would be brief and any move only temporary. This alas proved to be an illusion as those who left were to be permanently separated from their homes and lands.

Through generations of sacrifice the Palestinians had developed an ancient attachment to their property and above all to the extended family. Over the centuries their only investment had been to plough their savings into land and buildings. Houses were built with two aims, to raise income from rents and to provide security and accommodation for the younger generation. Visitors from Britain failed to understand the deep feeling Palestinian Arabs had for their homes, towns, villages and land from which they were evicted. Insensitively they asked, 'Why is there so much stress on property?', never having experienced unrecompensed loss themselves. After all, it was not a traumatic experience but perfectly normal for westerners to move house three or more times in a lifetime.

In the autumn of 1947 my friends the Markarians decided to move to the Katamon quarter of Jerusalem. It had become dangerous for them to remain in their property just off Princess Mary Avenue, close to the Jewish quarter of Nachlat Shiva. The move was short-lived, owing to a violent incident that shocked the residents of the Katamon quarter, deepening an already-present sense of fear and insecurity. In early January 1948 on a very wild, stormy and wet night a large explosion was heard above loud rumblings of thunder. The Semiramis Hotel, owned by the Lorenzo family, was blown up by the Haganah (Jewish underground defence forces), who believed it to be the

182 ARMENIANS OF JERUSALEM

headquarters of Arab guerrillas. In fact it was not. Most of the occupants of the hotel were killed, including many members of the Abu Suan family, who had moved there to be with their cousins, the Lorenzos. Two old aunts had just joined their relatives, as their own house at the junction of Julian's Way and the Shama'a was now in the midst of a battlefield. Ironically, they also perished that night in the Semiramis.

Jerusalem had now entered a state of anarchy. The Jewish forces had penetrated the Katamon hills, making it unsafe for all those who lived there. Next day, looking across the open fields towards the main Katamon road, I saw crowds of civilians weighed down with belongings, hurrying in a state of disarray and panic to escape to the relative safety of the Old City. This living scene reminded me of episodes in films – a mass exodus of civilians fleeing the ravages of war. It was not only Arab residents who were on the move, but Armenians, Greeks and others.

The Markarians had no time to enjoy their new home, abandoned their belongings and left in haste. The fashionable Katamon quarter, now practically devoid of its residents, most of whom owned their own houses, was being guarded by guerrillas from neighbouring Arab countries. Their headquarters was in the compound of the Greek monastery of St Simeon. Sniping between the Arabs and the Jewish Haganah now occurred daily, echoing throughout the Greek Colony.

It became increasingly clear that the mandatory power was adopting a policy of non-interference. The Jewish Haganah took complete control of certain towns and areas of Palestine, as did the Arab guerrillas in other parts, to give protection to their own people. This state of affairs developed months before the official departure of the British on 14 May 1948. Indeed, from early in 1948 the British authorities appeared to do little to influence the situation.

After the evacuation scheme, Operation Polly, many families of British government officials had not returned to Palestine. This was just as well, as early in 1948 all British personnel were given orders to leave the country by 15 April. We were informed that our family was to leave on Friday 27 February. I had already secretly made up my mind not to leave for England with my parents. I thought it was high time for me to break away and start a new life on my own. My parents were astonished at my decision but I explained that this was what I wanted to do and after much argument they let the matter drop for a while.

THE DISPERSAL 183

Actually to leave me behind in such a dangerous situation was inconceivable to them. I loved my parents deeply and had no wish to hurt them. They had done everything possible for us during our childhood and had sacrificed much to give us a good education and family life. However my overwhelming fear was exile from Jerusalem, which I found difficult to explain and which no one could understand. Above all I wished to remain with the people I had been so happily part of since childhood. My parents had also had an extremely happy life in Jerusalem. My father himself had lived there for over 30 years. For him, and even more for my mother, to be forced to give up their home due to political circumstances was a cruel experience.

Throughout February the house was gradually emptied of familiar objects and furniture. What was not disposed of was crated up and sent on to Birmingham. My parents still hoped that I would change my mind but I remained stubbornly determined to stay.

The day of departure arrived and there were many tears. A bus was sent to collect my parents, my sister and other passengers. Still not giving up hope, my father made everybody wait while he rushed back to the house and tried to convince me that I should follow later. He warned me that once the British had left there would be civil war, anarchy, murder, looting and violence and that the situation would become very dangerous. With the optimism of youth I did not take his warnings seriously and refused to believe that the violence he was predicting could possibly occur. To my mind human beings could not behave in such a way. Since I was full of illusions and had so much belief in the goodness of life, I was obviously unaware of what was going on around me. Disturbing reports of war just loomed as a mirage on the horizon and I did not take them seriously. I was determined to stay in Jerusalem whatever the consequences and my father was deeply disappointed at my decision. As it turned out, his predictions all came true and gradually unfolded before my eyes. At the time I did not know that this was to be our final parting; I was never to see him again as he died in England in 1950.

My parents left Port Said on the troopship SS *Scythia* on 28 February and arrived at Liverpool on 11 March, reaching Birmingham the next day. Their life was to be a struggle from then on. My father was 51 years old and prospects of finding a job were slight. It also took time to find a house, which meant there was another long stay with relatives. They eventually bought a house in Coal Valley Road, Hall Green, with a garden bordering on a railway embankment. My

184 ARMENIANS OF JERUSALEM

father put one of his talents to use, bought the necessary tools and set up as a clock- and watch-repairer. My sister Gertie, now aged nineteen, sensibly decided to join the WAAFs and was soon commissioned.

I planned to stay on in the Greek Colony house and intended to take in lodgers. The house was anyway too large for me and the additional income would help pay the rent. My parents had left me some furniture and other household necessities, but I would have to buy whatever else I needed. First I had to negotiate the lease of the house and find out if the *wakeel*, Archimandrite Thaddeus, would agree to my plans. I called on him in the Greek Convent and, although he thought it was most unwise, he let me take on the house at an increased rent.

I continued to work at Russell & Company but it was evident that many of our foreign clients were in the process of liquidation, others transferring their business out of the country. Army instititions were winding down and selling equipment cheaply. I managed to buy blankets, china and cutlery which I needed for my so-called guest house.

Before long my aunt Isquhie came to visit me from Ramallah. She herself had moved house, had bought new furniture and also intended to let a room or two during the summer months to supplement her earnings from sewing. It was still possible for her to make the hazardous journey back to Ramallah. I was extremely fond of her and never felt that her visits were an interference. Soon I was to have my first lodger. A former schoolmate, a Greek called Kareklas, moved in from the Katamon, bringing his piano with him. This was an encouraging beginning and provided me with extra income.

I continued to act as if things were normal, even though I soon realized that many Arab and foreign families were leaving. The consensus was that there would be bloodshed and turmoil for a while. Word spread that a move to a safer place for about two weeks was desirable. Those meaning to stay and stick it out started to lay in huge quantities of foodstuffs and fuel. Hysteria spread among the population, with a strong urge to buy and store as much as possible. Cellars and larders in every house were filled with sacks of rice, sugar, flour, lentils and other dry stores. Kerosene was stored in four-gallon tins and jerrycans, candles laid in and old lamps put into running order. I too laid in a quantity of tinned food, rice, sugar and flour. Life had become very difficult and it was increasingly dangerous to move about.

THE DISPERSAL

Looking back, I find it amazing how it was possible to adapt to the situation, with its uncertainty, news of daily killings, and the continual roar of gunfire that echoed around us daily. All over the country and in Jerusalem itself violent incidents occurred between Arabs and Jews. The commerical centre of Shama'a just below Mamillah Road, composed of Arab and Jewish shops, turned into a sea of violence. Most of the buildings were destroyed and the area remained derelict for the next 40 years.

All the shops in the Mamillah and along Julian's Way had shut down, including alas the Viennese Tearoom where we had passed many happy times. The offices of Russell & Company where I worked had also become inaccessible, and the directors decided that it was wiser to move out and operate from two locations. Jewish staff were transferred to an office in Sansur Building, in Ben Yehuda Street in west Jerusalem, while the non-Jewish staff were to work from the home of one of the partners, Mr John Scott-Smith, in the Greek Colony not far from where I lived. Equipment and files were divided and work separated between Arab and Jewish areas. After settling into our new office I was sent to wind up the accounts of the Jerusalem Sports Club. To me that was the sure indication that British rule in Palestine was really coming to an end.

By now the Katamon had become a battlefield. On 14 March 1948 houses belonging to the Shahin family and to Dr Freij were dynamited by the Stern Gang in the belief that they were Arab strongholds used by snipers. The explosions were horrific, followed by gunfire with the glow of tracer bullets lighting up the night sky. In turn the Arabs attacked the Jewish settlements of Yemen Moshe and Ramat Rahel.

On 9 April 1948 a dreadful event took place, which was to terrorize the Arab population more than anything that had happened so far. It resulted in a massive exodus from Arab towns and villages all over the country. At the village of Deir Yassin on the western outskirts of Jerusalem, men, women, and children were indiscriminately massacred by the Irgun Zvai Leumi. The inhabitants were driven out of their homes and over 245 were killed. More than 90 bodies, including pregnant women and children, were later recovered by the International Red Cross from a cistern where they had been dumped. Those who survived escaped to Silwan and other neighbouring Arab suburbs, some reaching the Greek Colony where I saw them wandering about defenceless and in a state of shock. What remained of the village was soon incorporated into the Jewish suburb of Givat Shaul.

186 ARMENIANS OF JERUSALEM

In reprisal for this horrific act, a few days later a medical convoy on its way to the Hadassah Hospital on Mount Scopus was ambushed and set alight as it passed through the Arab suburb of Sheikh Jarrah. Tragically, many brilliant young Jewish doctors and nurses perished. This was only one of many violent incidents sparked off by the cruel massacre at Deir Yassin.

In contrast to the horrors of war around us, spring arrived offering gentle balmy days with the occasional shower, birdsong, and an abundance of wild flowers in the fields around. That year five weeks separated the Western and Eastern Easters, the Orthodox churches celebrating Easter on 2 May. My aunt Isquhie, who was increasingly worried about me, decided that she would come and stay over Easter and use the time to complete some sewing for her clients in Jerusalem. My lodger, Kareklas, had already left, abandoning his hired piano, which was to be returned to a Jewish shop in Princess Mary Avenue.

There were still a few Greek families in the neighbourhood. On the Saturday before Easter one of them had brought back a lighted lamp from the ceremony of the Holy Fire, *Sabt el Nur*, in the Holy Sepulchre. From this flame we and our neighbours lit candles which by custom were to remain alight all night until Easter morning. Shooting and bombing started early that evening, so we lay on mattresses on the floor in the central corridor. At about 10.30 p.m. there was a tremendous blast followed by firing. The tiles on the roof rattled out of joint, windows, cupboards and doors blew open and the electricity was cut off. The only light we had was that of the candle – the *Nur*, Holy Fire – which miraculously had not been extinguished. Next day we heard that a truck full of explosives had been blown up on the main road of the Jewish settlement of Mikor Chaim only half a mile away. There were no casualties and little damage was done but the noise was appalling.

During April it became increasingly difficult even for foreigners to pass freely between Arab and Jewish parts of the city. Houses were blown up, road-blocks erected, streets that were open to traffic became daily more dangerous, there was sniping and street fighting. One frequently heard of the deaths of British soldiers, policemen and civil servants. Government services were gradually cut, with one department after another closing. Local postal services were suspended in mid-April, and by the 26th all airmail services in and out of Palestine ceased. Telephone links with abroad ended on 5 May and we were gradually approaching a state of limbo. All Arab shops and premises

THE DISPERSAL

187

outside the Jaffa Gate, in the Jaffa road and the Mamillah were already shut and boarded up by their owners before the end of April. It was not known what the future would bring, as the United Nations could not offer a substitute administration. The authorities strongly advised British residents to leave the country.

In spite of the strife around me I was still hopeful that things would return to normal, and assumed that after the British had departed there would be chaos but that law and order would soon be restored. My decision to remain aroused suspicion in some, but oddly enough I was totally unaware of this at the time as I considered myself to be part of the local scene and was prepared to sink or swim with everyone else.

Towards the end of April 1948 the situation deteriorated to the point where it was unwise to move about unless absolutely necessary. The population of the Greek Colony diminished daily, and friends and neighbours who had told me that they were going to stay slipped away unobserved. Families hired small trucks to take them, their baggage and chattels away. There was no time to bid farewell; people preferred to leave unnoticed in the early dawn. Mohammad, the milkman, stopped his usual rounds. His clients had left and it was too dangerous for him to venture out of the Old City. Villagers ceased to bring their vegetables and fruit. The Greek Colony was now practically abandoned, with only about five Greek families staying on. Houses were barred and shuttered, Greek flags pasted on doors (to paste a British flag on my house would have been folly) all in the hope that property owned by foreign nationals would be protected – after all it was generally thought that there would be a return in two or three weeks' time.

After a fierce battle for St Simeon's Monastery in early May, the Katamon heights fell to the Haganah and the Arab defenders had to withdraw to a line just west of the Greek Colony. The whole of the Arab suburb of Katamon was now under the control of the Jews and the few remaining residents had to flee to the Old City.

During a lull in the fighting unfamiliar sounds of banging reached us from the Katamon. News quickly spread that the Jewish forces were breaking into Arab houses to consolidate their position and to loot. They were surprised to find immense quantities of stores: food supplies, silver, carpets and other valuables. The houses were soon to be totally denuded of their contents.

It had now become dangerous for us to go out into the back garden

188   ARMENIANS OF JERUSALEM

to water plants and feed the chickens. The slightest movement there would invite sniper fire, exposed as we were by the open space between the Greek Colony and the Katamon. For the first time we began to think that we might follow the example of others and move out. A decision became all the more urgent when one of our neighbours, Mrs Kuttab, was shot dead by a sniper bullet while trying to escape. This incident convinced us that we must leave the Greek Colony and move to Isquhie's house in Ramallah, twelve miles north of Jerusalem, where we would be out of the fighting. I asked a taxi driver who had come to collect a neighbour to return in two days' time and take us to Ramallah. He agreed to do this for the exorbitant sum of 20 Palestine pounds, ten of which were to be paid then and there.

With great reluctance we started to pack. Furniture, bedding and other household chattels were pushed into one room and the iron shutters closed and firmly latched. We put all our food stocks into boxes but abandoned a sack of sugar and one of flour. To add to our problems I had some poultry in the yard and two broody hens sitting on twelve eggs each. What were we to do with our black cat, Sooty, to whom we were very attached? When the time came for us to leave she was not around and so had to be temporarily abandoned. The garden was full of plants and seedlings; the sweet peas grown from the seed brought from England were well advanced.

A very sad moment in my life had indeed arrived. Leaving home yet again was as wounding as it had always been under better circumstances. I dearly loved every aspect of the Greek Colony house – the garden, the trees, the shadows, the dawn and sunset, the very air, the birds, butterflies and wild flowers around it; the neighbours, our contacts with the local people, visitors, friends, hawkers, the sound of grasshoppers that lulled one to sleep at night, the bell of St Simeon's monastery ringing out over the valley every Sunday morning, and above all my parents and the interesting family life in which I was brought up. By staying on when everyone else was leaving, I was unconsciously trying to preserve something that had been a very happy experience. This wonderful dream was to be shattered on my departure from the Greek Colony.

The situation was even worse for thousands of Palestinian Arabs whose lives were being disrupted. The Greek Colony house was not my own property, but my deep attachment to it stemmed from the fact that I had lived in it for 22 happy years. My belongings were very modest, whereas others had to abandon complete households of

THE DISPERSAL

189

immense value. Most Palestinians owned the property from which they were being evicted: their loss was incomparably greater than mine.

We were all packed and ready for the car to come and take us to Ramallah when the telephone rang. It was my mother's cousin Nazouhie, who in her forthright way persuaded us to cancel our plans and come to join my great-aunt Arousiag, herself and her brother, Dr Krikorian. They had decided to stay on and protect their property in the Arab suburb of Baqa'a, less than a mile from the Greek Colony. 'Come straight here,' she roared over the telephone in her authoritative voice. 'The buildings are under the protection of the Red Crescent and Cross and we will be perfectly safe. I will tell you all later.' She also said that it would be dangerous to travel to Ramallah and that in any case hostilities would be over within a few weeks. We were too frightened to refuse, the telephone call had changed our destiny and we were plunged into an unexpected future.

I was secretly pleased that we would now be closer to the Greek Colony house and could return there at short notice. Unfortunately this was not to be.

For my aunt Isquhie the situation was much more complicated. Her house was in Ramallah; she did not believe that the war would be over so soon, and she had misgivings about the possibility of an early return home if she did not go at once. Her fears were realized, as she was to remain on the west side of Jerusalem (divided for nineteen years) in the new state of Israel for the rest of her long life. She had in fact sacrificed her home out of concern for me, but never once did she reproach me for the situation in which she found herself.

The taxi arrived, we told the driver of our change of plan and he agreed to take us the half mile to the Bethlehem Road in the Upper Baqa'a for the ten Palestine pounds which we had already paid. In such desperate circumstances there was no argument, exploitation was widespread and people were prepared to pay large sums just to get away. We packed ourselves into the car, livestock and all, and within a few minutes arrived at the house where we were to spend the period of 'Israel's war of independence' which was already under way.

We were greeted by my great-aunt Arousiag, now aged 75, a short, plump, good-humoured and shrewd woman with very poor eyesight scarcely helped by her thin-rimmed pebble glasses. A life of constant hard work, which had started at an early age in the household of Bishop Blyth, had formed her character. A *mandeel* of very fine muslin

190 ARMENIANS OF JERUSALEM

tightly covered her thinning hair. These headscarves were usually brown or purple imprinted with large roses or with sprigs of white prunus flowers, sometimes edged with *oya* (crochet) of violets, narcissi or other flowers. Under her ground-length skirts peeped strong leather open-heeled slippers. A brassiere was unknown to her, instead she wore a *sidriyyeh*, a tightly buttoned under-bodice to contain her generous figure. She told me that she had once worn a bustle when that was in fashion.

Aunt Arousiag did not suffer fools gladly, but was very tender-hearted and easily given to tears. Even though she knew the answer to a question she would often reply abruptly: '*Barafsh, bi khusnish*' (I do not know, it is not my business). After a stern reprimand she would console me with one of her sayings: 'I may chew you but you must know that I would never swallow you.' My great-aunt was an economical housekeeper and an excellent cook, producing a variety of delicious dishes, jams and preserves, with the aid of a primus and a small *fteeleh* (a paraffin stove).

Aunt Arousiag's hobby was gardening and she was indeed clever at growing plants, at grafting and taking cuttings. One of her great achievements was the grafting of a red shrub rose (which I later identified as Erich Brunner fils) on to a yellow *banksiae* climbing rose. Visitors were fascinated to find the pergola over the front veranda of the house covered by a climber that bore flowers of two different colours. Sprays of large crimson blooms mingled with the tiny yellow clusters of the host, the *banksiae*. This graft has survived almost 100 years, and still puts on a brave show of both types of flowers although weakened by lack of attention and pruning. Aunt Arousiag also grew red hippeastrum species in rows of earth-filled kerosene tins to provide flowers for the Armenian cathedral in June at the Feast of Pentecost. The flame-colour of these lilies and the shape of their petals symbolized the tongues of fire: Acts 2:3 'Then they saw what looked like tongues of fire which spread out and touched each person there'. She was deeply devoted to the Armenian Orthodox Church to which she belonged, read the bible daily, and I would often hear her calling upon the Lord and saints for help: '*Ya rab, mali gherak*' (O Lord, I have no one but Thee).

We unpacked our belongings and the hens joined others already there in the run. It was early May and revisiting the Greek Colony house was out of the question: anyone moving between the suburbs and the city was threatened with sniper fire from all directions. We

THE DISPERSAL   191

were to stay with my great-aunt in the first-floor flat of her brother
Hagop's three-storey house, which she now occupied alone since her
nephews and nieces had left. Next door her brother Soghmon's son,
Krikor, and his sister, Nazouhie, lived in their villa. The basement of
their house was to provide us with shelter during the war.

Both houses were surrounded by a high stone wall and well-kept
gardens which opened on to the main Jerusalem to Bethlehem
highroad. Opposite stood the *gazkhana* (petrol storage depot) and a
small distance away the Jerusalem Electric Corporation – both potential targets in time of war. A few hundred yards to the north on the
other side of the railway level-crossing the German Sisters of St
Charles Borromeo had their church and hospice. These buildings had
come under the protection of the Red Cross and the nuns had
reluctantly sheltered a few Arab families from the neighbourhood.
The enclosed order of the Clairice sisters in their convent a quarter
of a mile to the east off the Hebron road had done likewise. All
monasteries and convents were considered to be safe places of refuge
in time of war and many civilians sought temporary accommodation in
them. Others deposited valuables, Persian carpets and silverware,
before fleeing.

We found that only about 150 people out of a resident community
of thousands had opted to stay on. These included Armenians, Greeks
and a few Arabs. Some of the Arabs were members of St Paul's
'Anglican church in Jerusalem: the Sabas, the Ittayims, and the well-
known dentist Dr Ibrahim George and his sister Emma. They had all
taken temporary refuge in the German Hospice. A few of our
immediate neighbours also decided to stay and protect their property:
the Georgians, an old-established *kaghakatsi* family and the Krikorians
(no relations of ours, Yohannes being the son of the famous Jerusalem
photographer Garabed Krikorian). Next door an old Greek couple the
Polymedes had stayed and further up the road the Merguerians,
another *kaghakatsi* family. Nigoghos Georgian's daughter Marie, who
was married to a Scotsman, John Reid, also stayed with her three
young children. The fact that there was to be a Red Crescent and
Cross Society centre in the vicinity had perhaps encouraged them not
to move.

After the First World War Dr Krikor Krikorian had joined the
public health department and was later appointed senior medical
officer and deputy head under Colonel Heron, a post which he held
until the end of the British Mandate. He was a man of strong

192 ARMENIANS OF JERUSALEM

character, known for his integrity and well respected in the community. On 22 April 1948 the International Committee of the Red Cross proposed the setting up of 'lieux de Genève' in various parts of the city. He had been asked to set up one of these first aid centres to serve the area in which he was living. He agreed to do so and had converted part of the ground floor of his uncle Hagop's house into a Red Crescent and Cross station. The clinic and office were well stocked with medicines, equipment, uniforms, Red Cross brassards and stretchers. A large Red Crescent and Cross flag flew from the roof of the building.

I was to look after the office and type letters when the need arose. Dr Krikorian had also asked Shukri Nammar, one of the drivers in the public health department, to move in with his wife and two young children, Rasim and Ibtisam. They were given two rooms at the back of the ground floor flat. Vartivar, an Armenian from the Convent, had been asked to come in to act as guard and general help. He slept in the basement of the doctor's house next door. We could now see why Nazouhie had felt so confident when she rang up and told us that we would all be safe under the flag of the Red Crescent and Cross.

22 1948 WAR

The Baqa'a where we now lived was out of the firing line and seemed safer than the Greek Colony. We felt protected as British soldiers were nearby, guarding the *gazkhana* and the electric power station. Nazouhie would send me out after supper with a pot of hot coffee and biscuits for the men stationed outside the garden gate. They welcomed this and promised that as long as they were there they would keep an eye on us and the property. Meanwhile, sporadic firing continued, intensifying at night, and we were confined to our houses.

On 13 May British troops withdrew from positions around the Jewish Quarter of the Old City. The Haganah moved in, tension increased and an already dangerous situation was aggravated by continual sniping.

On 14 May General Alan Cunningham, the last British High Commissioner for Palestine, left Jerusalem. His heavily guarded convoy passed our house and we all went out into the Bethlehem road to view his departure. With him he took the carved British royal coat of arms which had hung at Government House: this he deposited at St George's Cathedral before flying from Kalandia airport to Haifa.

So ended 30 years of British rule in Palestine on the target day, 14 May 1948. The soldiers outside the gate left without saying a word. We now felt insecure, there was no authority to turn to for help and we were trapped in the southern suburbs. Shooting and the crash of mortars went on unabated, echoing all over Jerusalem. Rumours spread that small groups of the Haganah were seen on 14 May in the Greek and German Colony area which by then had been almost totally abandoned. It was far too dangerous for us to go out into the road: to get from one house to the other I now had to scale the boundary wall.

That same afternoon Goharig Merguerian, with her young son, old

194 ARMENIANS OF JERUSALEM

mother and another Armenian neighbour, who all lived a few doors away managed at great risk to reach our house. They asked aunt Arousiag if they might stay with us for a few nights in the security of the Red Crescent and Cross centre. They had left their menfolk behind to guard their property, a large two-storey house overlooking the street linking the Bethlehem and Hebron roads. Goharig was an old friend and aunt Arousiag readily agreed to her request, morbidly quoting the Arab saying: *Il maut ma' il nass rahmeh* (Death in the company of others is a mercy).

That night after shutting the wooden shutters we decided to sleep on mattresses on the sitting-room floor. The street outside, once a bustling thoroughfare, was now deserted and silent, which made us all the more frightened. Krikor and Nazouhie stayed in their house and next day told us that they had spent the night in the basement.

We continually followed all news bulletins on the wireless. On 15 May we heard that the new State of Israel had been proclaimed. This naturally was greeted with great celebration and rejoicing by the Jewish population. Nevertheless, throughout the day we could hear very heavy firing and shelling coming from the direction of the Old City which continued well into the night. To bolster our morale we decided to keep the electric lights on in the flat and on the balcony to show that the house was occupied. However in the early evening the lights gradually dimmed and we were finally plunged into darkness. Both the electricity and water supply had been cut off and we had to resort to lamps and candles. Lack of power meant that we could no longer listen to the wireless.

Meanwhile fierce battles raged and heavy shooting continued all night. It sounded to us as though there was fighting on the southern outskirts as well as in the besieged Jewish quarter of the Old City. That night the Haganah occupied the German Hospice, even though it was under the protection of the Red Cross. Soldiers manned the church tower and after searching the hospice took into custody the few remaining Arab men of military age whom they found there. The Red Cross protested and the Haganah left the building within a few days.

On the morning of 16 May Jewish forces took complete control of the Arab suburb of Baqa'a. There was no resistance of any sort; they just walked in, gradually taking over buildings in strategic places. Nearly every house was empty: set tables with plates of unfinished food indicated that the occupants had fled in disarray, haste and fear.

1948 WAR 195

In some kitchens cooking stoves had been left alight, reducing the ingredients of a waiting meal to blackened remains.

Next day I managed to creep up to the third storey flat and cautiously peered through the window-lights in the attic roof. Looking around I could see that the Merguerian house had been occupied and that armed soldiers were on their balcony. That day it seemed to us that the battles had intensified, bombing and firing had dramatically increased. The Haganah were trying to link up with their comrades in the Old City but a heavy attack on the Jaffa Gate at midnight was repulsed. Bullets whistled past the house and shells aimed at the electric power station and *gazkhana* fell all around us. Aunt Arousiag always feared that a direct hit on the loft would cause a fire. Every time there was a big bang she cried, '*Ya Kilkhateer*' (O head of St James, protect us) or '*Ya rab mali gherak*' (O Lord, I have no one but you). Her prayers were answered as apart from a few broken roof tiles and stonework shattered by bullets the house did not suffer major damage.

On 18 May another attempt was made to storm the Old City, this time through Zion Gate. The attack also ended in failure but Bishop Gobat School and the Dormition Abbey were occupied and from then on used as Jewish military posts. From the tower of the Dormition Abbey hundreds of shells poured into the Armenian convent and the quarter surrounding it. Later it was reported that by 20 June nine Armenians had been killed and 90 wounded as a result of the shelling and in exchanges of fire between the defenders of the Jewish Quarter and their Arab assailants. Those who died were hastily buried in alleyways and courtyards of the Armenian compound: Pergeech, their cemetery on Mount Zion, was now in no-man's-land and inaccessible.

West Jerusalem was also in a state of siege, cut off from the coast as the main road through Bab el Wad was under the control of Arab forces. Food, water and fuel for heating were in very short supply and the Jewish inhabitants suffered. We ourselves were unable to replace any of our stores, which from now on we used sparingly. We resorted to tinned food and the hens continued to supply us with a few eggs. We had no shortage of water; from the cistern under the house we pumped our supply up to the tanks in the loft.

The situation in the Old City was equally difficult and supplies were very short. A four-gallon tin of kerosene now cost the exorbitant sum of five Palestine pounds. The municipal water supply, the electric power station, all government offices including the general post office

196 ARMENIANS OF JERUSALEM

had fallen to the Jewish state. All these services had to be started again from scratch in the areas that remained under Arab control.

The Merguerians spent a few days with us and then decided to risk returning home. Goharig went down to the garden gate, where she attracted the attention of a passing Jewish soldier who agreed to escort the ladies back to their house. To their relief they found the menfolk unharmed, but part of the house was to remain a military post for months to come.

Fierce battles continued to rage and Krikor and Nazouhie advised us to spend nights in their basement where we would be all together. Aunt Arousiag refused the offer and stubbornly opted to stay on alone in her room in the flat upstairs. One evening at about 9 p.m., above the roar of firing we heard screams for help from next door. It was aunt Arousiag who was too scared to stay alone any longer. To join us meant climbing the boundary wall, as it was far too dangerous to come round by the garden gates on the street. The wall was about seven feet high and she needed my assistance. I found her downstairs waiting for me and after much heaving and pushing, no easy feat as she was so heavy, I managed to raise her to the top of the wall. From there she was helped down on the other side by Vartivar and Krikor. We were all very angry at her obstinacy, especially Nazouhie who, fearing broken bones, lost her temper and fiercely reprimanded her; but aunt Arousiag kept silent. From then on she spent the daylight hours upstairs in her flat, meekly joining us via the gates at about four in the afternoon. Unwillingly she spent nights with us on mattresses on the floor in the basement.

Between outbursts of shooting a deathly silence prevailed, only to be broken by the barking of dogs and the braying of an abandoned donkey shut in its shed. It was heartrending and we wondered how many more animals had been trapped in the same way, but we could do nothing about it. Cats and dogs that had been left by their owners roamed the streets, painfully emaciated and in a wild state. Many of them came to our basement window searching for food. Night after night they would gather, quarrelling amongst themselves for the scraps that we could spare. Krikor's own dachshund, Vicky, growled resentfully at these starving night visitors.

As our neighbourhood was now under the control of the Jewish forces we had to adapt to a new situation. The Red Crescent and Cross centre had come to a halt as there was no longer any fighting in the area, no freedom of movement and so no patients to treat. We

1948 WAR   197

thought it wise to remove the crescent from the flag in case it provoked hostility. Dr Krikorian's telephone was not cut off and he was still able to contact Dr Jacques de Reynier and the staff of the International Red Cross. At the time it seemed that there would be no interference with the inhabitants who had opted to remain. However after an extensive search of the area by Jewish soldiers, Arab residents who were found in hiding in the Baqa'a were arrested, imprisoned, then sent across the lines to the Old City.

On 19 May Arab Legion soldiers joined Palestinian irregulars in a massive attack on the Jewish Quarter of the Old City. In a desperate attempt to relieve their comrades two Jewish planes flew over and dropped food and other supplies on the quarter. Shelling of West Jerusalem from the Mount of Olives began simultaneously. The Jewish settlements of Mikor Chaim, Talpiot and Ramat Rahel to the south of the city were besieged and changed hands two or three times during fierce fighting.

In the meantime we tried to occupy ourselves as best we could during daylight hours, while continuing to sleep in the basement night after night to the roaring of cannon and rifle fire. What scared us most was the crack of exploding dumdum bullets just outside the basement windows. It was difficult to locate the sound, at times it seemed a few yards away and the next second appeared to come from a distance, giving us the impression that someone was firing at close range from the garden.

On 22 May there was an unexpected and alarming development. At about 6.15 p.m. the Jewish forces rounded up most of the remaining inhabitants of Baqa'a, men, women and children. The very old were left behind. We too were ordered to join the group but Krikor adamantly refused to allow any of us to leave the house, on the grounds that we were under the protection of the Red Cross. He shut us into the clinic and locked the door. After a heated argument the soldiers left us alone. Those arrested were marched away in single file to the Katamon quarter. There they were told that they were to be held hostage until the captured Jewish defenders of Kfar Zion, a settlement on the Hebron road, were released. In the event their names were taken and some hours later to their great relief they were allowed to return home, although considerably shaken. Our Red Cross centre had escaped this episode, which afterwards drew adverse comment from those who underwent that frightening experience.

On Friday 24 May 1948 after a brave fight the occupants of the

198 ARMENIANS OF JERUSALEM

Jewish Quarter of the Old City surrendered to the Jordanian army. Soon after, Abdallah el Tal, who commanded the attack, invited a team of Red Cross and United Nations personnel to supervise arrangements for evacuating the survivors. It was estimated that between 1,000 and 2,000 civilians, as well as 600 armed men had been in the siege since early May. Krikor was visited by a representative of the International Red Cross and asked to participate in the negotiations: his advice and views would be valuable as he was well-known and trusted by both sides in the conflict. He agreed to do so and was picked up at the house and driven away in a jeep identified by a blaze of fluttering United Nations and Red Cross flags. A local truce was agreed upon and the convoy travelled through a stretch of no-man's-land to get to the Old City.

The team met in the Armenian school of The Holy Translators which was used as local headquarters for the Arab Legion forces. There it was agreed that all able-bodied fighters except women, of whom there were many under arms, should be taken as prisoners of war and sent to Amman. Women, children and old men were transferred to the neighbourhoods of west Jerusalem now under Jewish control. There they were accommodated in abandoned Arab houses in the fashionable suburbs of Katamon, the Baqa'a, the German and Greek Colonies. They arrived exhausted and in a state of shock. Although their ordeal was now over it was to be another twenty years before they could return to their homes in the Old City.

Krikor came back safely and told us about his experiences. He brought news of my aunt Malakeh, who with her husband, Sahag, and son, Morris, had moved down to Jericho. He said the Armenian convent was packed with refugees. His brother, Yerevant, and wife, Peggy, as well as Anna, his sister, who left the Baqa'a house to shelter in the convent, had already left for Beirut.

Patriarch Guregh Israelian had allowed between 3,000 and 4,000 Armenians from all over the country to shelter in the convent. Refuge was also given to some Muslim families from the Nebi Daoud area, who for centuries had been on good neighbourly terms with the Armenians. Every room was filled and tents had been erected in many of the courtyards. The arrangement was supposed to be temporary but to the present day many Armenian families who arrived in 1948 are still there, unable to reclaim their property in West Jerusalem.

On 1 June Krikor was informed by the Red Cross that there was to be a truce between the warring parties: the United Nations had sent

1948 WAR

Count Folke Bernadotte to the area with a plan for peace. We were filled with hope but to our ears it sounded as if the bombing and shooting had intensified. Indeed between 4 and 10 June there was heavy cannon fire every night, the house shook constantly and each morning we picked up large pieces of shrapnel in the garden. Our siege had already lasted for almost three weeks and our food supplies were running low.

We had been confined since 15 May, unable to move outside the premises. Jewish soldiers patrolled the streets around us and we saw no one else, not even the neighbours who had remained in their homes further up the road. However, one morning footsteps broke the silence and to our surprise we saw Soeur Marie-François of the Convent of the Clairice. She had been given permission to go to the German Hospice to collect food and medicines for those sheltering in her own convent. Soeur Marie-François was indeed a spectacular sight, wearing her formal habit with a topee over the flaps of her coif to protect her from the hot sun.

On 10 June a truce was announced to take effect the following morning, Friday 11 June. This fragile truce was to last for a month, during which time the combatants were not supposed to reinforce their positions nor to build up their armaments. It was also hoped that negotiations could start and an agreement be reached during the month. However on the night of the 10th all hell was let loose and both sides of the city were pounded with shells and gunfire. It was difficult for us to imagine that the truce would take effect. Our hopes revived, however, when the guns fell silent next morning after 27 days of open warfare.

A few days after the truce came into effect my aunt Isquhie bravely decided to walk over to the Greek Colony house. She wore nurse's uniform with a Red Cross brassard on her arm as protection. Eventually she returned and all she brought back was a lovely bunch of sweet peas from my garden. She told us that she saw no one, apart from a few soldiers who did not question her. She also said that the house had been broken into.

Even though a truce was in force shortages of food, water, fuel and medicines were becoming acute. The road from Tel Aviv to Jerusalem, the lifeline of the city, was still blocked at Bab el Wad. All attempts by Jewish forces to break through with convoys of supplies failed. The population of the new city was experiencing tremendous hardship. Rationing was introduced, a black market flourished and everyone had

200 ARMENIANS OF JERUSALEM

to tighten their belts. The situation was alleviated by the large quantities of food looted from Arab houses. Water from the many cisterns beneath these abandoned houses was pumped up into tankers and taken to the Jewish suburbs for distribution. It was well for us that we were able manage on our own stock of food and water, as we seemed to have been forsaken by the outside world.

The truce held, although from time to time there were isolated skirmishes and sporadic shooting. Our movements were restricted but Jewish residents from the western suburbs and elsewhere were allowed to circulate freely. During this time looting of Arab houses started on a fantastic scale, accompanied by wholesale vindictive destruction of property. First it was the army who broke into the houses, searching for people and for equipment that they could use. Next came those in search of food, after which valuables and personal effects were taken. From our veranda we saw horse-drawn carts as well as pick-up trucks laden with pianos, refrigerators, radios, paintings, ornaments and furniture, some wrapped in valuable Persian carpets. Stores of food and fuel were found in unimagined quantities and removed. In the Wa'ari quarter not far from where we lived a small water cistern had been emptied by the owners and refilled with paraffin: this was soon pumped out and taken. Safes with money and jewellery were prised open and emptied. The loot was transported for private use or for sale in West Jerusalem. To us this was most upsetting. Our friends' houses were being ransacked and we were powerless to intervene. In fact there was a vacuum, there was no law and order and chaos prevailed.

This state of affairs continued for months. Latecomers made do with what remained to be pillaged. They prised off ceramic tiles from bathroom walls and removed all electric switches and wiring, kitchen gadgets, water-pipes and fittings. Nothing escaped: lofts and cellars were broken into, doors and windows hacked down, floor tiles removed in search of hidden treasures. Rooms were littered with piles of rubbish and as winter set in rain poured into these derelict houses. At night the wind howled and the banging of windows and doors echoed through the lifeless buildings, a haunting sound in an already ghostly scene. It was unbearable to pass these houses, so familiar, but now within six months become so strange, with overgrown gardens, front doors and windows smashed or wide open and above all void of their inhabitants. We lived in the middle of a sea of destruction.

However, some things did not change. At daybreak we continued to

1948 WAR   201

enjoy the usual chatter of sparrows, the raucous call of crows and the tender song of bulbuls, all apparently unaffected by the turmoil.

Our only link with humanity was the sound of bells from the German Hospice and the convent of the Clairice sisters announcing Tierce, Nones and other hours of prayer. When the wind was in the north-east we could faintly hear the bells of the Old City, each one distinctive and familiar: the deep sound of the Greek bells of the Holy Sepulchre, the European pealing of the bells at the Latin Convent and the solitary note struck on the bell of the Armenian convent, aptly described by the *kaghakatsi* community as *hanoun* (compassionate). The bells of the Church of the Dormition had been silenced since the tower became a Jewish military post. Our emotions were so easily played on that the sounds reverberated in our minds, giving us a sad sense of isolation. Aunt Arousiag was often moved to tears. However, we were safe, for the looters made no attempt to interfere with houses that were still inhabited – although we watched what was going on around us with trepidation, fearing that our turn would come.

In an attempt to instill order two military governors, Joshua Simon and Colonel Maurice Bassam, were appointed to our area. It was a relief to know that there would now be somebody in authority. They made their headquarters in a building in the Greek Colony, previously the offices of the Arab Higher Committee. Joshua Simon was well known to me, as for many years he had worked for the American Colony in Jerusalem in their souvenir store inside the Jaffa Gate. I had often been sent there by Russell & Company to carry out the audit. Later on when I went to him with a serious problem he was of great help to us.

23　UNEASY CALM

Jerusalem was now divided by a belt of no-man's-land extending from Sheikh Jarrah in the north to Ramat Rahel in the south. The main road to Bethlehem was blocked near the Orthodox monastery of Mar Elias. The imposing French hospice of Notre Dame outside the New Gate, now occupied by Jewish forces, served as a main base for attacks on the Old City. Arab Legion soldiers manned the Citadel at Jaffa Gate and the Old City walls and were able to snipe at anyone moving in the western suburbs. Barbed wire was put up everywhere to prevent the unwary from straying into mined stretches of no-man's-land.

It was in mid-June that we were to be confronted with another vital decision. Krikor, convinced that there was no hope of a change in the situation for a long time to come, proposed that we should all leave for the Arab side of Jerusalem. He felt that he was contributing nothing by staying under an Israeli regime, and that to protect a house, 'stones and mortar' as he put it, was not a sufficient reason for remaining totally cut off from colleagues and relatives. Krikor made it quite clear that we were included in his plans, telling us that arrangements for our transfer to the Arab side could be made through the Red Cross. He thought that I would easily find a job, that aunt Arousiag would join her sister Heghnoug in the family house in the Armenian Quarter, and that Isquhie would return home to Ramallah.

We were habitually in awe of Krikor's authoritarian personality, as indeed were all other members of the family; one word from him was usually enough to exact obedience. News of this plan shattered poor aunt Arousiag who had made up her mind not to leave. She loved the house and gardens where she had spent most of her life and was determined to preserve it. Out of compassion for her age and near-blindness, Isquhie and I also rejected Krikor's plan and decided to stay and support her.

At the time looting was at its wildest and we were certain that, if we all left, both houses would suffer the same fate as those abandoned around us. We explained this to Krikor and Nazouhie and they reluctantly accepted our decision. At the time we were naïvely hopeful that they would soon return but this proved to be wishful thinking: neither Krikor nor Nazouhie, nor any other member of the family, was ever able to return home. When I look back I fail to understand how we had the courage to stay on in such a dangerous and uncertain situation.

Representatives of the Red Cross arranged to collect Krikor and Nazouhie on the morning of 15 June to escort them across the battle lines. Vartivar, the general factotum, was to go along too, and so was Vicky, the dachshund. We were very sad to see them go. They were taken to Government House on the southern outskirts of Jerusalem, by then in the hands of the United Nations, and from there they walked down to Silwan and then on into the Old City. What little luggage they took was carried on donkey-back. Behind them they left a house packed with furniture and belongings, some of which they were storing for their very good friends, Colonel and Mrs Pedretti.

Before leaving, Krikor had made arrangements for the dentist, Dr Ibrahim George, to take over the Red Cross centre. Shukri Nammar, the driver, and his family decided to stay on as they had no other place to go to. Along with everybody else they had lost their house only half a mile away near the former Jerusalem Sports Club of British Mandate days.

Krikor's presence and his contacts with the International Red Cross had given us a sense of security. We were now on our own, responsible for two large buildings comprising four households, each full of personal effects belonging to various members of the family. We soon had doubts as to the wisdom of our decision.

Krikor was able to telephone us just once from the Old City, giving news of their safe arrival, but soon afterwards the telephone was cut off. Subsequently we learned that he worked for a time with the medical services of the Jordanian army and later moved to Beirut. There he was appointed director of the laboratories of the American University of Beirut hospital, a post he retained for the rest of his working life.

We continued to follow our usual routine and spent our nights in

204   ARMENIANS OF JERUSALEM

the basement of Krikor's house. It was a great relief when electricity was reconnected, even though for only a few hours a day. At every opportune moment we listened to news on the wireless, switching from station to station to catch every bulletin. Our food stocks were now getting very low and my aunts were sacrificing their portions at meals to give me the lion's share. They assured me that being young I needed more food than they did but in fact we all had to do without. There was plenty of tea and sugar which we found sustaining, but not much remained in the way of staple foods and we lacked fresh fruit and vegetables. To overcome this I sowed the seeds of tomatoes and runner beans which I had brought back with me from England the previous autumn, and soon we had a bumper crop of fresh vegetables. As the weather cooled we planted lettuce. Both my aunts helped me with the watering, aunt Arousiag at the pump and Isquhie carrying the cans. The hens were still laying but their store of grain was running alarmingly short.

Bad news and uncertainty created tension, but gardening and other ploys distracted us for a while and gave relief. Aunt Arousiag occupied herself in sawing the wood of an old mimosa tree that had blown down: quite a feat for a woman of her age. She proudly told us that her nephews would soon return and would use the logs to fuel the bathroom geysers. Isquhie cooked for us, cleaned the house and always found sewing to do.

One morning while I was working in the garden two armed men dressed in military uniform approached me via the garden gate. I took fright but all was well when I recognized Simon Schurr, chief clerk of Messrs Russell & Company. We chatted over a cup of tea and he told me of the extreme shortages of food, water, fuel and medicines in west Jerusalem. Before leaving he asked if I could sell him some eggs and a couple of chickens and I agreed to do so.

The truce ended on 9 July after a month of relative calm and hostilities resumed. Jewish forces again tried to break into the Old City but without success. The noise was unbearable and for the first time we felt that we were in immediate peril. Shells and bullets were falling around us and we had to stay indoors. Battles raged near the New Gate, Jaffa Gate, and Zion Gate. On our wireless we heard that the shelling had been so heavy that many more of the inhabitants of the Old City had left for Jericho and East Jordan. The war continued all over the country with the fall of many Arab villages and towns, including Lydda and Ramleh, to the Jewish forces. In Jerusalem the

UNEASY CALM

situation did not change: both sides held their positions. The stalemate was intriguing and the intensity of fruitless daily bombing aroused suspicion. Rumours soon spread that perhaps after all there was a secret agreement between the sides and that the noise we heard was only a sideshow for the benefit of the population. The Arab Legion was accused of using ammunition filled with bran and sawdust intended to cause minimum damage to the enemy.

On Saturday 17 July we heard that a second truce had been arranged in Jerusalem and that it was to apply to the rest of the country within 48 hours. From then on an uneasy though welcome calm prevailed, during which time it was hoped that a permanent solution to the dispute could be found. The United Nations mediator, Count Folke Bernadotte, presented a peace plan to both parties. His efforts came to naught: he was assassinated by the Stern Gang on 17 September 1948. This cruel murder shattered all our hopes for peace and it gradually became clear that the present state of 'no war, no peace' would continue for ever.

In early August the military authorities appointed our neighbour, Mr Georgian, to be *mukhtar* of our area. Any requests and complaints could be taken to him and he in turn would discuss them with the governors, Simon and Bassam. Most urgent was the scarcity of food as we had no access to the markets in west Jerusalem and there were no shops around us. With permission, Mr Georgian opened a small store in a garage in the German Hospice where rations could be bought. We were only able to go there in the mornings when the curfew was lifted for two hours. We would often return empty-handed as supplies had either run out or not yet arrived. At the beginning the daily ration consisted of a quarter of a loaf of bread and a little margarine. Once we were told to bring a jar as jam would be issued next day, but this turned out to be just a large spoonful per person. At Christmas each family was allowed to buy half a frozen chicken. Families who were in desperate need of medicines, shoes or clothing, were able with difficulty to obtain permission to make a single trip to the shopping centre in west Jerusalem. However they had to be accompanied by a military escort wherever they went.

In mid-September the Israeli authorities decided to enclose a small area to form a security zone patterned on the cages created by the British towards the end of the mandate. The aim was to keep closer control over the non-Jewish inhabitants of Baqa'a. A barbed-wire fence was erected enclosing an area of about half a square mile. The

206 ARMENIANS OF JERUSALEM

fence, which ran along the Bethlehem road, passed our gate and continued to the German Hospice, giving us access to the shop but restricting us to the width of the pavement. We were now allowed to move freely inside the zone during daylight hours and soldiers were posted around the wire perimeter to protect us from marauders.

The creation of the zone was not good news for the few who lived outside it. They were told that for their own protection they had to move into an abandoned house of their choice within the fenced area. This affected about five families including an Armenian couple, Mary and Vahé Ohannessian, who were made to leave their home and move across the road to be within the perimeter. The order did not apply to Greek citizens, of whom there were quite a number in the Greek colony and elsewhere. They had their own *mukhtar* and a consul to fight for their rights. Arab families had no one to represent them, so they had to obey and unwillingly leave their homes.

Trucks were provided by the authorities but the physical lifting and carrying of furniture and effects was to be done by 'volunteers' from within the zone: the *mukhtar* called upon us to help. Along with others I was sent to the nearby Nammar quarter to move the furniture and belongings of Dar Richa. The head of the family, who had previously owned a large grocery store in Mamillah, was now in military custody. Another family, the Ittayims, who lived in the same area, were also obliged to move. There was no room for their upright piano on the truck so it had to be rolled downhill as far as the German Hospice. These operations were fraught with emotion for those forced out of their own property, and for those obliged to assist.

Other families who had taken asylum in the German Hospice and in the Convent of the Clairice sisters were also pressed to leave and move into abandoned houses within the zone. It was then that I met the Andrés, Joseph and Thérèse and their five daughters, who since May 1948 had sheltered with the Clairice sisters. They were moved into a house near the railway line allocated to them by the military governor. Their own property, which they dearly loved, had fallen into no-man's-land on the way to Bethlehem.

The wire perimeter proved ineffective, as looters often breached the fence and entered to steal what they could. The answer was to have our own guards, with a rota drawn up by the *mukhtar*, Mr Georgian. Two men armed with wooden batons were to go out on patrol duty every evening. Much to my aunts' dismay my turn soon came round. My companion was to be a young Armenian neighbour,

UNEASY CALM

Vramshapouh, a tailor by profession and the brother of Goharig Merguerian. He was generally called Chabuk – meaning 'quick' in Turkish – referring to his nimbleness in tailoring. Luckily, just after we had been to collect our batons and report for duty we were told that the project had been cancelled. Apparently the previous night the guards had used their batons effectively against intruders, but this was considered too provocative. The fence now served only as a psychological barrier and soon fell into disuse.

The second truce seemed to be holding. During the first few weeks of October we were visited by military personnel carrying out a census of all non-Jewish inhabitants. On 12 October we were issued with a temporary identification card by the military governor of Jerusalem with the words in French: 'Ce document est simplement une carte d'identité et n'accord aucun droit de circulation au titulaire.' We were described as residents of the Baqa'a zone, Jerusalem. The cards were signed by Maurice Bassam, were valid until 31 December 1948 and renewable for a further three months. It was then that I realized that to be a British subject was no longer a privilege and I was an alien along with all those others now trapped in the suburbs. British policy towards the new Jewish state was considered hostile. Second to Hebrew, French replaced the English language on official documents, identity cards, passports and street signs.

At the end of October 1948 the rules were somewhat relaxed. We were allowed to go out for longer periods every morning, although restricted to the streets in the immediate neighbourhood. We were not permitted to visit the centre of Jerusalem, but at least the inhabitants of the zone could visit each other more often to exchange news.

For the first time in five months I was able to walk over to the Greek Colony house. On the way a strange feeling overcame me, I was dazed and bewildered to find everything had changed. The house had indeed been 'broken into' as Isquhie had reported earlier. It was in a pathetic state – doors and windows wide open, furniture smashed, family photographs scattered all over the floor, volumes of Bach's organ works left for me by my father thrown out into the garden. The cellar and attic had been broken into even though they contained nothing. The cisterns had been opened and emptied of their water and the house now stood in the street, as the garden wall had been torn down and the stones used in barricades. I wandered through the silent, dusty rooms in a frightened and disorientated state, expecting

208   ARMENIANS OF JERUSALEM

to be pounced upon at any minute. I can only compare that visit to the Greek Colony house with Scarlett O'Hara's return to Tara in *Gone With the Wind*. The Greek Colony was all but deserted. Every uninhabited house had been broken into and ransacked, the rooms piled with rubbish.

In spite of the destruction that confronted me, I still had hope of putting the place in order and returning to live there soon. Just as I was leaving my black cat, Sooty, whom we could not find when we left, suddenly reappeared. She had a wild look about her but nevertheless recognized me, purring loudly and rubbing herself against my legs. The plants on the veranda were long since dead: I salvaged the pots, gathered them up and wheeled them back through the German Colony in a discarded perambulator which I found in the street. Next day I returned to clean the house and secure the doors – the whole operation futile as it only encouraged looters to break in again. Sooty was waiting for me this time, and with a little food I coaxed her into a sack to take her back – again in my only means of transport, the perambulator. We were surprised at the way she settled into her new surroundings, but this happy state soon ended when she strayed into the road and was shot dead, along with many other animals which were becoming a nuisance.

Autumn was upon us and figs were plentiful in abandoned gardens around. I went out and collected baskets-full with which we made fig jam. This we resorted to nightly at suppertime when all else we had was bread and a cup of tea. Whenever I brought the jar of fig jam to the table Isquhie would thankfully say, '*saglikolsun tatli il qutein*' – in Turkish 'never mind – as long as we have fig jam'. The fig trees grew in a small unharvested field of wheat sown the previous autumn. Here was a good chance for me to provide grain for the chickens. I gathered the ears of corn into a small sack and took them home, where my aunts cleverly managed to thresh them by beating the sack vigorously with an iron rod. The contents were then scattered before the chickens chaff and all, for them to extract what they could. In another abandoned garden I came across a large locked wire cage which had been the home of about 25 pairs of pigeons of various breeds, obviously much cherished by their owner. Unfortunately they were all dead, having been without food and water for days and unable to fly free to fend for themselves. Some had died sitting on eggs or young in their nests, a scene which haunts me to this day.

Five months had already passed and we looked for signs of a change

UNEASY CALM
209

in the situation. Our funds were running out, Israeli currency had been introduced and it was against the law to possess foreign money. Life was becoming very difficult and we could not tell what the future would bring. We had stayed on strongly believing that my cousins, the rightful owners of the property we were protecting, would soon return. Our only news of the family came in occasional brief notes on Red Cross forms from my aunt Malakeh in the Old City. From time to time she was able to send us food parcels in the same way.

My aunts were visited by some of our immediate neighbours but seldom went out themselves. In the afternoons we would sit on the back terrace of Krikor's house and have tea surrounded by a vigorous hydrangea that grew in a big wooden packing-case. It always produced masses of pink blooms, sometimes well over a hundred, and had to be protected from the hot sun by a temporary awning of canvas. In various other tubs and pots, colourful geraniums and fuchsias abounded. In the evening we watered the garden and the tubs. Attracted by the damp, toads left their hiding-places at nightfall and hopped about on the terrace, delighting us with an occasional deep croak.

Religious freedom was a sensitive matter for the new Israeli authorities. Towards the end of summer 1948 permission was granted to Christians in the community to go to church on Sundays. The only Protestant church within reach was St Andrew's Church of Scotland, situated above the valley of Hinnom in a front-line position facing the Old City. To get there we were issued with passes, and in order to keep out of sight of snipers were marched to church under armed guard along the now-disused railway line. The route took us past the government printing-press and a large Arab khan and we went into church through the back garden of the Scottish hospice. The Reverend William Clark-Kerr, minister temporarily in charge, had remained to protect the buildings. The hospice attached to the church had been briefly occupied by Jewish forces and in spite of his protests the domestic staff, all Arabs, had been arrested and taken away.

The minister's movements were limited and at first he was only allowed to exercise for a few hours a day in the gardens behind the church. He was acutely aware of the hardships that we were going through and voiced his opinions whenever possible, but to no avail. He particularly objected to our arriving at church on Sundays under armed guard. I was asked to play the organ, which I willingly did for the rest of my stay in west Jerusalem. The congregation, who attended

210 ARMENIANS OF JERUSALEM

faithfully, belonged to various denominations, Anglicans, Lutherans and others, among them American marines, UN observers and YMCA staff. Roman Catholics had access to chapels at the German Hospice and Terra Sancta College. Members of the Greek Orthodox community attended the liturgy at the Church of St Simeon in the Katamon. No such arrangements were made for the only remaining Muslim family, the Nammars, left behind in the Red Cross centre. We all looked forward to going to church on Sundays, as it was our only opportunity to make contact with friends from outside our immediate area.

On 29 November 1948 all Anglicans within the perimeter were invited to the house of Mr and Mrs Iskander Saba, who were leading members of St Paul's Arab Anglican congregation. Their church, even though on the Israeli side of the line, had been closed. The Anglican Bishop in Jerusalem, Weston Henry Stewart, had crossed over from St George's Close to visit us, the remnant of his flock now being stranded in Israeli west Jerusalem. He came through the newly established official crossing point, the Mandelbaum Gate, where diplomats, consular and United Nations officials and religious dignitaries were now able to pass after obtaining permits. The gate took its name from a Mr Mandelbaum who owned property near the narrow strip of no-man's-land between the two sides.

The bishop brought news of friends and relatives. After much discussion of the present and the future, he told us that he did not think that there would be any change and that we should accept the division of Jerusalem as a permanent fact. This was devastating news and filled us with gloom and despondency. Soon after, many of the community lost hope and decided to leave. Through the Red Cross they arranged to rejoin their families, who were now making a new life in Amman or Beirut. So the community was gradually eroded. The bishop, who knew me and my family well, told me that if I decided to move he might be able to find a niche for me at St George's or in one of the mission schools. I was grateful to him for this suggestion and kept it in mind.

In December we were visited by Mr James Sutton, an American Quaker who had known us in Ramallah when he was headmaster of the Friends' School. He was now acting general secretary at the YMCA while Mr and Mrs Alva Miller were on leave in the States. His sympathetic and jovial disposition cheered us up no end and he promised us any help we might need. We were also visited by Father

Patrick Coyle, who resided at the Terra Sancta College in west Jerusalem and was in charge of Latin church property, much of which had suffered war damage. Both he and Mr Sutton had permission to move about freely in west Jerusalem and we were always very glad to see them.

Late in 1948 it was agreed that a few Christians would be granted permits to cross to the Old City for the Christmas services in Bethlehem. However the only people allowed this privilege were foreigners: consular officials, US marines, United Nations personnel and members of religious orders. No local people were allowed to cross.

24 ADAPTING TO REALITY

By the end of 1948 all unoccupied houses in the Arab suburbs had been totally vandalized and nothing was left in the way of worthwhile loot. Winter had set in and to add to our hardship it was unusually cold. Nerves were frayed and, as one observer said, we were living 'as it were in a concentration camp on the edge of a battlefield'.

In January 1949 the United Nations appointed Dr Ralph Bunche to mediate between Israel and the Arab states. Meetings took place on the island of Rhodes and a series of armistice agreements were signed separately between 24 February and 20 July. Egypt was the first Arab country to sign, followed by Lebanon, Jordan and lastly Syria. Iraq, which had taken a prominent part in the 1948 war, did not sign, on the grounds that she had no common frontier with Israel.

Mixed armistice commissions under UN chairmanship were established between Israel and each of the four Arab signatories. These MACs were to supervise the armistice, and deal with problems of prisoner exchange and border adjustments. However this did not mean Arab recognition of the new State of Israel. It was not until March 1979 that the armistice with Egypt was to be converted into a peace agreement. More than 40 years have passed and the other Arab states have yet to make peace with Israel, which they consider a colonialist intrusion created in their midst.

It gradually became clear that Palestine had been permanently divided. The Old City and the part of the country that remained under Arab rule were now referred to as 'the other side' and had become inaccessible to the inhabitants of west Jerusalem and the rest of Israel. We had to satisfy ourselves with a distant view of old Jerusalem, barricaded within its ancient walls, cut off from us by a belt of ruined buildings and a mined and deserted no-man's-land. This

ADAPTING TO REALITY

derelict area gradually became a haven for wild birds and animals and the barbed wire a host for climbing plants. Below the Jaffa Gate a mound of earthenware pots and jars, stocked for sale and left lying there by their owner, remained untouched for over twenty years.

Travel to surrounding Arab countries was impossible, and there was no communication by post or telephone. This unnatural situation was tragically difficult for those with family living on both sides of the line. They had to rely on foreign acquaintances who, often reluctantly, took verbal messages across to the other side.

On 18 January 1949 another census was held and we were issued with official Israeli identity cards, but this did little to change our status as we were still not allowed to move about freely.

On 9 February the weather took a turn for the worse and we had severe snow storms, the temperature fell to well below freezing point and snow lay on the ground for three days. Water pipes burst and all temperate-loving plants such as jasmine, bougainvillaea (known in Arabic as the *majnouneh* – the mad – owing to its rampant red flowers) and citrus trees were cut to the ground. That year it even snowed in the Jordan valley 1200 feet below sea-level, an unusual event which caused much damage to citrus and banana groves as well as to many tropical trees. The cold added to the misery of the thousands of Palestinian refugees who had settled in vast tented camps put up by the UN Relief and Works Agency around Jericho.

One evening during this very cold spell there was a loud knock at the front door of Krikor's house. At first I refused to open up but I was roughly told that the door would be broken down if I did not. In fear I obeyed and was confronted by six villainous bearded armed men in uniform. In broken English they told me they had orders to search our house, and that we had been reported for protecting enemy property and hiding arms. We were well aware that this was a pretext and that they came to loot. My immediate reaction was to argue with them and I lost my temper, was defiant and fiercely rude, which almost caused my arrest. My aunts growing increasingly worried intervened and tried to pacify me saying, 'Let them take anything they want, John.' The men were amazed at the vigour of my outburst but after going through some of the rooms they left empty-handed. Before leaving they told us that they had not finished with us and would return next day.

We were thrown into a state of confusion but after discussion decided that the best thing was to remove valuables, silver and other

214 ARMENIANS OF JERUSALEM

objects and hide them in the garden. We worked late into the night. Early next morning we buried antique copper and brass ornaments, some of which we packed into a Russian samovar. Cutlery and silver, placed in hessian sacks wrapped and sewn up by Isquhie, were concealed in a pergola thickly covered with creepers and evergreen shrubs. There they remained undiscovered for a whole year until it seemed safe to bring them back into the house again. We later learned that other families living inside the zone were also constantly visited, usually after dark, by gangs who accused them of sheltering Arabs. This was only an excuse to enter and extort what they could – money, jewellery and valuables.

After this incident we were unmolested for a few days, but early one afternoon aunt Arousiag appeared at the window of her upstairs flat and frantically called out for help. I dashed up to find another band of armed men confronting her in the house. They told me that they belonged to *Lehi* (an underground group of fanatical Jewish terrorists, part of the Stern gang) and that they had orders to search the house. We had already heard of this group and of their brutal activities, which made us all the more scared. They cross-examined me closely, demanding to know who had lived in the flats. For fear of inflaming them further I thought it wiser to conceal the fact that the top floor had been occupied by a Muslim family. I tried my best to explain away the two pianos and large amount of furniture in the two other flats, but matters were complicated by my cousin Vahan's large sealed wooden crates, a dozen of which were stored in one room ready to be transported to Armenia, where he planned to settle. They suspected that the boxes contained weapons, and after much argument insisted on breaking into some of them. Others were not touched when they had satisfied themselves that we were telling the truth.

The unoccupied top-floor flat did not escape attention and the men ordered us to hand over the keys of the front door. After completing their search they came down and told us that they would return next day to take possession of all the contents. They warned us not to go in or to remove anything. In the flat aunt Arousiag had left a sack of Nablus soap under one of the beds. As she had a spare key she insisted that I fetch it for her, trusting it would not be missed.

Next day at about four in the afternoon a truck stopped outside the front gates. Five armed men made their way to the top floor. We remained indoors and watched as they threw mattresses, cushions, bedding and other unbreakable items through the windows down to

ADAPTING TO REALITY

215

the garden below. Furniture they carried by the staircase. The last man to leave took the *oude* which he had found on top of a cupboard. The looters threw the keys back at us contemptuously and showed no regret for their actions. As soon as they were out of sight we went upstairs to tidy what was left in the ransacked flat, much shaken by this threatening experience and dreading what would happen next.

I sought for ways to grapple with this continuing menace and the *mukhtar*, George Georgian, advised me to go and see Joshua Simon, the military governor. I went to his office and told him that we were constantly marauded by armed gangs. He was sympathetic and gave me notices in Hebrew, signed and stamped, to the effect that we and the property were from now on under the protection of the military governor. I pinned the documents forbidding unauthorized entry on the front doors of each house and from then on we were no longer visited by gangs.

When Mr Sutton of the YMCA next visited us we told him about our nightmarish experiences. Eager to be of help, he offered to house Aram's Sweighoffer grand piano and arranged for it to be taken to the YMCA on a truck under cover of darkness. The piano was to remain there in room 110 where it was used for social events and prayer meetings. Twenty years later I was asked to confirm that Aram owned the piano, and payment was made to him in Beirut.

In June 1949 Mr Albert Cohen was sent to take charge of the petrol depot opposite our house. We came to enjoy his friendship and he often joined us on the veranda in the afternoons. Aunt Arousiag he found engaging and referred to her as 'ya Mama', chatting to her in Arabic, which he spoke well. Mr Cohen offered to post our letters, and to do small errands for us in town.

The situation was gradually returning to normal but food supplies were short and our movements were still restricted, although we were no longer under curfew. Word spread that in the Arab village of Beit Safafa three miles south of Jerusalem it was possible to buy meat, eggs and vegetables. When fighting ceased the whole village had remained under the control of Arab Legion forces. However, when making frontier adjustments the mixed armistice commission had ruled that Beit Safafa should be divided down the middle by a barbed-wire fence. The Arabs were to relinquish half of their village to enable the Israelies to reopen the railway line from Jerusalem to the coast. There was stiff resistance from the angry Beit Safafa inhabitants but the

216 ARMENIANS OF JERUSALEM

decision was implemented by force early in May 1949: the northern half of the town came under Israeli rule, the southern under Jordanian.

Beit Safafa was half an hour's walk from the Baqa'a through uncultivated open fields. The wire fence dividing the village had been breached in a secluded place and a meeting point had been established. The scene was full of emotion as friends and relatives were briefly reunited. At this point food supplies were brought in from the Arab side and sold at high prices. To visit Beit Safafa was fraught with danger, for there was always the possibility of encountering mines in the fields or arrest if discovered in a forbidden area. However people disregarded the risk and set out under cover of darkness, returning laden with provisions by mid-morning. Only once did I join a group on a visit to Beit Safafa. Luckily we were not observed and I returned home safely with provisions from what seemed a daring adventure.

Soon afterwards Isquhie decided that she too would join friends who were planning to go to Beit Safafa to buy food. The expedition was a disaster, for the party were spotted by a military patrol, arrested, herded into open trucks and driven to police headquarters at the Moscobiyyeh (Russian Compound) in Jerusalem. After much questioning their supplies were confiscated, but they were allowed to return home with the warning that they should not attempt to go to Beit Safafa again. Isquhie came back in the early afternoon flushed, shattered and empty-handed, refusing to talk about her experience. Later she admitted that her purchases had included a leg of lamb. From then on we were deprived of our only contact with the Arab side, as the authorities tightened their control over the area and sealed the border.

In September 1949 the inmates of the zone were affected by a catastrophe. The André family had obtained permission from the military governor to visit their house, close to no-man's-land in the vicinity of the Greek convent of Mar Elias. Joseph André and three of his young daughters set off one morning to walk the few miles through open fields. Unfortunately one of them triggered off a landmine and they were all blown up. The explosion was so loud that we heard it as far away as Baqa'a. Two of the girls, Lise and Fabbi, died as a result, but Denise and their father survived. This incident cast a cloud of gloom and sorrow over us; a close-knit family had been stricken with life-long grief.

Our quest for food had to continue and we lost no opportunity to

ADAPTING TO REALITY

search for it ourselves. After a very cold winter, especially one with snow, the olive crop is usually abundant. In a large grove owned by the Greek Orthodox patriarchate situated between the railway station and the YMCA in full view of the Old City walls, we found trees heavily laden with olives which, unpicked, had turned from green to dark purple. The owners were unable to come from the Old City to harvest them. In spite of the danger from snipers, I went to the grove with some of our neighbours and brought back baskets full of olives. I myself rarely ate olives, but they were aunt Arousiag's favourite accompaniment to a meal. Our illicit outings came to a sudden end one afternoon when a volley of shots rang out aimed at us from the Old City walls. We hid for a while then hurried home thankful that no one was hurt.

From November 1949 restrictions on our movements were lifted and we were permitted to go into town and to move about the country. The Baqa'a zone was abolished, the wire fence dismantled, and so ended a year and a half of confinement within the perimeter. The term 'Israeli Arab' was now commonly used for those who had stayed in the country, but their freedom of movement was restricted and visits to Arab countries technically at war with the new state of Israel were prohibited. This situation still continues, with one exception: travel is possible to Egypt since the conclusion of the peace treaty signed on 26 March 1979.

My priority was to contact Mr Schurr at Russell & Company and find out whether I could get my job back. I walked over to the office in Sansur Building, Ben Yehuda Street, where I was warmly welcomed by the staff. This was my first visit to the centre of town since long before May 1948, and it was a strange experience after such a long period within the confines of the Baqa'a. There was no immediate vacancy for me but I was asked if I would go and tidy up the long-abandoned temporary office in the house of Mr Scott-Smith in the Greek Colony. I agreed to do this and went to work there for a few mornings a week, sorting out piles of documents thrown out of their cabinets, lying among heaps of rubbish. It took me many days working on my own in a ransacked building in bitter cold, in rooms which had been used as latrines. The silence in the neighbourhood was broken only by the familiar cawing of black hooded crows in the trees around: that at least had not changed. I was once disturbed by a group of would-be looters who asked me what I was doing. Luckily files and papers were of no interest to them and I was left alone. It was not

218   ARMENIANS OF JERUSALEM

until February 1950 that I started work again in the offices of Russell & Company. I was now the only non-Jew on the staff; the office closed for the Sabbath and we worked on Sundays.

Isquhie continued to be busy with housework and sewing. She used spare linen curtain material to make herself a dress. To earn money she took in sewing, mostly repairs and alterations. Aunt Arousiag had cash of her own. With a sparkle in her eye she claimed that it was safe from thieves and if the devil himself came he would be unable to find where she hid it. I gardened and did odd jobs for Mrs Shukri Deeb, an Arab Orthodox lady living close by. In return she gave me tinned food and a suit that had belonged to one of her sons. Isquhie earned very little from sewing, and decided that she would apply for a job at the Jerusalem YMCA, which would give us a regular income. She was accepted and put in charge of the hostel linen room, a post which she held until the late 1960s when she was obliged to retire on grounds of age.

While we had been kept within the perimeter I had put in hours of daily piano practice. I longed to have a teacher again and was now told of one in the German colony – Frau Imberger, a Templist who had decided to stay on with her family after their release from internment by the British during the Second World War. Frau Imberger was a large woman who wore daunting pince-nez, but I soon took to her. She lived in a flat over a wool shop once run by the Eppingers and long since closed. As children, when visiting the shop with my mother, we were always fascinated by a bell which rang out loudly over our heads as soon as we opened the door. The interior of the shop, well-stocked with wool, exuded an overpowering smell of moth-balls. Frau Eppinger, an elderly lady, was always referred to by the Arab inhabitants of Jerusalem as the *poursianiyyeh* (the Prussian woman).

I enjoyed working with Frau Imberger, who told me she perceived that my playing was influenced by my love for flowers. However this delightful interlude came to an abrupt end when one day I arrived and found to my horror that the door of her house had been sealed and she was no longer there. It seemed that all remaining Templists had been ordered out of the country and offered a home in Australia. The ending of our musical rapport was a blow to me.

As the armistice agreements of 1949 were holding, it was now safe for Jewish families to move into the Baqa'a and other Arab suburbs. After the signing of the Rhodes agreements, clashes between the two armies facing each other in Jerusalem were few, but from time to time

ADAPTING TO REALITY 219

we heard gunfire and the occasional explosion. Many buildings close to the armistice lines now became accessible to looters. A prime example of this was the ophthalmic hospital of the Order of St John of Jerusalem, standing on the Hebron road just above the valley of Hinnom within sight of the Old City walls. The medical staff and patients had been evacuated to the Old City early in the war. After the armistice the buildings were looted and from St Andrew's Church we saw piles of furniture and equipment from the wards and clinics out under the olive trees, waiting to be collected. It was sad to see a hospital which had contributed so much good to the people of Jerusalem since its establishment in 1882 come to such an end. Part of the hospital had been occupied by the Israeli army throughout the fighting. They had installed a cable from there across the valley to Bishop Gobat School. This served as a conveyor-belt for arms and equipment to their outpost on Mount Zion.

All abandoned houses in the Baqa'a, Katamon, Greek and German Colonies were gradually taken over by new Jewish immigrants, mostly from north Africa. These houses were in a bad state of repair as a result of looting and deliberate damage and had to be patched up. Elegant flats and villas were divided to accommodate two or three large families, even though they were originally built for one. Verandas were enclosed with breeze-blocks and concrete to provide extra rooms. The result was architecturally disastrous. The orderly, well-kept and fashionable suburbs were transformed into a ghetto of slums where beautifully planned gardens reverted to a wilderness of weeds and rubbish. These neighbourhoods became unrecognizable to those who had known them in days past. Our Greek Colony house did not escape. It was shabbily divided into two flats and the verandas where we had spent so many lovely summer afternoons were built up. For reasons unknown to me the pine and pepper trees were chopped down and the garden was totally neglected. The house was now named Villa Shanghai. I found myself frequently going to the Greek Colony just to gaze and evoke fond memories. I kept my thoughts to myself, remained unobserved and never made contact with the occupants, whom I secretly resented. I still considered the house to be mine and hoped to go back there one day.

To me the saddest part was the lack of familiar faces. I would wander through neighbourhoods that I had known so intimately but which were now so strange: strange people enjoying themselves on the verandas of friends' houses where I had been a frequent visitor. It was

220   ARMENIANS OF JERUSALEM

as if I had been in the underworld for a long time, had come back and was desperately trying to recapture a past that had been good and lovely. I strongly felt that injustice had been meted out to a community of innocent people, and I was aware of their suffering, which I found impossible to ignore. Why I inflicted such pain on myself I do not know, but pain it was.

Bus services to the suburbs were now running, routes No 4 and No 6 were retained but taken over by the Israeli transport service, Egged. Kiosks and shops opened up, even though food and other commodities were still in short supply. I now had a working postal address and was able to write to my parents in Birmingham after a silence of about eighteen months. My father wrote back to say that all was well with them and they were settled in their new house in Coal Valley Road, but they had been worried about us. My cousin Vahan also wrote from Cyprus to enquire about his aunt Arousiag.

By the summer of 1950 all Arab houses in our area had been occupied by Jewish immigrants. With so many empty rooms on our hands it seemed more than likely that we would soon be forced to take people in. The top flat was empty and aunt Arousiag rattled about alone on the middle floor. The Nammars had already taken possession of the whole of the ground-floor flat and remain there to this day. We, aunt Isquhie and I, continued to live in Krikor's house.

That summer aunt Arousiag was visited by a priest from the Armenian Convent in the Old City, who had crossed through the Mandelbaum Gate. As there was no Armenian church in west Jerusalem he was looking for a room to convert into a chapel. He asked her if she would consider offering her large sitting-room for this purpose and she readily agreed as she felt it would protect the house. An altar was set up and after a dedication ceremony services were held once a month for the few Armenians living in west Jerusalem. This arrangement was to last until early in 1951, when the Armenians were given the use of the Templist church in the German Colony together with its out-buildings. They named it Surp Krikor (Saint Gregory) and services are conducted there to this day.

Other problems faced the Christian community in west Jerusalem. One was the inaccessibility of their cemeteries on Mount Zion, now in no-man's-land. With the passing of time many old people died. Permission was given for Greek Orthodox, Armenians, Anglicans and other denominations to be buried in a cemetery belonging to the American Christian Missionary Alliance in the German Colony.

ADAPTING TO REALITY

Members of the Roman Catholic community were buried in the grounds of the Ratisbonne monastery in west Jerusalem.

The presence of the chapel did protect the house for a short time but the empty rooms on our hands were a constant worry. This was eased when Vahan wrote from Cyprus to say that a good friend of his, Mr Hikmeh of Barclays Bank, was willing to give us help and advice. He did so, and arranged for a Polish immigrant family to move into the flat with aunt Arousiag. She was to retain two large rooms only, with use of the toilet but no access to the kitchen.

We got on well with our new neighbours and their little son, Ulig. His mother, Bianca, worked in the house all day on a noisy machine repairing nylon stockings – a trade now obsolete. Later the top-floor flat was let to an elderly English missionary, Miss Bernstein, who came out to propagate the gospel among the Jews. To many the creation of the State of Israel was the fulfilment of Old Testament prophecies. Missionaries of different sects flocked to Jerusalem and several other cities hoping to witness the millennium, which they thought was round the corner. Aunt Arousiag did not care for Miss Bernstein but Isquhie got on well with her, repaired her clothes when necessary and sold her fresh eggs from our hens. After she returned to England Miss Bernstein frequently sent food parcels to Isquhie.

We had no trouble with the authorities over Krikor's house as he had not been absent on 15 May 1948. In the summer of 1950 he authorized Mrs Dora Pedretti, a life-long friend, to take possession of the house and contents and to look after it for him. Isquhie and I continued to live there for a while but it was obvious that we had to move out. By that time there were no empty houses left in the neighbourhood and we realized that perhaps after all we had made a big mistake – we should have moved, as others had done earlier, into an abandoned house of our own choosing.

In 1952 the problem was solved when Miss Bernstein returned to England for good. It was agreed that Isquhie could take over the top flat on payment of key money. She would otherwise have been homeless, as she had long since lost her house in Ramallah. She lived in the flat until her death in 1989, although legal attempts were made to remove her. This was the gratitude we received for protecting our relatives' property.

Aunt Arousiag thought that the renting arrangement made by Mr Hikmeh would be temporary, and in optimistic mood said, 'We will ask the tenants to leave once the family come back.' She felt that she

222 ARMENIANS OF JERUSALEM

had saved the house from falling into the hands of squatters. The rents she received, although small, were of great help to her, but she was soon to be confronted with legal problems.

After the end of the British Mandate new laws with regard to property were passed by the Israeli authorities. All persons residing in an Arab country at the time of the creation of the State of Israel on 15 May 1948 were automatically considered absentees. Bank accounts were frozen and all other assets, including houses and lands, were confiscated and put under the control of the Custodian of Enemy Property. Forty-two years later the situation regarding property has not changed. During this time lands and houses have been sold over the heads of the rightful owners, without any payment of compensation. Title deeds no longer gave right of possession; yet they were carefully preserved by their owners. Arab refugees who have lived in camps since 1948 still tragically show foreign visitors the keys to their front doors as well as the title deeds to their homes. The only people to whom this law did not apply were the small number of Palestinians living in America, Europe or non-Arab countries on 15 May 1948. The majority of displaced residents of Palestine were affected, as they had taken refuge in neighbouring Arab countries. In no way was it possible for these unfortunate people to claim their rights, the law was so inflexible and tightly framed.

This law finally caught up with aunt Arousiag and she was informed by the Custodian of Enemy Property that she had no rights in the house. She was to be treated as a tenant, and a demand for rent was sent to her for the two rooms which she occupied; furthermore, rents collected by her were to be handed over to the Custodian. The owner had been her late brother, Hagop, and her two nephews and two nieces were recognized as joint heirs to the property. Two of them were considered absentees, the other two not. This news caused much worry to us, and we sympathized with aunt Arousiag who in vain kept on explaining that the house was really hers. She had lived there since it was built by her brother at the turn of the century, and had ploughed most of her earnings into the building. Unfortunately her pleas fell on deaf ears.

Soon after, aunt Arousiag was served with a summons to attend a court hearing of her case. We needed a lawyer and decided to appoint our Armenian neighbour, John Merguerian. As with most court cases in Jerusalem there was considerable delay until the hearing. I of course had to accompany her to the courts in the Russian Compound,

ADAPTING TO REALITY

a new experience for me which I did not relish. On arrival we were ushered into a waiting-room on the second floor of the building, where we sat for hours before we were called in, only to be told that the proceedings had been adjourned indefinitely – which in a way was a relief.

Aunt Arousiag, who was nearing 80 and who always refused the help of a proffered arm, was naturally exhausted by the affair. On leaving the building she tripped and rolled down a flight of some 30 steps to the garden below. One minute she was beside me, and the next had vanished. I looked down and saw her in a heap at the bottom of the stairs. I followed, expecting the worst, but true to her resilient nature she suffered only shock and a few bruises. Later that summer Vahan and his wife, Sirarpie, came over from Cyprus to try and deal with the problems of the house, and to arrange transport of their personal effects stored in the crates which had caused us so much trouble with the looters.

25 A PERIOD OF CHANGE

Jinneh balla nas ma tindas (a paradise without people is not worth stepping into) says the Arabic proverb. This was the unhappy situation that I found myself trapped in. Whereas in days past I used to walk about and chance on people I knew, I now encountered a sea of unfamiliar faces, a reminder of my visit to Birmingham in 1947. The population of the suburbs we grew up in were no more there. A touching poem by Krikor Naregatsi (AD 951–1002) from his *Book of Lamentations* well describes the scene:

> I am the city which has neither towers nor gates
> I am the house which has no hearth in the winter
> I am the bitter spring useless for the parched
> I am a garden left dry and uncared
> I am a meadow choked with weeds
> I am the wheatfield which God intended for his own
> But whose earth has been turned upside down.

Even though life in west Jerusalem might have appeared normal, it was not so for us. We were cut off from what was now called 'East Jerusalem' with which there were no telephone or postal links, so near yet so far. Use of the single crossing point between the two halves of the city – the Mandelbaum gate – was restricted to the UN and foreign officials with permits. There was only one concession for Arab and other Christians, they were given permission to cross to east Jerusalem briefly to join relatives for Christmas. Easter visits were not allowed. Forms had to be filled in weeks ahead and submitted to the District Commissioner, Mr Raphael Levy, in the Gencrale Building, Jaffa Road. A stay for 24 hours was allowed, but when Christmas Day

A PERIOD OF CHANGE

fell on Friday or the Sabbath and the crossing point was closed, extra nights were permitted. Orthodox Christians and Armenians crossed on their respective Christmases, 6 and 18 January. Permits were only given out on the morning of departure, which kept everyone in a state of suspense, and many applicants would find that for unknown reasons they had been turned down. Those with permits were allowed to purchase £1 sterling at a bank, a ridiculous amount which put a heavy burden on the hospitality of friends and relatives in the Old City. The Israeli lira was valueless and illegal on the Arab side of Jerusalem and in the Arab world.

Muslim Arabs were treated differently. They were prevented from crossing into the Old City and were not allowed to go on the *hajj*, the annual pilgrimage to Mecca. However, an arrangement could be made through the International Red Cross for divided families to meet on opposite sides of the armistice lines. There they stood at a distance from each other separated by no-man's-land and barbed wire, speaking through a megaphone. This sad state of affairs lasted for twenty years.

Radio programmes entitled 'Messages to Families' broadcast nightly from both sides of the line were another form of communication. Letters on Red Cross forms were permitted, but were limited to a few words, and the reply, equally short, had to be written on the reverse side.

Working on Sundays, which I was now expected to do at Russell & Company, went against the grain. I was obliged to ask for time off to go to St Andrew's Church of Scotland where I played the organ for the morning service. I needed a change and applied for a job at the Jerusalem YMCA where I was offered work as a night telephone operator. I accepted, although at a reduced salary, and joined the staff in May 1950, there to spend four happy years.

At the time the General Secretary was Mr Alva Miller, who had been in charge for many years, accompanied by his gracious wife, Mildred. During the 1948 war the building came under the protection of the International Red Cross and most of the staff had been trapped there when the fighting began. As it was an American institution directed by the international committee of YMCAs in New York, the Israeli authorities did not interfere but kept a watchful eye on what went on. The majority of the staff were Arab, both Christian and Muslim, with one or two Jews. As soon as conditions allowed, young

226 ARMENIANS OF JERUSALEM

men from Beit Safafa were taken on to work as janitors, also in the soda fountain, dining-room and physical-training department.

My work at the switchboard did not require much skill, but I found it enjoyable as it put me in daily contact with people. The YMCA was a centre of culture and provided a stimulating environment. I worked in a small office next to the reception desk, and was given a room in the hostel on condition that I could be called when necessary by the night watchman, the Hajj whose forebears came from Babylon.

In the summer of that year Mr Miller retired and Mr J. Leslie Putnam was appointed General Secretary. Some months later Mr Herbert L. Minard came out as Programme Secretary to direct cultural actitivities. Their wives, Rena Putnam and Marcella Minard, added much to the congenial atmosphere of the YMCA, to which they were devoted. They were of great help to stranded families confronted with problems in the aftermath of the war. Both couples were a pleasure to work with. It seemed as if we were living and working together on a large ship with everything provided, but a ship sailing through turbulent waters to an uncertain future.

My capabilities and interests were soon discovered. I was moved to reception and within a few months appointed head of the main office, where I was responsible for a staff of four receptionists, hostel bookings and all that went on at the front desk. When needed I moved to other departments, including the accounts office, which I ran when the accountant went on annual leave. After a few lessons I played the carillon in the tower for half an hour each Sunday evening, then rushed down to the lobby for vespers, where I accompanied hymns on the fine Ibach baby grand piano. At Christmas I played the organ in the auditorium for a joint carol service attended by the various Protestant groups in west Jerusalem.

The YMCA was the centre of a musical world, its auditorium put to full use with weekly orchestral concerts and piano recitals. Many of the musicians stayed in the hostel, where I had the privilege of meeting them – among others the pianist Pnina Salzman, whose playing and repertoire I much admired, and the conductor Georges Singer, who became a friend. Some of the young musicians who were making their debuts needed special attention before playing – a bowlful of hot water to make fingers supple, or gentle conversation to reduce tension. It was a relief that shared interests in music and the arts could override political divisions.

I was eager to start piano lessons again and was taken on by Mr

A PERIOD OF CHANGE

Yohanan Boehm, who later became music critic of the *Jerusalem Post*. He then recommended me to Mrs Sonia Valine, a renowned Russian-born teacher and a great musician, who was to have a deep and lasting influence on me. I loved working with her and willingly absorbed all the knowledge she imparted.

My interest in flowers was put to good use and I was given responsibility for decorating the lobbies for special occasions. On United Nations Day in November when a large reception was held, I provided pots of exhibition-bloom chrysanthemums from my garden at Krikor's house in the Baqa'a. For events in the auditorium I also created large-scale flower arrangements.

Transient visitors came from all over the world, among them a group of American Indians with colourful names – Mr and Mrs Old Coyote and Mr and Mrs Swallowtail. In permanent residence were French UN observers, US marines, and a group of British engineers from Vickers in Barrow-in-Furness who had come to help build a cement factory. A group of Arab students from Nazareth who were studying at the Hebrew University were also given lodgings during term-time. Meanwhile, membership of the YMCA had changed: before the 1948 war 90 per cent were Palestinian Arabs, but the tables had turned and by 1950 90 per cent of the members were Jews.

At Christmas the hostel would be full of Christian Arabs from Nazareth and towns in the north, hoping to collect their crossing permits to the Old City. As Nazareth and other Arab towns in Israel were under military rule, they also required permits to enable them to travel even to Jerusalem. This situation was to last until 1966, when restrictions on their movements within the country were lifted.

I did not apply for permission to cross to the Old City until Christmas 1951 and it was a new and strange experience for me. Hundreds of people were waiting anxiously on the Jordanian side; many asked us if we had seen their relatives queueing to cross over. Taxis and porters offered their services while vendors of fruit, cakes and drinks lined the way in an atmosphere fraught with emotion. It was indeed a different world.

I headed for the Armenian Quarter, where I was to stay with my aunt Malakeh. That evening I was invited to a cocktail party at the British consulate and there I met my old school friend Issam Nashashibi, whom I had not seen for years. Time passed all too quickly and after visiting a few friends and buying provisions that were in short supply in Israel, aunt Malakeh saw me off. I knew too well

228 ARMENIANS OF JERUSALEM

that although we were living in one city I would not see her again until next Christmas.

In September 1950 I received news of my father's untimely death at the age of 53. He had been ill for some time and had to undergo an operation at the Queen Elizabeth Hospital in Birmingham. I immediately asked for a month's leave to go and visit my mother and make arrangements for her future. I found her devastated, to the point that it seemed that her life had ended with my father's death. She half expected me to come and settle in England but I adamantly refused. My sister Gertie, commissioned in the Waafs, was stationed in Germany and engaged to be married. We decided that it was best to sell the house in Coal Valley Road and my mother would then return to Jerusalem and join us in the Baqa'a.

My mother settled her affairs in Birmingham but had to wait endlessly for permission to return to Jerusalem. With difficulty she was granted a temporary visitor's visa to re-enter the land where she was born, where her forebears had lived for centuries and where her two sisters were living – albeit one on each side of the armistice lines. She came back in the spring of 1952 and aunt Arousiag agreed to rent us one of the two rooms that she was allowed to retain for herself in the middle flat.

In July 1952 I took leave and spent a month in Cyprus with my cousin Vahan and his family. Through the Lebanese consul, who was his friend, I obtained a visa to travel to Beirut to visit Krikor and Nazouhie. I changed passports and flew from Nicosia to Beirut and went straight to Krikor's house in rue Bliss, where I was warmly welcomed.

After a few days Krikor and Nazouhie drove me to the Sabtiyyeh just above Beirut, to show me plots of land where they intended to build new homes for themselves. By now I realized that they had indeed given up all hope of a return to the Baqa'a, a feeling generally shared by those who had moved to Beirut from Palestine. The land was planted with umbrella pines and had a wonderful view of Beirut and the sea far below. 'There is no better view than this in all the world, John,' Krikor said; but Nazouhie thought otherwise and with tears in her eyes told me, 'We will give up these plans today if only we can go back to our home in Jerusalem.'

I thoroughly enjoyed my stay in Beirut, '*kütchük* Paris' (little Paris) as it was known. I went to visit the medical school where my mother and aunt Malakeh had studied, wandered about in the *suqs* and spent

A PERIOD OF CHANGE 229

hours admiring the flower market around Bab Idris. To me the atmosphere evoked memories of Jerusalem in past days, as most of the Palestinian Arab families I knew and grew up with were now living there, and for me it was indeed like old times. After ten happy days I flew back to Cyprus, changed passports again, spent another two nights in Nicosia and left for Lod airport In Israel.

The staff at the YMCA, many of whom like me were in their early twenties, were congenial to work with. A family atmosphere prevailed, including quarrels and friendly backbiting. During our time off we regularly met over coffee in the soda fountain, took meals in the dining room and played canasta, a new card game introduced by Herbert and Marcella Minard. Day trips to the coast and other sites around the country were organized, many to Tiberias where the YMCA owned a rest house, 'Peniel by Galilee' (Gen. 32:30). With Armenian colleagues we went for weekends to Jaffa. I had not been there since the 1948 war and was horrified to see such change – the *bayyarat* (orange groves) so neglected. A sea of green had been converted into a desert of dead trees, dried up after their Arab owners had fled, mostly by boat to Beirut. In any case all the water pumps serving these groves had already been stolen. In Jaffa we were the guests of the priest in charge, Hair Papken, at the ancient Armenian Convent of Saint Nicholas on the sea front. We dined in a room once used as a bedroom by Napoleon Bonaparte when he landed in Jaffa in 1798.

After a short holiday in Peniel in the summer of 1953, I returned to Jerusalem to find that aunt Arousiag had had a stroke which left her bedridden. A doctor was called but could not do much, and we arranged for a German sister from the clinic of the Hospice of St Charles to visit her daily. My mother and Isquhie had the difficult task of looking after her, and it was obvious that long-term arrangements had to be made. Poor aunt Arousiag, she was sorry for herself and it was pitiful to see a strong and independent person smitten down. All my attempts to cheer her up were in vain.

After a few weeks her nephew Vahan came to see the situation for himself and arranged that I was to fly with aunt Arousiag to Cyprus. In the meantime he disposed of what family belongings were left and put the house in the hands of a lawyer. It was subsequently sold for £4,000 sterling, half of which went to the Custodian of Enemy Property as two of the four heirs were living in the Arab world in May 1948. In fact the house went for next to nothing and from now on aunt Isquhie had to pay her rent to a lawyer.

230 ARMENIANS OF JERUSALEM

No one can imagine how difficult it was for aunt Arousiag to leave Jerusalem and her home, but she was very brave. On the day of her departure she was carried downstairs in a wicker chair and we were driven off to the airport where we were given facilities for an invalid. At Nicosia airport we were met by an ambulance and driven to Vahan's house, where we were greeted by his wife Sirarpie and his two small sons, Krikor and Ara. I did not stay with them as I had arranged to go to friends in Kyrenia. Aunt Arousiag lived for a few more months and died at the age of 82.

Towards the end of 1953 I grew restless and decided that perhaps it was time for me to move on. I felt that there would be no change in the political situation, Jerusalem was divided and there was no future for me at the YMCA. Besides, like Krikor, I wanted to work among the people I grew up with. I consulted Bishop Stewart when he came over to our side of Jerusalem and he offered me the post of secretary-accountant at the Bishop's School in Amman. I readily agreed, and the bishop promised to arrange for the necessary permits to enable me to leave Israel and take up residence in Jordan. I was expected to be there for the start of the new term in September.

The decision to move had put me in a quandary. It meant leaving my mother and aunt Isquhie behind and the interesting life of which I was part at the YMCA. Strangely enough, neither my mother nor my aunt stood in my way, as they thought a move would be better for my future. They reassured me that it would be good for them too, as they could perhaps follow later when I was settled.

I gave in my notice but then there was a seemingly insurmountable hitch. The Jordanian authorities at first refused to give me permission to cross from Israel to take up work in Amman. I was devastated at the delay, but was allowed to continue working at the YMCA until my papers came through. Thanks to the influence of one of the Bishop's School teachers, Mr Jiryes Halassa, a senator in the Jordanian parliament, my application was finally accepted. In February 1954 I had a message from the bishop to say that I should be ready to cross the lines on 4 March. As a friend commented, my move was to be 'on the most commanding day of the year': but filled with sadness and doubt this was no encouragement to me.

Crossing the lines from one side of the city was not easy and there were many restrictions. I was to be allowed to take my clothes and the sum of US$10 only. A kind friend in a consulate was of help and offered to transport a few of my belongings – ornaments, books, a small radio and a little money. In many ways it was a very sad day for me. My mother and aunt, as well as many colleagues from the YMCA, came to see me off at the Mandelbaum Gate. I handed over my Israeli identity card to the authorities and walked into the unknown.

26 AMMAN THEN BACK TO JERUSALEM

To reach the Jordanian post on the other side of no-man's-land I had to pass bombed-out buildings standing ghost-like in the middle of a heap of rubble. My papers were ready but the point of entry into Jordan was not stamped into my passport. This was to cause a problem later on. I looked around but no one had come to meet me so I hired a porter and walked to St George's Close, where I asked to see Bishop Stewart. He told me that Colin Sharp, the headmaster in Amman, was awaiting me and that I should make my travel arrangements through his driver, George Bazuzi.

I was to leave for Amman in the afternoon, so with time on my hands I set out to make contact with aunt Malakeh. She had been appointed matron of the Red Crescent Society maternity hospital in the Old City and during lunch she told me about the hard time they had all gone through during the 1948 war and since. While in Jericho during the war, she had involved herself in nursing and midwifery among the thousands of displaced Palestinians now living in difficult conditions in camps around the town. Many women had to give birth on a straw mat on the floor, for lack of maternity facilities.

Unemployment was high all over the country, and there was much poverty. She went on to tell me that the refugees still hoped to return to their homes now under Israeli occupation. Soon after the exodus of 1948 groups would hire buses and be driven to the hills overlooking their former towns and villages, many now only recognizable by surviving cactus hedges surrounding the ruins. One popular vantage point for refugees from the Galilee area was the town of Umm Qeis (biblical Gadara) in northern Jordan, where they had a clear view of the lake and the surrounding countryside. In the Old City of Jerusalem people clambered on to the roofs of tall buildings or climbed the

AMMAN THEN BACK TO JERUSALEM 233

Mount of Olives to glimpse their property in the southern and western suburbs, now in Jewish hands.

Deep in thought I walked back through the Old City to St George's to start the journey to Amman. The drive took two hours and it was dark when we arrived at the Bishop's School. I was shown into a room on the ground floor in the boarding house, and told that the headmaster and his wife expected me for supper. The Sharps were very kind, and after enlightening me on the work I had been appointed to do spoke to me about Amman and the country around.

After the comfort of the YMCA I was now faced with austerity: the room was furnished with bare necessities; an old discarded army bed, a cupboard, small table and a chair. A bedside lamp was considered a luxury and there was no carpet on the floor. I started talking to myself, and decided to use the little money I had to make my living conditions more tolerable. The school carpenter, Sahag Kankashian, a *kaghakatsi* from Jerusalem, offered to make new furniture and help me to buy whatever else I needed. In time I made my room attractive and comfortable. Bathroom facilities were primitive, to say the least, and in the morning hot water had to be collected in an empty jam tin from the boarders' washroom. This was it: I had already been told that 'missionaries on the fringes of the desert should not expect more'.

For the first few months I was very depressed and wondered if I had made the right decision. I would lie on my bed and constantly take myself back in thought to the Greek Colony in Jerusalem and my lovely life there. I imagined the long evening shadows in the garden, heard familiar birdsong, and the banging of my bedroom door when the wind suddenly came up as it usually did in the late afternoon. I felt nostalgic when the clouds blew in from the west, knowing that they had passed over Jerusalem, but I knew that I could not return there and had to make the best of my new situation.

The school office I was to work in lacked modern equipment. On an antiquated Underwood typewriter, the keys of which were so long that they threatened my eyes, I was expected to produce letters and all exam papers. Duplicating was done by rolling stencils over trays of black jelly, which was a very inefficient and dirty job. I was also in charge of the accounts, billing and collection of school fees. I complained about the equipment and was authorized to buy new machines and reorganize the office.

School funds were limited and we ran on a strict budget, the deficit of which was made up by the home office, the Jerusalem and the East

234   ARMENIANS OF JERUSALEM

Mission. Salaries were low and expatriate staff worked for 18 Jordanian dinars per month plus board and lodging, which was estimated at 12 Jordanian dinars. However when we went on leave we forfeited the amount estimated for board and lodging at the school.

I made contact with a few friends who had moved to Amman from Jerusalem just before the war, and they were most hospitable and helpful. I got on well with the staff, both Arab and English, and made new friends, particularly a young Englishman Nicholas Dobree, a Cambridge graduate who came out to teach literature. He had a note of sternness about him and was a disciplinarian who could control classes of mature pupils, no easy feat in the Middle East. By the end of the summer term he had trained a group of Arab students to put on Shakespeare's *Richard III*, a great achievement for boys whose mother tongue was Arabic. The performances were well-attended by parents and their friends.

Nicholas was drawn to the desert and we often went on day trips to various sites around Amman, capturing the atmosphere and enjoying the scenery. Like me he loved Jerusalem, and whenever possible we drove over in the school car to spend a few days at St George's Hostel. Sadness overcame me when we reached Ras el Amud overlooking Jerusalem. From there on the skyline to the west I could see the convent of the Clairice sisters, so close to the house in the Baqa'a where my mother and aunt Isquhie were living – but inaccessible to me.

During the summer holiday we took a trip, visiting Damascus first and then going on to Ain Anoub in the Lebanon. We travelled by service taxi and at the Syrian frontier there was a delay when I was asked why there was no stamp in my passport to indicate my point of entry into Jordan. Since the Syrians were at war with Israel there was no question of my owning up that I had entered through the Mandelbaum Gate. I argued with them in voluble Arabic and the amused officials issued me with a Syrian visa.

We spent two nights in Damascus at a guest house run by an American missionary. Visits to the ancient mosque and colourful *suqs*, riding in a 'diligence' down the Street called Straight, eating frogs' legs for the first time at Socrates restaurant, were all part of an enjoyable visit to this great city.

We travelled on to Ain Anoub, a Druze village in the mountains nine miles south of Beirut overlooking the Mediterranean. We stayed in the Anglican bishops' school, then run by Miss Phyllis Shepherd;

AMMAN THEN BACK TO JERUSALEM

during the school holidays for a ridiculously small fee the buildings were used as a resthouse for mission staff. This was indeed a lovely place, the creation of Canon and Mrs Worsley, who had come out in the 1880s to look for the descendants of the ancient Hittites. They had arrived at the village in a pantechnicon driven by their coachman, Mr Webb, and were stopped in their tracks when a wheel fell off the vehicle. They believed the incident was a sign from God that they were to settle among the Druze people of Ain Anoub and preach the Gospel to them. However, before she even started on her mission, the villagers made it clear to Mrs Worsley that, though she might convert some, a Druze born would always die as a Druze. This did not deter her. Twelve acres of land were secured, on which the Worsleys built a school for girls and a house for themselves, known to this day as Beit Worsley. The Worsleys died at Ain Anoub and were buried in a vault in the grounds. As they had no heirs there was long controversy over the inheritance. Eventually the property was handed over to the Jerusalem bishopric, who continued to run it as a school.

Our stay at Ain Anoub was memorable. We were looked after by Garabed, the Armenian caretaker, whose black dog, Harith, accompanied him everywhere. We took our meals in the garden under the canopy of umbrella pines buzzing with cicadas. In the afternoons we walked down to the beach for a swim at Khaldeh, after which the long climb back through wooded hills brought us home as dark fell. On other days Miss Shepherd would drive us to Beirut, skilfully negotiating steep and winding roads in her old Morris Minor car with one of the doors tied fast with a piece of old ribbon.

During my year in Amman Colin Sharp retired and was succeeded by the Rev V. H. Hambling, whose first task was to improve staff living conditions. I did not stay long enough to enjoy the improvements as in November 1954, after I had lived in Amman for nine months, Bishop Stewart transferred me to Jerusalem.

I was appointed accountant at St George's Close and was simply delighted at the thought of going back to the Jordanian part of divided Jerusalem. As this was a local appointment I was not given accommodation at St George's Hostel like other British staff. My aunt Malakeh came to the rescue and said I could use her house in the Armenian Quarter. She was living at the maternity hospital and her husband, Sahag, now regional manager of the Singer Sewing Machine company, was away in Amman for most of the time. Her son, Morris, had emigrated to the United States and was never to visit Jerusalem again.

236 ARMENIANS OF JERUSALEM

This arrangement was temporary and I was constantly on the look out for a permanent place to stay. Miss Mary Thompson, the warden of St George's Hostel, often let me use a vacant visitor's room for a few days, then would tell me it was booked and I had to move on. In the summer Stewart Perowne, who was in charge of the bishop's relief fund projects, let me use his rooms while he was on leave. On his return Mrs Rittel, the matron of St George's School, allowed me to sleep on a couch in the clinic. When she in turn asked me to move I went straight to the bishop and told him that I had no alternative but to resign. By then I had made myself indispensable and so was given a permanent room in the hostel.

Many of the Arab staff at St George's had known me and my parents over the years. Both George Bazuzi, the bishop's driver, and Emile Bajjalli, the bishop's *kawas*, had worked in the public works department with my father. For the first time I met Mr Najib Bawarshi, Abu Raja, now the bishop's agent and in charge of works and repairs. With a twinkle in his eye he told me how fond he had been of my mother when they worked together at Dr Paterson's hospital in Hebron, winding bandages on spools all those years ago. He became a firm friend. Mass'ad Ghazawi, the carpenter, had been the first Palestinian refugee to be employed at the close. In his workshop hung a large framed photograph of himself and his colleagues at the port of Jaffa, where he had worked during the British Mandate. Among the gatemen one stands out: a Kurd, Ahmad Barazani, who liked to be called Jack. Neat in his military clothes, with a large greyish moustache, wearing gold-rimmed glasses, he had an imposing presence. He proudly told everybody that he had been a guard at the famous meeting between Churchill, Stalin and Roosevelt at Yalta. We could not verify this but nevertheless were impressed with his story. Hajj Hassan, the gardener who had been there since Bishop Blyth's days, was still growing dahlias, zinnias and other flowers. We all worked as a team for a period of twenty years, sharing good and bad times including the ordeal of the 1967 Arab–Israeli war.

The Rev Harold Adkins had recently been appointed sub-dean of the cathedral (the bishop himself was the dean), after serving as chaplain at All Saints, Beirut. In addition to his duties in the cathedral, he was an admirable headmaster of St George's School.

Canon and Mrs Edward Every were also on the staff. Canon Every, a scholar of the Eastern Churches, acted as liaison between Anglican and Orthodox ecclesiastics in Jerusalem. Mrs Every had worked with

AMMAN THEN BACK TO JERUSALEM

Arabs, first at Bir Zeit school and then in an eye-clinic at el Feheis in East Jordan, where she was known to all as Sitt Adela. They both gave a sympathetic ear to local people in difficulty and helped distressed individuals more than anyone will ever know.

Miss Elinor Moore, former vice-principal of the Jerusalem Girls' College and a historian, was on the bishop's relief committee. She was also in charge of the college records and her knowledge was invaluable to her former pupils when they required copies of documents and certificates lost during the war.

I was to take charge of the mission accounts, which I found to be in some muddle. There were curious notes, such as 'Beware, this column has been carried forward incorrectly', pencilled in the ledgers. Whereas my predecessors had all been women untrained in accounts, and had laboured full-time, it was not so for me. I made no attempt to change the old-fashioned system of double-entry bookkeeping with ledgers and journals, which I treated as an artistic creation. All I seemed to lack was inkpot and quill. The work was varied, dealing with returns from schools and institutions throughout the diocese, drawing up budgets and paying subsidies, wages and salaries. We used the Ottoman Bank, which since the division of Jerusalem had moved to offices in a Greek convent in the Via Dolorosa, built on a site believed to be *habs el masih* (the prison of Christ). What a dramatic address for a bank: The Prison of Christ, Via Dolorosa, Jerusalem. Russell & Company, now with headquarters in Beirut, were still auditing the accounts at St George's. Their area representative, Mr Emile Safieh, whom I already knew, was a most pleasant colleague to work with again.

Extra voluntary work was heaped on me: monthly bookkeeping for the blind home run by Miss Ketchejian, payment of pensions on behalf of the World Council of Churches to East European refugees in Jerusalem waiting to be re-settled in France, treasurer of St George's Cathedral.

Soon after I arrived the bishop asked me to draw up an inventory of medical equipment at St Luke's Hospital in Hebron, now to be handed over to UNRWA, the United Nations relief agency. St Luke's had developed from Dr Paterson's hospital where my mother and aunt had started their nursing careers. The matron of St George's School, Miss Ferguson, who had been a nurse with the China Inland Mission, accompanied me and helped by naming all the instruments.

The work in Hebron over, the bishop put me in charge of the

238 ARMENIANS OF JERUSALEM

diocesan refugee fund. Considerable sums of money had been collected abroad to assist Palestinian refugees. Projects included a milk and soup kitchen in Bethany, a sewing centre in the chapter-house at St George's and an antenatal clinic at Latroun. Help was also given to frontier villages such as Beit Suriq and Beit Duqqu, whose inhabitants were not technically refugees but had no access to their farm lands beyond the armistice line. Funds were allocated by the relief committee and the work adminstered by Mrs Stewart and a team of ladies. Stewart Perowne was in charge of the largest project, the building of new villages on the outskirts of Jerusalem to re-house refugees. From then on I was to work in a small office in the gatehouse of the close, where I was accessible and in contact with all who came and went.

St George's Hostel where I now lived had been started in 1923 by Canon Stacy Waddy in the former choir school founded by Bishop Blyth. Its aim, as recorded in an early minute of a committee meeting, was 'To keep body and soul of a pilgrim together'. Nothing much had changed since then. The rooms were sparsely furnished, with horse-hair mattresses on bedsteads over which hung iron hoops holding mosquito nets. Each room had a dresser with a matching china bowl and jug for washing, and a chamber pot for use at night. Hot water, heated on primus stoves at 5 a.m., was brought to the rooms in jugs by the maids at 6 a.m. to enable visitors to attend matins in the cathedral. Toilets and bathrooms were concentrated in a corner of the building and visitors crossed the open quadrangle to get there. Bath-nights were allocated by the warden; permanent staff were allowed two a week, my days were Tuesday and Saturday.

We took our meals in the charming vaulted dining-room which ran parallel to the cloister outside. Seated at a long table with the warden at the head, we met and exchanged views with the visitors, and were waited upon by the domestic staff. It was here that I was still to be pestered by the devious questions familiar from my childhood: 'How long have you lived here?' or 'Where do you come from, Mr Rose?' I knew at once that they were intrigued and wanted to find out my background. I would put them at ease immediately, telling them I was half English, half Armenian and born in Jerusalem.

The food was good with a limited repertoire of English and Arabic dishes, and meatless days observed on Wednesdays and Fridays. Grace was said before every meal and casual clothes never worn in the dining-room. It was all very proper.

AMMAN THEN BACK TO JERUSALEM

From 1948 to 1967 the cathedral and close buildings were a few metres away from the armistice line dividing Jerusalem. The Nablus road that passed the close gate, the lifeline to the north, became a busy thoroughfare, whereas St George's Road beyond the school was silent and inaccessible. A high wall with a narrow overlapping gap manned by the Jordanian army served as a barrier between the two roads. Behind the barrier United Nations observers had made their offices in a large building which became known as 'MAC House' (Mixed Armistice Commission house) and are still there to this day. The view looking west from the hostel garden was one of dereliction; barbed wire everywhere, mounds of rubble dominated by a row of collapsed buildings which belonged to the *awqaf* (Muslim Supreme Council) now serving as a shield between the two warring sides. In the spring this harsh scene was softened by the beauty of almond trees draped in shades of white and pink blossom.

Life in Jordanian Jerusalem was very pleasant. The Old City was clean, not over-crowded, had retained its Arab character and was not caught up in the modern world. It was safe to travel to outlying villages, go for walks in the country, and above all to enjoy a simple life. Everyone was friendly, hospitable and always willing to help.

In the early 1950s salaries and wages were low but so was the cost of living; there was plenty of home-grown produce and a variety of imported goods in the shops. Visitors could stay at the hostel for the equivalent of 70p per night including three meals, with tea and cake served morning and afternoon as well. Electricity and water were a problem as the main sources, now under Israeli rule, had been cut off since the division of Jerusalem in 1948. For some years people resorted to lamps and cisterns until a new power station was built, and water was once again piped from Ain Fara and Solomon's Pools.

There were always interesting people living in the hostel or paying visits from time to time. Teachers and missionaries from all over the Middle East, Save the Children Fund staff and members of archaeological digs would come for weekends. For a time John Allegro, who was working on the newly discovered Dead Sea scrolls, made his headquarters with us. Stewart Perowne added much interest and colour to our life at the close and was always ready to shock. On one occasion when a group of pink-faced elderly missionaries returned from a trip to the Dead Sea he exclaimed, 'Gracious, the sea has given up its dead.' They overheard him and were not amused. One Christmas Day while driving over to Amman he stopped at a busy cafe

240 ARMENIANS OF JERUSALEM

in the town of Sweileh and ordered the owner to tune his radio to the BBC so that he could listen to the Queen's speech. The stunned patrons were deprived of their Arabic songs and forced to listen too, without understanding a word. In the winter he wore a long grey coat lined with the fur of local foxes especially shot and cured for him by Arab villagers, who affectionately called him *'abd el faqir* (servant of the poor).

Stewart befriended me and included me in visits to places of interest in and around Jerusalem, to archaeological sites, to see the new refugee villages built under the auspices of the Anglican bishop, and to religious ceremonies. On Saturday evenings we often walked down to vespers at the Russian church of St Mary Magdalene in Gethsemane. Listening to the singing of the service interspersed with that moving response *Gospodi pomilyi* (Lord have mercy) was indeed a spiritual experience. On Good Friday at the Burial Service we were given banners to carry in the procession round the church. At midnight on Easter Eve the priests, nuns and congregation wait silently outside the closed church door until the bells of the Holy Sepulchre are heard ringing out across the Kidron valley. The solemn atmosphere changes to one of joy, the priest repeatedly greets the people with the words '*Christos voskrese*' (Christ is Risen) to which all present reply '*Voistinu voskrese*' (He is Risen indeed).

The Church of St Mary Magdalene on the slopes of the Mount of Olives had been built in memory of Tsarina Maria Alexandrovna, wife of Alexander II, and consecrated in 1888 in the presence of the Grand Duke Sergei and his wife, the Grand Duchess Elizabeth. The Grand Duchess Elizabeth, who became a nun after her husband's assassination, was murdered during the Russian revolution. Her remains were brought to Palestine in 1920 and buried in the crypt of the church. In May 1982 the Grand Duchess Elizabeth was canonized and I was present at a splendid service when her remains and those of her companion, Sister Barbara, were brought up from the crypt and placed in the main body of the church.

Frequent visits were made to the Trappist monastery at Latroun, where we were looked after at lunch by Père Marcel, the guestmaster, the only monk allowed to speak to us. We often stayed for the service of Nones, sitting in the visitors' gallery. On Corpus Christi we drove over to see the carpet of oleander petals which adorned the floors of the cloisters.

The monastery of Latroun was precariously close to the dividing

AMMAN THEN BACK TO JERUSALEM 241

line between Jordan and Israel, but visitors were officially allowed access. From the wooded grounds we could look across the plains deep into Israel and discern the once-busy Jerusalem to Jaffa highway overgrown with weeds, snaking its way through no-man's-land. Below the monastery walls lay the ruined village of Latroun, again only identifiable by its cactus hedges. Close by, a Jordanian army post (in one of the Tegart forts the British police had put up all over the country), towered over the village of Imwas. Even though on the edge of no-man's-land, the villagers went on living there until the 1967 war, when they were driven out and their houses blown up to make way for what is now Canada Park.

I settled into my new life quite happily. My mother came over for Christmas through the Mandelbaum Gate and stayed for 24 hours. She was trying to join me permanently in Jordan as she was not allowed to renew her visa to remain with aunt Isquhie on the Israeli side of Jerusalem. Although the British consulate tried their utmost to obtain permits for her to cross over, they failed and she had to go back to join my sister Gertie in England. On 18 January, the Armenian Christmas, aunt Isquhie came over also for 24 hours. I saw them off, first one then the other disappearing through the gate, knowing that we could not communicate again for another year.

When I arrived in Jordan the political situation was calm, but in November 1955 objection to the Baghdad Pact sparked off riots and demonstrations. King Hussein's position was threatened until the army was called out to restore order. There was trouble in Jerusalem and we were advised to stay within the close compound. In Jericho violent mobs demonstrated for three days against British imperialism. The riots developed into an attack on Boys' Town, the training centre for refugees founded by Musa el Alami. He was away in Beirut and on return he found the farms, workshops and other buildings totally ransacked. Undaunted, he built the project up again.

In 1956 the Suez crisis caused instability and anti-western feeling in Jordan yet again. The crisis loomed for some time while Gamal Abdel Nasser planned to take control of the canal. There was danger that war would break out, and all British subjects in Jerusalem were constantly advised to leave the country. At first I resisted, but so much pressure was put on me that this time I decided to leave with the other members of staff. For guidance Miss Ferguson held out to us her box of rolled-up biblical texts to choose from. The one she pulled out herself quoted 1 Sam. 17:47, 'Stand fast. The battle is the Lord's.'

242 ARMENIANS OF JERUSALEM

This convinced her that we should not leave, but in the end she too was made to go.

The British consulate had arranged that we should be evacuated to England through Israel, as all other routes out of Jordan were closed. The sub-dean, Harold Adkins, and I were the last to leave the close and we crossed the lines through the Mandelbaum Gate on the afternoon of 1 November. The bishop was away and Canon Every, as his commissary, with Mrs Every and Miss Elinor Moore stayed on in the close and were ably assisted by the Arab staff.

We crossed over in the late afternoon and it felt strange to be back on the Israeli side of Jerusalem. We were to stay at the YMCA, where I had many friends whom I had not seen since I left eighteen months before. A total blackout was in force. Next morning I went to visit aunt Isquhie, who could not believe her eyes when she saw me. It was a short and sad meeting.

We spent two nights in Israeli Jerusalem and were then flown out on an El Al plane to London. Harold went on to his parents' home in Quorn and I stayed in London before going to my sister Gertie, now married with two tiny children. She lived in Stafford, where she had been joined by my mother. And so another exile, albeit short, had begun.

Within a month the débâcle of Suez had blown over and I made preparations to return to Jerusalem. The only route available was through Baghdad and I had to obtain an Iraqi visa from the embassy in London. First I had to change my passport yet again as it had been stamped by the Israeli authorities when I left Lod airport. No difficulty over that, but at the Iraqi embassy there seemed doubt as to whether I was to be given a transit visa. When I detected this I burst upon the clerks in Arabic and they were so amazed that they stamped my passport on the spot. I was also able to obtain a visa for Harold, who was to return with me. We flew to Baghdad. I was airsick and an alarmed Chaldean lady made the sign of the cross over me to speed my recovery. After one night in Baghdad we flew on to Jerusalem in an almost empty plane on which one of the passengers carried a pair of turkeys, each strapped into a pannier beside him.

On my return I was put in temporary charge of the hostel as the warden, Miss Mary Thompson, was not coming back and no one else had been appointed to the post. I was also asked to play the organ regularly for the cathedral services – another voluntary duty.

In 1957 Bishop Stewart retired after years of service, first as

AMMAN THEN BACK TO JERUSALEM

archdeacon in Palestine and then as bishop in Jerusalem since 1943. Both he and his wife, Alison, had seen tragic changes in the country and had been of help to many after the 1948 war. With his departure the diocese was reconstructed, and an archbishop in Jerusalem appointed to preside over an episcopal synod including the dioceses of Egypt and Libya, the Sudan, Iran, and the new diocese of Jordan Lebanon and Syria, each under their own bishop.

The first Anglican archbishop in Jerusalem, Angus Campbell MacInnes, arrived on 7 August 1957 with his wife, Joy. He was the son of Rennie MacInnes, bishop in Jerusalem from 1914 to 1931, and had been born in Cairo. For many years he was headmaster of Bishop Gobat School, then served as archdeacon in Palestine up to and including the 1948 war, when he was wounded. Mrs MacInnes, daughter of Dr Masterman, head of the London Jews Society hospital, was born in Jerusalem and herself trained as a doctor.

The archbishop and Mrs MacInnes knew my parents well, and Mrs MacInnes had taught us as children in Sunday school in the Templist meeting-house in the German Colony. They had many friends in Jerusalem, especially among the local population, who were pleased at the appointment.

Soon after his arrival the archbishop appointed me warden of St George's Hostel and organist at the cathedral, writing in the October 1957 quarterly magazine of the Anglican Archbishopric in Jerusalem:

Our accountant, John Rose, has since his return after the Suez crisis acted as warden of the hostel. He has a real flair for decoration, has done wonders in the garden and greatly increased the comfort of the guests and is an admirable host. I am therefore appointing him warden in succession to Miss Thompson who so nobly carried on the work until she was evacuated last November.

The organ has been in need of rebuilding for many years. That it still provides our music is in no small measure due to John Rose's father who during the days of the Mandate used to come to the cathedral day after day when his work was over, to see that it was in good repair. John Rose has acted as our organist for some time past. I am now asking him officially to become the organist at St George's. His three jobs, accountant, warden and organist, seem to fit in with one another, and it is

244 ARMENIANS OF JERUSALEM

good to have in him someone who has been born and brought up almost within the shadow of the cathedral.

A hard-working, varied life was to begin. I had fallen into a niche where all my interests were fulfilled, and the work made easy by my knowledge of the Arabic language, the country and the people.

For me the first big event at the organ was to play for the enthronement of Archbishop MacInnes at the end of August. The following year Canon Najib Cub'ain was consecrated as the first Arab Anglican bishop of Jordan, Syria and Lebanon. After a moving service a tea party was held in the hostel garden attended by Arab Anglicans from all over the diocese. A large chocolate cake with sugar figures of priests and monks dotted all over it was flown in from Cairo. The reception was attended by Muslim and Christian dignitaries and many friends. The new bishop was true to his calling. He was kind, and always found time to listen to the many problems and requests brought to him daily, helping whenever possible. People in all walks of life were treated with the same courtesy. Both he and his wife, Sitt Lydia, were hospitable, constantly inviting friends to partake of meals at their table. At the time the bishop was living in the hostel compound and he showed great interest in the renovations I was carrying out and always encouraged me. During my twenty years at St George's I had the most amicable relations with him and all the Arab clergy.

27 WARDEN OF ST GEORGE'S HOSTEL

When I was officially appointed warden of St George's Hostel in 1957 I inherited a domestic staff of women, and it was new to them to have a man in charge. Latifeh Kawas, the head maid, a widow who came from Jifna, was a stabilizing influence who gave me support from the start. She was a favourite amongst the visitors and it was a sad day when she left the hostel ten years later to join her son and daughter in Kuwait. Nothing has been heard of her since the Gulf war.

Vera, the cook from Beit Jala, remained difficult and made it clear that she hated interference in the kitchen. She jealously guarded her recipes and always prevented Dahud, the *marmiton*, from learning them. When I took the grocery shopping out of her hands she resigned.

Hajj Hassan, the bishop's gardener, continued to shop for vegetables and fruit in the Old City, while meat and other stores were delivered to the hostel. Fresh eggs were brought in every week by Mrs Wilson, an English lady who had a farm near Rachel's Tomb. She had come to Palestine as a circus performer and animal tamer. Once, when the circus animals were being paraded through the town, an elephant stopped in its tracks in Princess Mary Avenue. The circus performer came to the rescue: she whispered into the elephant's ear and the procession moved on. A policeman on duty, Mr Tug Wilson, was so impressed that after a short courtship he married her.

I replaced Vera with a chef, George Mansur (Abu William), who had worked in the kitchens of the Latin convent. I gradually widened his knowledge of cooking until he became one of the best cooks in Jerusalem. After a while I only needed to dictate a new recipe once (often out of my 1890 edition of Mrs Beeton) for him to reproduce it perfectly. We made all our own jams, apricot, quince, plum, and the

246   ARMENIANS OF JERUSALEM

orange marmalade (a Mrs Beeton recipe) served for breakfast became famous. At Christmas Abu William made puddings, mince pies and plum cake. As ready-made suet was unobtainable we made our own, successfully rendering down the fat surrounding beef kidneys.

I was intent on retaining a Middle Eastern atmosphere at the hostel, producing a variety of Arab dishes for lunch, for supper serving good European food. Meatless days on Fridays and during Lent were still observed and *mujaddara*, a dish of lentils and rice known as 'Esau's mess of pottage', was sometimes served. I noticed that hesitant visitors fell upon it and found it delicious when I referred to its biblical connotations.

Our repertoire was extensive and no dish was repeated within two or three weeks. Abu William was constantly complimented by the guests, who found every meal at the hostel table of party standard. A note written by Noel, Countess of Mayo, visiting the hostel, illustrates this: 'Your sweet tonight was delicious. I must congratulate you on your extensive well thought out menu.'

Another guest sent a cutting from her local paper which describes the scene:

It will be a long time before I forget the long high vaulted room at St George's hostel in Jerusalem where we enjoyed some exotic oriental dishes. Glass plates in green and ultramarine glowed on wooden shelves behind my chair, glass that had been fired and hand-spun in Hebron as it had been for thousands of years. The water jugs and fruit bowls on the long table were of the same glass, and the luncheon mats were of heavy linen with crimson embroidery. The food was Middle Eastern modified to suit the western palate but not altered beyond recognition. It was delicious and of infinite variety, and the desserts were delicious too.

Once during dinner a visitor, the sixth Marquess of Northampton, commented in a loud voice, 'Mr Rose, you provide an excellent bill of fare at St George's.' What more of a compliment could one want?

I soon realized that I needed a team of men to take charge of the dining-room. My first applicant was Mousa Khalil (Abu As'ad) from Bethany. He spoke English and had worked on the domestic staff at Government House when Sir Harold and Lady MacMichael were in residence. He talked affectionately of them, and always mentioned

WARDEN OF ST GEORGE'S HOSTEL

Miss Araminta and Miss Priscilla. I employed him on a trial basis; he proved to be efficient, was of great help to visitors and is still there today. His brother Yusef later joined the staff as gardener, although the cultivation of plants was new to him. We worked together, and created a garden that became known for its beauty and variety.

The courtyard which became the garden had over the years been neglected. It was gravelled over, had a few flower beds, and laundry hung out in one corner. The gravel was replaced by natural paving stones winding among flower beds in which we grew many plants from seed. Others we acquired from the Franciscan garden at Gethsemane, where Father Eugene Hoade had a rare collection of plants. The centrepiece was an old white oleander which had with age developed into a tree fifteen feet high, a spectacular sight in bloom especially on moonlit nights when it gleamed in palest blue. A plant of great interest was the twining moonflower (*Ipomoea bona-nox*) whose heavily scented furled white flowers could be watched opening in slow motion as night fell, ready to attract moths. It became the most photographed plant in the garden. Another was *Hibiscus mutabilis* with double white camellia-like blooms which darkened to crimson by the end of the day. Visitors were intrigued to see flowers of two different colours on the same bush.

We dug out a small pond and used an ancient well-head given to us by the Assyrian Convent of St Mark as a basin for a fountain. Frogs were brought in from the Wadi Qelt but proliferated and were so noisy that they became a nuisance. Every spring we depleted the population by catching as many as we could, letting them loose in the Pool of Siloam. The pond attracted different birds, including Syrian nightingales and the tiny glittering blue Palestinian sunbird which flitted among the flowers in search of nectar. Antiquities of stone and pottery stood about the garden, some found on the premises, other brought in by Stewart Perowne, some given to me by Abuna Philipos in Jericho. Groups of pilgrims and visitors would visit the garden before or after attending cathedral services.

Two other gardens rivalled ours, one at the American Colony and the other at the residence of Katy Antonius (Mrs George Antonius). Mrs Antonius had converted her house into a fashionable restaurant, The Katakeet, where the food was of the highest standard and her own antique furniture and ornaments added to the charm. It was claimed that she was the only person left to hold a 'salon' in Jerusalem and she also enjoyed inviting the young to lavish parties at The

248 ARMENIANS OF JERUSALEM

Katakeet. Just before the 1967 war she decided to sell up and leave for good. Before going she invited me to help myself to choice plants from her lovely garden.

Gardening was a time for meditation and thought, especially in the cool of the evening when passages of the Quran, *dhikr* (reminders), are recited before the *adhan* from the minaret at Sheikh Jarrah inviting the faithful to prayer from field, village and town. During Ramadan in the early hours we would hear drummers going around the streets alerting those fasting to prepare for their last meal before sunrise.

Omar Suleiman, another member of staff, had a tragic beginning to his life. During the 1948 war his parents with their young children were forced to flee their village, Beit Mahsir (now Beit Meir), which lay to the west of Jerusalem off the main highway to Jaffa. His mother, Hajjar (Umm Ali), carried her baby, Omar, on her back and walked for miles to Jericho where the family took refuge. They later moved to 'Aqbat Jaber, a large refugee camp run by the United Nations Relief and Works Agency. Aunt Malakeh, who frequently visited the camps as voluntary nurse and midwife, met them and arranged for Abu Ali to come and tend her orange grove.

The family moved into a room in the garden and aunt Malakeh took charge of Omar, who as a result of his unsettling experience did not speak for over three years. She was extremely patient and kind to him, and taught him basic housework. When he was about fifteen years old she pleaded with me to take him on at the hostel, saying: 'John, he has to work among friends, where he will be treated kindly.' I finally agreed and aunt Malakeh brought him to the hostel. To build his confidence I sent him to the Old City with Mousa to buy a set of new clothes. First he worked in the laundry, then moved to the dining-room where he became a good waiter. He had a flair for cooking, filled in on the cook's day off and eventually became a cook himself.

The staff worked harmoniously and my relationship with them was enviable. I was drawn into their family problems; we were the best of friends, treating each other with respect but without familiarity. Raised voices, which sometimes alarmed foreign visitors, did not mean a quarrel was in progress but were a way of holding a normal conversation in the Middle East.

The hostel was not subsidized nor was it expected to make a profit. It was to raise enough income from visitors to cover daily expenses and to enable missionaries to stay at cut prices. No funds were available for capital expenditure. I ran it without outside interference:

WARDEN OF ST GEORGE'S HOSTEL

a supervising committee formed when I took over was buried after the first meeting. However I always consulted the archbishop over major decisions.

A new phase began when the Hon Richard Hill, later Lord Sandys, gave £100 sterling to the hostel. He had lived there while working in the bishop's office and realized that there was scope for improvement. With the money I renovated three guest-rooms, making them attractive and comfortable. An Armenian seamstress, Azad, came in to sew curtains and bedspreads from striped *qumbaz* material. A different colour was used for each room and the result was charming. As money came in I managed to renovate all the rooms.

Any profits made by the hostel I ploughed back into improvements. A new hot-water system was installed, with running hot and cold piped to washbasins in each room. The kitchens were modernized and a new scullery put in; previously the maids had washed up in a draughty passage outside the kitchen, using a cement sink with a bucket underneath.

While renovating I had to be very careful not to spoil the original architecture of the building. All the rooms were domed, and haphazard alterations could destroy their beauty. In 1964 I had made enough money to complete the inner hostel cloister. An old tiled awning, which had been there since the days of the choir school, was replaced with stone arches in keeping with the rest of the building. Once glassed in, the corridors became an attractive passageway. On the window-ledges we grew pots of hyacinths, cyclamen, primulas and African violets, all rare on our side of Jerusalem at the time. The inner walls were decked with oriental hangings and copper ornaments, while from the ceiling hung hand-painted glass lamps brought from Damascus.

St George's Hostel became a popular place to stay on a visit to Jerusalem. It gained a reputation for good food, an English college atmosphere, attractive decor, lovely gardens and pleasant staff, and above all it was inexpensive. Applications poured in from around the world and it was often difficult to find a room. The visitors included teachers, missionaries, bishops and clergy, and embassy staff from surrounding Arab countries. Mission workers from Israel, United Nations personnel, staff from embassies in Tel Aviv, were now able to cross over to spend weekends in East Jerusalem and return. Tourists were only allowed a one-way crossing between Israel and Jordan, which complicated travel arrangements.

250   ARMENIANS OF JERUSALEM

The original purpose of the hostel had been to provide the right setting for pilgrims and missionaries visiting the Holy Land. I was soon criticized for taking in embassy staff and others who could afford to stay in modern hotels. I overcame this by contributing 500 Jordanian dinars yearly from the hostel's profits towards bursaries for Arab refugees at St George's School.

Over the years I accumulated a file of flattering letters from visitors. From John Raven (botanist and philosopher):

A line to thank you and all your staff for the extraordinary kindness which you showed us through all our comings and goings. I meant what I more than once said to you – that we have never stayed in a more delightful place than St George's hostel, nor ever received more unfailing kindness of hospitality from everybody we met.

Another guest, Richard Martin Taylor, wrote:

St George's hostel was all and more than we had been promised. We loved the garden and the decoration and the friendly and efficient way in which it was run. You were so calm and unruffled in the face of your daily invasions.

One departing guest told me that staying at the hostel was like attending a course at a finishing-school. Guests admired the high standard of service: at meals, the starched napkins formed into bishop's mitres and the quaintness of brass finger-bowls (sometimes with jasmine floating in them) intrigued many, especially American visitors who had not come across them before. Every Sunday the archbishop brought his house guests over for lunch. He presided at the table and enjoyed talking to those around him.

St George's Cathedral had a succession of American chaplains on the staff since 1922, appointed by the Protestant Episcopal Church in the USA: in 1960 the Rev John David Zimmerman (J. D. Zee to his friends), a biblical scholar who had been a navy chaplain, was appointed, accompanied by his wife, Lilian. They were a great addition to the life of the close. Lilian Zimmerman was a gracious hostess who made friends easily and did much for young expatriate wives. Sitting at the head of the hostel table she looked out for the lonely and introduced people to each other. She also organized church school on

WARDEN OF ST GEORGE'S HOSTEL

Sundays and was responsible for beautiful flower arrangements in the cathedral. As a trained dietician she was of great help to me in the hostel and efficiently took over when I went on leave. J. D. Zee, whose dry sense of humour was appreciated by those who shared it, was installed as a canon of the cathedral. He was a meticulous librarian, always on hand to help students of biblical archaeology. They were sorely missed when they left the close in 1970.

Jerusalem has always attracted eccentrics, some of whom stayed in the hostel. Two young Englishmen came to witness the Second Coming, which they believed was imminent. They stayed for a few days and against all advice moved into a cave near Absalom's tomb to wait. After a week they returned, hungry and dishevelled, and having no further means were repatriated by the British consulate. An elderly Swedish lady, clad in a gabardine uniform covered with badges, arrived without a booking. I asked her how long she wanted to stay, and in broken English she explained that she was 'waiting for somsing' – this also was the Second Coming. She gave up after a while and crossed into Israel to stay at St Andrew's Hospice above the Hinnom valley, where she hoped the event would take place before her eyes on Mount Zion.

Bus tours for tourists had not yet been introduced and the hostel advised visitors on how best to use their time. We were in contact with reliable guides and also a chauffeur, Samir Khayo, who was dependable and well-thought-of. As for the guides, they provided some amusement. Once a loud American voice called out from amongst a group visiting the Damascus Gate 'Is this AD or BC?' The guide answered 'For you, madam, *kulshi*!' (everything). Another middle-aged lady reported her guide for attempting to kiss her at Gethsemane. I reprimanded him, but he was one up on me, saying: 'Mr Rose, there is nothing wrong in demonstrating the Kiss of Peace in the Garden of Gethsemane.'

In the 1950s many institutions which had been obliged to abandon their work and property on the west side of Jerusalem made new beginnings, now that the city seemed permanently divided. Buildings went up for a new YMCA and YWCA for the youth of Arab Jerusalem. In October 1960 St John's ophthalmic hospital moved to new buildings in the Sheikh Jarrah Quarter. On Tel el Nijm (star mountain) a complex of buildings was put up to serve as a leper home. Talitha Cumi, my mother's old school, reopened in new buildings in

252 ARMENIANS OF JERUSALEM

Beit Jala south of Jerusalem. Schneller's orphanage started again in Zerqa, east of the river Jordan.

New institutions were opened: Dar el Awlad (boys' home) for orphans and refugee children by Mrs George Antonius, Rawdat el Zuhur (garden of flowers) for young girls by Miss Elizabeth Nasir. The Four Homes of Mercy founded by Mrs George Siksik expanded and moved to Bethany. A new vocational training centre for blind girls, Helen Keller House, was built in Beit Hanina. These projects all relied heavily on donations from abroad.

A new shopping and commercial centre sprang up in the vicinity of Herod's Gate. Hotels opened, a post office and telephone exchange were built and the Ottoman Bank moved out of the Old City into new premises. The Muhafizah (governorate) and law courts were built in Salah el Din Street not far from St George's. We were, however, constantly reminded of the division of the city by a high stone wall which ran from the Damascus Gate to a point along the Street of the Prophets, beyond which damaged buildings formed the demarcation line.

In 1959 the leper home at Tel el Nijm was dedicated by Bishop Najib Cuba'in, Anglican bishop in Jordan, Syria and Lebanon, in the presence of a large group of well-wishers. Sister Johanna, a Moravian, had devotedly cared for lepers in Jerusalem for many years. After the 1948 war the home, Jesushilfe in west Jerusalem, had to be abandoned and she escorted her patients across the lines to primitive buildings in the village of Siloam. In her inaugural speech she mentioned the ten lepers 'that stood afar off' (Luke 17:12), asserting that with modern medicine they were no longer a threat to anyone. In their new homes within the compound her patients would lead normal lives.

On 18 April 1962 the foundation stone of St George's College was laid by Bishop Stephen Bayne, to be built between the school playing-field and the cathedral. For some time Archbishop MacInnes had hoped to found a theological college in Jerusalem, primarily to serve students from Africa and the Middle East. Short courses, with lectures and visits to biblical sites, would also be available to students from all over the world. During vacations the college rooms were to be used for hostel visitors. The building was completed within ten months and dedicated on 25 February 1963.

In 1960 my mother returned to Jerusalem. I rented a room and a kitchen for her from aunt Malakeh's neighbours, the Simounians. Aunt Malakeh was then working as a nurse in the Anna Spafford baby

WARDEN OF ST GEORGE'S HOSTEL 253

home run by Mrs Bertha Spafford Vester of the American Colony. At Mrs Vester's request she went to nurse Lady Glubb, mother of Glubb Pasha of the Arab Legion, who had broken her hip while staying in the Colony hostel. Her work at the baby home was to be Malakeh's last nursing post in an institution, although she still acted as midwife to the local community and was frequently consulted in matters of gynaecology.

My mother did not stay long in the Armenian Quarter. As she was getting on in years, I decided to move her to two rooms which I rented in the Nuseibeh house opposite St George's, where she was able to have meals in the hostel whenever she wished. Guests found her interesting and sought her company. Of an afternoon she would be seen sitting in the hostel garden chatting to visitors and the domestic staff. If ever I had a misunderstanding with one of the staff, they always appealed to her to act as mediator.

In the summer of 1960 my cousin Nazouhie came from Beirut to visit relatives. She was dressed in black, mourning for her brother, Krikor, who had recently died. Nazouhie asked me to come with her to the Armenian convent where, from the roof, we had a view of their house in the Upper Baqa'a, easily identified by the cypress trees in the garden. We gazed and gazed and came sorrowfully away.

One of my duties, accompanying the cathedral services on the organ, was for me a serious responsibility. I never seemed to get over the initial state of nerves that overcame me every time I sat at the keyboard. The instrument, an English organ of tender tone, had been damaged during the war of 1948 and had had no regular attention since my father left Jerusalem. However, it served its purpose and kept the music going in the cathedral. As in days past at services on Sundays and saints' days, versicles, canticles and psalms were sung. We used Merbecke's setting for the Communion service. In time I mastered the accompanying of the psalms and knew most of them by heart. I was inspired by their poetry and treated them as a spiritual exercise.

The choir was made up of blind girls from Miss Siranoush Ketchejian's school which she had called 'Ebenezer', but to satisfy an objection from the Jordanian authorities had renamed 'Hitherto Hath the Lord Helped Us' school. Later it became the Mary Lovell Home for Blind Girls. The girls sang well and performed anthems at Christmas and Easter. With their acute sense of timing, rapport between the choir and organ was no problem. Every Friday afternoon

254   ARMENIANS OF JERUSALEM

I went with Harold Adkins, the dean, to the school in Shua'fat for choir practice. Until Braille hymnbooks were available, the girls sang everything by heart.

The organ featured prominently in many important events in the cathedral – enthronement services for archbishops and bishops, Te Deums for archbishops of Canterbury and York while on visits to Jerusalem; ordinations and the installing of deans and canons, weddings and funerals. Meticulous preparation for these services was made by the dean, and all passed without a hitch. I was sometimes called upon to play for the Arabic service in the cathedral, which meant reading their music from right to left, and demanded immense concentration.

The dean, Harold Adkins, was very musical and formed a choir of expatriates and members of the Arab community. We gave concerts in the cathedral and among other works put on the *St John Passion* by Schütz. The choir later developed into the Jerusalem Choral Society under the baton of Miss Salwa Tabri, teacher of music at the Women's Training Centre, Ramallah. During Easter week a religious drama, *Eyes on the Cross*, was produced in English and Arabic by Dr and Mrs Kenn Carmichael. The Carmichaels, who belonged to the Presbyterian church in the USA, had professional theatrical experience and drew the best out of an amateur team. They were a great addition to the close and everyone loved working with them.

Eminent English visitors to Jerusalem in the 1960s included Prince Philip, the Duke and Duchess of Gloucester and Princess Alexandra who all attended cathedral services. The Shah of Iran, President Bourguiba and other Arab heads of state were brought to Jerusalem by King Hussein and taken to the Haram. In their honour we were directed to put up a triumphal arch in the Nablus road outside the close. These arches were decked with flowers and greenery surrounding a large photograph of King Hussein. School children were given a holiday to line the streets, waving flags as soon as the motorcade passed. There were so many visits that we decided to put up a permanent arch of metal poles painted in the Jordanian colours, which we decorated when required.

On 4 January 1964 Pope Paul VI came to Jerusalem. He flew from Rome to Amman, then drove to Jerusalem and stayed at the residence of the Apostolic Delegate half way up the Mount of Olives. Two weeks before his arrival I was asked to lay out the grounds leading to the residence. I was told that I could spend as much money as I

WARDEN OF ST GEORGE'S HOSTEL

needed, employ gardeners, import good soil and help myself to plants from the Franciscan nursery in Gethsemane. It was a daunting task and time was limited, but with the help of Yusef, my gardener, and others I managed to put the area between the main gate and the house into some order. It was a bad time of year for gardening and I had to go to Jericho, where in the mild climate a few herbaceous plants were still in bloom. On his return from Rome the Apostolic Delegate brought two flowering camellias which he asked us to plant at the front of the house. We had done our best, but whether the Pope would notice was another matter.

The fact that an Anglican was asked to carry out work for a Catholic institution was taken as an exercise in ecumenism. I was bombarded with letters, articles about the venture appeared in the British press and I was interviewed for the Home Service of the BBC. *The Daily Telegraph* wrote:

Anglicans in Jerusalem are playing an unexpected part in the welcome to the Pope on his forthcoming visit. To beautify the approach to the house of the Apostolic Delegate at which he will stay, Mr John Rose, warden of the hostel attached to the Collegiate Church of Saint George, is busy transplanting flowers and shrubs from the Protestant garden.

In a BBC report Alan McGregor said:

In this atmosphere of renewed Christian concord, the Church of England has given emergency help to the Catholics in a rushed job to get the garden of the Apostolic Delegate's residence into a fit condition to meet the Pope's eyes. The garden of the house, which is about half way up the Mount of Olives, has been long neglected. Once the immediate excitement and jubiliation over the announcement of the Pope's coming diminished, one Catholic's first thought was: 'What about the garden?' In desperation the Catholics turned to the best-known amateur gardener in Jerusalem, Mr John Rose, organist, and accountant at the Anglican Cathedral and hostel of St George. He agreed to help and was given a taskforce of a dozen gardeners. 'I was told I could take anything from the Garden of Gethsemane,' he said. The garden is now a mass of evergreens,

256 ARMENIANS OF JERUSALEM

young cypress, and carnations. 'The Vatican gardens could not do better,' commented a priest admiringly.

From the Secretary of the Council of Christians and Jews, the Rev W. W. Simpson:

> I am delighted to read that you have been asked to reorganize the gardens at the Apostolic Delegate's house. This, apart from being a delightful piece of ecumenism, is an honour well deserved, for I have the most vivid and happy memories of the wonderful garden at St George's when I was on a visit in June 1962.

The whole of Jerusalem, rich and poor, Muslim and Christian, nuns and priests, turned out to greet the Pope. The visit was interpreted as a good omen – that peace might return to the Holy Land. After a stop at the Place of Baptism at the Jordan river, the motorcade continued to Jerusalem, pausing at Bethany where His Holiness was greeted by the Muhafiz, protector of the Holy Places. The day was bitterly cold, but the area around the Damascus Gate was crammed with expectant people waiting as though to get a glimpse of a saint. It was an extraordinary moment of hope and joy, which we shared standing by the wall of the municipal gardens outside the Damascus Gate.

When His Holiness arrived there was an awed silence while he was carried shoulder-high into the Old City. He went first to the Church of the Holy Sepulchre, where Mass was celebrated. During his stay the Pope exchanged visits with patriarchs, and was called on by Christian and Muslim leaders. On a short trip to Galilee in Israel the Pope visited Nazareth and other Christian sites. Unprecedented permission was granted for cars with Jordanian drivers to cross the lines carrying members of the entourage. Samir Khayo, our hostel driver, who had never been to Israel before, was one of these.

The visit over, I received a letter from Lino Zanini, Apostolic Delegate, dated 13 January 1964:

> The beautiful garden that with so much painstaking care you have prepared for the coming of the Holy Father invites me to thank you and to assure you that everybody has been delighted with the wonderful work that has been carried out by you. Rest

WARDEN OF ST GEORGE'S HOSTEL 257

assured of my gratitude while I implore upon you and all you have at heart God's choicest blessings. Kindly accept the little souvenir I enclose herewith as a memento of the happy event.

The mementos mentioned were a papal medal, a key-holder with the papal arms, and a signed photo of the Pope.

In 1962 Nancy Drew, the archbishop's secretary, resigned and left to get married. She was succeeded by Montagu Lucy Buxton, who came out for three years. I was attracted to her from the moment I set eyes on her and in time we struck up a friendship based on shared interests. In our spare time we would go into the country botanizing and visiting archaeological sites. I introduced her to some of my favourite childhood haunts, above all Khalet el 'Addas near Ramallah and the hills around Jifna, where in the spring there was an abundance of wild flowers.

We were invited by the hostel staff to their villages, particularly during the olive-picking season when we picnicked with them on the terraces. When the Archbishop's gardener, Hajj Hassan, retired after many years of service we frequently went and visited him in his home at Beit Iksa. We sat on the balcony chatting away, in the distance the minaret of the mosque at Nebi Samwil dominating the countryside. Before offering us tea in fine teacups (given years ago by Bishop Blyth) the Hajjeh used to go out, tin can in hand, to milk her unruly goat.

We often drove to the Wadi Shu'eib in east Jordan to see the black irises and the fritillaries that grew in the valley there. We never tired of walking down the Wadi Qelt to the monastery of St George Couziba perched high on the side of a cliff and surrounded by hermits' caves. In the little church we visited a favourite ikon (Our Lady of Tenderness), said to have been discovered in a cave. We would sometimes take a precarious path to Jericho. On the way we silently passed a hermit reading his bible outside his cave on a ledge below. We followed the wadi until we reached aunt Malakeh's house. After a rest we returned by bus to Jerusalem, in itself a fascinating journey. Looking south to the Dead Sea, the headland on the west concealed the Qumran caves. At one point along the road the minarets and domes of the Nebi Musa would appear for a moment on the distant skyline, then disappear into the desert landscape. In the late afternoon groups of gerbils used to leave their burrows and stand

258 ARMENIANS OF JERUSALEM

upright, sniffing the cool air and inquisitively viewing the scene around them.

During the winter we regularly visited Jericho and spent the afternoon relaxing in my aunt's house and garden, where she lived from October to May. As soon as the citrus came into season in December Abu Ali, the gardener, would have sacks of fruit ready for us to take back to the hostel. Before Christmas aunt Malakeh gave us large sprays of red poinsettias for decorating the cathedral.

Christmas was a busy time at the close. On Christmas Eve after an early supper pilgrims would leave for Bethlehem by bus, accompanied by the clergy. There carols were sung in the courtyard of the Greek Orthodox Church in accordance with the permission granted by the patriarch years before. On return it was time for the sung midnight Eucharist, for which the cathedral was always full. On Christmas Day the archbishop preached in a packed church beautifully decorated by Lilian Zimmerman and her team. For all these services I prepared Christmas music and Miss Siranoush and her choir of blind girls sang a selection of carols.

After a delicious Christmas Day lunch prepared by Abu William, the domestic staff were sent home. That afternoon Canon and Mrs Every would invite friends for tea and to listen to the Queen's speech. In the evening the archbishop and Mrs MacInnes would invite the staff and all visitors staying at the hostel to a buffet supper. This was followed by charades, usually organized by Canon Edward Every. The evening ended with the singing of carols chosen by the guests.

In April 1965 Monty and I announced our engagement – an event that was expected but nevertheless caused a stir. Some missionaries had the old-fashioned notion that we were disloyal, as once working for the church we should be committed to our jobs for life as they were.

Our wedding took place on 29 May 1965 at St George's Cathedral. We were married by Archbishop MacInnes, Harold Adkins was best man and Augustin L'ama, organist at the Church of the Holy Sepulchre, played for the service. Here was another example of ecumenism. Mrs Zimmerman made the arrangements for a reception in the hostel gardens, a cosmopolitan affair made up primarily of Armenians and all the Arab staff of St George's. Monty's brother, stepmother and aunt came out for the occasion, together with a friend, Katharine Butler. My mother was away in England and aunt Isquhie was shut off on the other side of Jerusalem, but aunt Malakeh took

WARDEN OF ST GEORGE'S HOSTEL

their place, looking well in a smart dress and hat instead of her usual drab nurse's uniform. And so started what proved to be a very happy life. When we returned from a honeymoon in Greece Monty continued to work in the archbishop's office for a while until the new secretary, Miss Jean Waddell, arrived in September. For a while longer our busy and interesting life at the close went on, but somehow it was too good to be true. At the time we were scarcely aware that clouds of war were gathering over the country once again.

28 THE 1967 WAR AND ITS AFTERMATH

Towards the end of 1966 it looked as if the Middle East was indeed heading for war. The fragile situation of 'no war, no peace' which had lingered since 1948 was becoming intolerable. Over the years there had been many hostile incidents, but matters were brought to a head on 13 November 1966, when the Israeli army launched a massive attack on the undefended Arab village of Samu' in the Hebron hills. Many villagers died and the destruction of property was immense. The incident provoked riots all over the West Bank of the Jordan as well as in Amman. King Hussein nearly lost his throne and the army was brought out to restore order.

Discontent among the Palestinians had been brewing for some time. They felt that the king was not doing enough for them militarily or economically, and many in the West Bank and refugee camps wished to be independent of Jordan. The inhabitants of border villages criticized the Jordanian army for failing to protect them against Israeli incursions. In fact it was widely believed that Jordan wanted to keep in line with the policies of Britain, America and Israel. I myself was a great supporter of the king and argued with my Palestinian friends that it was far better to remain under Jordanian rule until a political settlement was agreed.

Early in 1967 border clashes resumed and on 7 April there were serious skirmishes in the demilitarized zones on the eastern shore of the Sea of Galilee close to the Syrian frontier. Against United Nations ruling the zones had been illegally occupied by Israeli forces, a cause of constant unrest in the area. By 14 May rumours had spread that there was to be war between Syria and Israel. Many foreign residents, especially those with young children, began to leave Jerusalem and tourism dwindled.

THE 1967 WAR AND ITS AFTERMATH

It was feared that war would spread and involve Jordan, panic set in and there was a mad rush to purchase food – dry stores, cooking oil and tinned products. Again candles were laid in and lamps put into working order, tins of paraffin filled and bidons of butagaz stocked. At St George's I laid in a huge store which included sacks of flour, potatoes, onions and tinned vegetables. Fresh meat, poultry, frozen fish packets and butter were packed into the deep-freeze. We already had a large supply of home-made jams and marmalade. In case of emergency we had three full rainwater cisterns within the close compound.

It was hoped that these precautions would not be necessary. For the moment there was no outward sign of a build-up of Jordanian soldiers in Jerusalem, no organized training for civil defence or first aid. Tension was heightened by rumours, and the ensuing preparations were not new to me: I had been through it all in the months preceding the 1948 war.

On 18 May Egypt called for the total withdrawal of UN forces from Sinai, where they had been stationed since the Suez crisis. On 21 May Sharm el Sheikh was occupied by Egyptian forces and the next day the Straits of Tiran were closed to Israeli shipping bound for the Red Sea port of Eilat.

On 30 May 1967 King Hussein of Jordan followed Syria and signed a defence pact with Egypt. Our hopes for peace were raised when President Nasser agreed to send Vice-President Zakariya Muhieddin to Washington on 7 June, to negotiate and settle the thorny question of the Straits of Tiran. This news, combined with our trust in the United Nations, relieved our immediate fear of war.

On Monday 5 June it was business as usual in east Jerusalem. As a precaution the boarding-house of St George's School had closed the previous Friday, and 40 boys, many of whom came from surrounding Arab states, had left by bus for Amman. However on Monday morning many pupils came in to sit for GCE exams, while teachers were busy correcting papers and writing reports.

I was out shopping in the Old City when I was told that the Egyptian air force had been totally destroyed on the ground and war had started. Destruction of Syrian, Jordanian and Iraqi planes followed, opening the way for Israeli forces to over-run the Sinai, the West Bank and part of the Golan Heights. The Arab forces were now unable to put up any defence.

So far there was no attack on east Jerusalem, but the atmosphere

262 ARMENIANS OF JERUSALEM

was very fragile and tense. As soon as news of the attack on Egypt was received, the headmaster, Harold Adkins, closed St George's School just in time for the boys and Arab teachers to leave for home before all transport came to a halt. The few remaining British staff and the headmaster, together with one pupil, Samir Mahir, who was unable to get away, moved into the hostel. Jordanian soldiers, who had briefly been stationed on the roof of the school building, left in a hurry and the compound which lay on the front line was deserted.

By late morning there was an eerie silence in the streets, no traffic moved and we could hear occasional gunfire. I managed to go across the road to bring my mother into the close, and to my amazement found she was unaware of the disastrous turn of events and only reluctantly agreed to come with me.

The archbishop had given permission for George Bazuzi, his driver, Emile Bajjali, the *kawas*, and 'Issa Kitaneh, the works foreman, to move into the scouts' room in the basement of school house with their families. They were joined by my mother's landlady, Umm Zaki Nuseibeh, and her three children, making a total of 24 people. The archbishop and Mrs MacInnes stayed in their house with their domestic staff, Abdu, Jamileh and Lydia. Hajj Hassan, the gardener, with his wife, the Hajjeh, had gone home to Beit Iksa. Miss Margaret Aplin, domestic bursar of St George's College, stayed on in that building, together with the housekeeper, Miss Abla, and Umm Saleh, the washerwoman, who was unable to return to her village. Bishop and Mrs Najib Cuba'in, who had for some time lived in the ground-floor flat of the college, did not move. In fact 65 people were now trapped in the close.

As lunch was about to start there was an enormous explosion nearby and most of the windows throughout the close were shattered. Piles of jagged glass built up in the hostel cloisters. For weeks we were too shocked and preoccupied to do more than sweep them to one side. By then all but three of the domestic staff had left for home without saying a word to anyone. The acting cook, Dimitri, Abu Karim, the marmiton, and Omar stayed on. The dish of the day was meatballs in tomato sauce. While Dimitri was carrying the food from the kitchen to the diningroom he slipped and fell, and his white uniform was covered with red sauce. We heard the crash, thought he had been wounded by a sniper and rushed out, but found he was unharmed and amused at our concern. Later Dimitri and Abu Karim were not to be found: they had disappeared through the back door, again without

THE 1967 WAR AND ITS AFTERMATH 263

saying a word. They had taken a desperate risk to join their families in the Old City, which we well understood. The only member of staff left was Omar, cut off from his wife, baby and relatives, who were living in 'Aqbet Jaber refugee camp in Jericho.

We were caught by surprise and had made no preparations against attack. At the eleventh hour Omar suggested filling sacks of earth to barricade the slit windows (at ground-level on the Nablus road) in the cellar which we planned to use as a shelter. That afternoon our neighbours the Larssons (Herbert, Titty and their three daughters, as well as old Mrs Edith Larsson), rushed into the close and asked if they might stay. Their house was in the firing line and their garden backed on to the Mandelbaum Gate. They brought with them their maid, Fatoum, a survivor of the Deir Yassin massacre. Her past experience had left her in a state of terror at the thought of an Israeli attack. Soon after, Mrs Musallam, wife of Dr Musallam of Nablus hospital where she was the matron, came into the close with her daughter, Margaret, who had been sitting her GCE exams at Schmidt's Girls' School. We now had a nurse with us in addition to Mrs MacInnes, who was a doctor.

After evensong the archbishop and Mrs MacInnes joined us for a light supper in the hostel dining-room. Monty and I assisted Omar with serving and clearing up, which we continued to do from then on. All the while we could hear distant gunfire, which at nightfall came closer and developed into heavy shelling. Most of us went down to the hostel cellar to take shelter but my mother, whose experience of warfare went back to 1914, refused to join us. She stayed in a room on the ground floor, changed and went to bed as usual. Canon and Mrs Zimmerman, Miss Elinor Moore and the Larsson family stayed up all night in the stair-well of the clergy house where they thought they would be safe.

The noise was deafening, the electricity failed and the shelling intensified throughout the night. It was terrifying – first a distant rumble and seconds later a crash. In the early hours of the morning we heard tanks rolling along the Nablus road directly outside our cellar window and soldiers talking in Hebrew. Footsteps in the cloister above alarmed us still further, and we were convinced that if discovered we might all be shot dead. One of the school teachers was so terrified that he shut himself out of sight in a wall-cupboard. Our only hope was that at daybreak the senseless shelling would cease.

The night seemed endless and we got no sleep. As dawn broke on

264 ARMENIANS OF JERUSALEM

6 June the sparrows in the pines in the garden burst into their usual song and then fell silent at one stroke. All the noise and banging had failed to change their habits. I climbed the cellar stairs cautiously and looked north towards the American Colony, only to see the loft of the Nuseibeh house in flames. On the hostel roof the laundry hung out the previous morning was riddled with bullet holes.

At about 8 a.m. the shelling eased and I crept up to our rooms above the cellar. Unseen, I peered through the Venetian blinds at the Israeli tanks in the Nablus road below. The headmaster's flat over the school across the way had received a direct hit and was on fire. Worst of all, there were many bodies of Arab soldiers lying dead in the street.

The close and hostel buildings shielded us from sniper fire, enabling Omar and me to get to the kitchen and fetch food to the cellar. We found that there was no water, for our large tank on the roof had been punctured by shrapnel. The municipal supply had also been cut off and we resorted to the cisterns.

Our telephone was dead but later that morning to my astonishment it gave a ring. I found it was Haidar Husseini, manager of the Arab Bank in Jerusalem, who was sheltering with many others in the telephone exchange in the basement of the post office at Herod's Gate. Although the exchange was out of action, one of the engineers had cleverly made the connection. Haidar urgently asked for the archbishop to contact the Red Cross and the United Nations, since the group, all civilians including women and children, had been without food and water for 24 hours and were prevented from leaving. As he finished speaking the telephone went dead again, and remained so for a long time. I passed the message on to the archbishop, but there was little he could do, as he himself was unable to communicate with anyone outside the close.

Battles in and around Jerusalem intensified and towards evening heavy shelling resumed. Jordanian guns were firing from the vicinity of the Mount of Olives on Jewish positions in the west of the city; the fire was returned. Most of the shells flew over our area but two crashed into the south-west corner of the quadrangle demolishing a buttress and beheading a *banksiae* rose. The cathedral also suffered damage: an unexploded phosphorus shell fell into the north transept, scattering its contents. Later, when sweeping up, the brooms caught fire.

For us in the cellar it was another terrifying night and we did not think we would see the light of day again. On 7 June we heard on the

THE 1967 WAR AND ITS AFTERMATH 265

radio that east Jerusalem had surrendered to the Israelis. The Jordanian army had withdrawn and there were only small pockets of resistance left. After consultations between the mayor, the Supreme Muslim Council and other religious dignitaries it had been decided to accept defeat as the only way to save the city from further destruction. On hearing this news I thought it prudent to make a white flag from an old sheet and hang it out from the back entrance of the hostel. The wooden door had been reduced to matchwood and there was blood all over the corridor and on the floor of two of the guest rooms.

Outside, in Salah el Din street, stood a dreadful symbol of war. A small Red Crescent ambulance carrying four stretcher cases had been incinerated by napalm. The intense heat had blackened and crumbled the stones of the outer wall of the hostel building. In the streets around, and on the school playing field, lay many bodies of Arab fighters. With the heat, the stench soon reeked throughout the close and became intolerable. In spite of repeated requests from the archbishop, more than a week passed before their removal. When this happened we watched through the hostel windows as masked men removed identity cards from the bodies, which were then carried away on trucks.

The war did not stop with the surrender of Jerusalem, the West Bank was over-run and one Arab town after another fell. There was stiff resistance in the north before the Jordanian army retreated. Once over the Jordan river they blew up the Allenby Bridge behind them. On the evening of 8 June the whole of the West Bank was under the control of the Israelis and a new era had begun.

The Egyptian army in Sinai had been routed, with 10,000 dead and 13,000 captured. On 7 June the Israeli forces had reached Sharm el Sheikh overlooking the Straits of Tiran and by 9 June the banks of the Suez Canal. Israel now turned to Syria and on 10 June, after fierce battles, the Golan Heights were captured, Kuneitra sacked and 17,000 inhabitants made homeless. A ceasefire went into effect but two days later the Israelis seized the stronghold of Mount Hermon which became an important listening-post for them.

Now that war had ended on all fronts we were able to return to our rooms upstairs and take meals in the dining-room, regularly joined by Archbishop and Mrs MacInnes. As there was no electricity, meal times were changed and evensong was said at four in the afternoon. Mrs MacInnes arranged for Jamileh, one of her staff, to come and

266 ARMENIANS OF JERUSALEM

cook for everyone. Fatoum, the Larssons' maid, kneaded dough for our bread.

A total curfew was in force, confining us to the close, but we were at last able to contact our colleagues in the college and scout room. We found them shattered but safe. They had heard calls for help from a wounded Arab soldier but were unable to reach him. He now lay dead in the school courtyard and all we could do was to cover his body with a blanket.

The 24 inmates sheltering in the scouts' room had run out of food, but we arranged for Abu Albert, the works manager, to collect their daily needs from my store in the hostel. Luckily the deep-freeze had not been defrosted for a long time and the thickness of accumulated ice preserved the contents until power was restored.

We were still cut off from the outside world. Towards the end of the week a group of people led by Père Couasnon, a Dominican father, carrying a white flag, arrived at the main gate. They had taken refuge from the shelling in the gardens of the Ecole Biblique, and spent several nights in the open under the trees. Their food had run out and they were now attempting to return to their homes. Among them was Mrs Mattar, wife of the warden of the Garden Tomb. She told us that very early on 6 June her husband had responded to a knock on the gate, opened up and was shot dead. Mrs Mattar and a young secretary, who were both in a state of shock, stayed with us for a while until they were able to leave the country.

One morning Israeli officials arrived to register the inmates of the close. Abdu, the archbishop's cook, who was Egyptian, was arrested, taken away to prison and later deported to Egypt. Soon after, Druze soldiers attached to the Israeli army were put on duty around the compound to observe our movements. We did not get a sympathetic smile out of them. The main entrance to the close remained shut and we were given a poster to hang on the gate which read, in Hebrew, English and Arabic: 'Holy Place. Unauthorized entrance forbidden.' These posters were issued to every religious institution in east Jerusalem.

After a week loudspeakers announced that the curfew would be lifted for a few hours every afternoon. On the first day Monty and I went straight to the Old City to see what had happened to aunt Malakeh and Sahag. Warily we walked down to the Damascus Gate, threading our way through fallen telephone and electricity wires, on a road strewn with spent cartridges which crunched under our feet like

THE 1967 WAR AND ITS AFTERMATH 267

shingle on a beach. We could see that the people we passed on the way were dazed, but greetings were exchanged by everyone, friend and stranger alike: '*Hamdulillah bisalameh*' (Thank God for your safety). It was indeed very touching. Just past the Garden Tomb a pile of bodies lay covered up with blankets. Hundreds of people were trying to get into the Old City through the gate which was now manned by Israeli soldiers. Identity cards or passports had to be shown before anyone was let through.

All the shops in the *suq* were shut and groups of people who had lived in the Jewish quarter in the Old City since 1948 were moving out in haste with as many belongings as they could, to become refugees yet again. Aunt Malakeh and Sahag were very pleased to see us and told us how they had sheltered under the dining-room table during the bombardment. They were worried about their house in Jericho, but were not in urgent need of anything and we promised to come again soon.

The people of Arab east Jerusalem and towns in the West Bank had decided that this time they would not leave their homes and run away in the face of war. This in spite of the fact that they were informed through loudspeakers that the Allenby Bridge, though damaged, would be open for a few days. Buses to the bridge were to be provided by the Israeli authorities from the Damascus Gate. However, many did leave to join their families, amongst them Fatoum who wasted no time in getting away.

Before the curfew was completely lifted we had an unexpected visit from aunt Isquhie. Herbert and Marcella Minard of the YMCA brought her over to St George's. My mother was delighted to see her, but Isquhie could not stay long and we were so overwhelmed by what had happened that it was difficult to put our feelings into words. We promised that as soon as possible we would visit her in the Baqa'a.

On 26 June residents of east Jerusalem were issued with temporary identification papers and were instructed to present them later in exchange for Israeli identity cards. Telephones were linked to the main post office in west Jerusalem and new post box numbers allocated. Israeli driving licences were issued, and special car number plates differentiating residents of East Jerusalem from Israel or the West Bank were distributed.

As soon as we could we drove Omar to Jericho to find out what had happened to his family. Monty came with us and we went down the familiar road through Bethany, now littered with reminders of war.

268 ARMENIANS OF JERUSALEM

Our papers were checked once at Khan el Ahmar, the Inn of the Good Samaritan. All along the road were burned-out Jordanian tanks. At intervals small trucks full of personal belongings had been strafed and private cars had been flattened while making their way to Amman. Where were the occupants now, we wondered? Ironically, wooden crates marked with clasped hands of friendship, the American flag and the words 'Gift of the United States of America' lay in piles beside the road, still full of ammunition. To add insult to injury, at the entrance to Jericho a pair of military boots was hanging from a sign welcoming visitors to the town.

As far as the eye could see flame trees covered in red flowers lined the road to Jericho and beyond. We found the 'Aqbat Jaber camp deserted. Panic had set in when flares were dropped and almost all the 3,000 inhabitants had fled across the Jordan river before the Israeli army arrived. Omar directed us to the part of the camp where his family had lived. One of his cousins appeared and he told us that Umm Ali, her daughters and sons, with Omar's wife and baby, had all left. This was the second time the family had become refugees, and to this day they live in a camp outside Zerqa in east Jordan.

The empty house was a sorry sight. In the garden a pen full of rabbits had been abandoned. All were lying dead except one, which Omar retrieved. This scene brought back memories of the cage of dead pigeons I had come across in the Baqa'a in 1948. As we could hear gunfire from the direction of the Jordan river and the road was crowded with military patrols we did not go into the town, and returned to Jerusalem before dark.

After the curfew was lifted shops reopened and the Jewish inhabitants of west Jerusalem poured into the Old City, mainly to visit the Wailing Wall which they had been unable to do for the past twenty years. Souvenir shops did a roaring trade: antique copper from Damascus, carpets and silverware were quickly lapped up at low prices. Israeli currency was introduced and the population had to exchange Jordanian dinars at a very unfavourable rate.

The hostel staff started to trickle back. Not much cleaning had been done since they left and they worked hard to put everything in order. Mousa, my right-hand man, and Yusef, the gardener, did not return: they had fled to Amman and to prevent further hardship I continued to pay wages to their families each month. Towards the end of the year Yusef suddenly reappeared and returned to work in the garden. Not long after there was great rejoicing when Omar received

THE 1967 WAR AND ITS AFTERMATH

news that Halimeh, his wife, had managed to return with their baby and was sheltering in Jericho. Mousa, who had found work at the Terra Sancta College in Amman, did not come back for over two years, when with great difficulty Archbishop Appleton managed to get a permit for his return.

Apart from the permanent hostel residents, we had very few visitors from abroad. The situation was still tense and sporadic gunfire, especially at night, continued for a long while. We took the opportunity to repair war damage and to replace broken glass. One morning the Israeli army informed us that they were going to blow up all the ruined buildings to the west of St George's in what had been for the past twenty years no-man's-land. We took precautions and opened all the windows but this was not enough. The explosions were so thunderous that all the glass was shattered once again, cracks appeared in ceilings and walls and lumps of plaster fell to the ground. Blasting, bulldozing and levelling went on day after day all around Jerusalem. It took us some months to repair all the war damage to the close, cathedral, hostel, college and school. Once done, the cost was reimbursed by the Israeli Ministry of Religious Affairs.

Damaged buildings outside the walls in the Jaffa Gate area were cleared away and in time gardens put in their place. The ancient city walls were now exposed to view. The demarcation wall dividing the city, built in 1948 outside the Damascus Gate across Suleiman's Way (renamed Paratroopers' Way), was demolished along with many buildings bordering Prophets' Street in the Musrara area. Traffic lights were installed, and traffic flowed again between east and west Jerusalem.

In 1968 an 'open bridge' policy was agreed by Jordan and Israel. This enabled residents of the West Bank to obtain permits to cross into Jordan for short periods and back again. The rule did not apply to people who either had been trapped over there or had moved to east Jordan during the war. They were not allowed to return.

No Arab bank reopened after the war. Our bank, the Ottoman, now held all clients' accounts in Amman. Until money was transferred from our London headquarters, we had to draw on mission funds at Barclay's Bank in west Jerusalem. Early in September 1968 I was given permission to accompany the archbishop to Amman where we were to arrange for the mission funds to be released. As accountant my signature was required before the transaction could go through. We left early, driven by George Bazuzi, and spent two nights at the

270 ARMENIANS OF JERUSALEM

Ahliyyeh Girls' School. When our business was successfully completed we paid a short visit to Miss Coate, who since 1948 had been working among Palestinian refugees. Discovering water in the desert near Zerqa, Miss Coate organized a new farming co-operative named Abdulliyyeh where many families were settled. On our return to Jerusalem I gave back my temporary British passport to the consulate and I never crossed over to Amman again.

Religious dignitaries were allowed through with their cars, but for Arab residents of the West Bank and Jerusalem the crossing of the Allenby Bridge was a long-drawn-out ordeal. For fear of terrorist acts, even stricter Israeli security regulations were imposed – long waits, humiliating searches and the confiscation of personal belongings. Many people, especially the elderly, could not face this experience and had to rely on others to do business for them in Amman. When aunt Malakeh needed to withdraw money from her savings account she had to rely on agents who charged a high fee for their services.

As things returned to normal we had applications from Jewish visitors who came to stay in the hostel. We were also visited by Jewish friends, some who had worked with me at Russell & Company, others who had been at St George's School. I was anxious to make contact with my former piano teacher, Mme Sonia Valine, and was told I could do so through the Rubin Academy of Music in west Jerusalem. I went to a concert there and found she was in the audience. It was a lovely meeting and from then on we resumed our musical rapport. She agreed to give me a lesson a week and we worked happily for the next eight years until I left Jerusalem.

Monty had never been to west Jerusalem, and as soon as this was possible we walked over to the Baqa'a to visit aunt Isquhie. I was also eager to show her the Greek Colony house. On the way we met many residents of the Old City setting out to visit their property in the Arab suburbs.

Aunt Isquhie was in the garden, just returned from the German Hospice where she had been working in the linen-room since retiring from the YMCA. She was delighted to see us. The place was still the same. The garden gate made its familiar creak on opening, the scent of lemon blossom and other shrubs still filled the air and chickens strutted about in the run. The middle flat, like Krikor's house next door, was now occupied by a Jewish family. Dar abu Rasim were still on the ground floor. The whole visit was like a dream.

We walked over to the Greek Colony house which I had not seen

THE 1967 WAR AND ITS AFTERMATH 271

for the past thirteen years. The surrounding area was in a delapidated condition with overgrown trees, many of them standing dead in untended gardens. The mud road, which had been such an annoyance to the residents of the Greek Colony, had been tarred. The fields where as children we had picked anemones and cyclamen had disappeared under a mass of high-rise buildings. These tenements, which stretched out to encompass the Arab village of Beit Safafa, obliterated the view between the house, the Katamon and the Bethlehem hills. I felt as though I had been long-since dead and was desperately trying to recapture a lovely life which had vanished. In the 1980s our Greek Colony house was pulled down and replaced by another high-rise building. The scene where I had been able to dream of the past had been removed and perhaps it was a good thing.

In November 1968 Archbishop MacInnes retired and was succeeded by George Appleton, former Archbishop of Perth, Western Australia. He was enthroned in the cathedral on Sunday 23 March 1969 on a bitterly cold day. The ceremony took place in the presence of many dignitaries, including this time a representative from the Israeli Ministry of Religious Affairs. Archbishop Appleton had the difficult task of formulating the future shape of this province of the Anglican church. The Jerusalem and the East Mission was to transfer its work to the Arab church led by their own bishop in Jerusalem. It took five years to accomplish this.

Life in Jerusalem changed rapidly. We were now geared to the Israeli economy and the Arab population in the 'occupied territories' adapted to a modern way of life. There was plenty of work in Jewish factories and farms, and above all in the construction sector where skilled Arab stonemasons and builders were much in demand. Living conditions improved, there was money around and many people could afford cars and other luxuries. The Old City of Jerusalem was losing its Arab character. Shops were modernized and many traditional trades vanished, making way for the sale of souvenirs, soft drinks and snacks to the thousands of visitors that poured into the city daily. New suburbs with high-rise buildings quickly went up on the hills around, encircling the city with a noose of concrete. However this did not mean that the population had accepted as permanent the Israeli occupation of their land and towns. On the contrary, as time dragged on we were plagued by uncertainty, strikes and violence: for us this meant that we were unable to go on long botanical walks into the surrounding country, or to visit our favourite haunts.

272 ARMENIANS OF JERUSALEM

Discontent was expressed by owners of property in the Arab suburbs of west Jerusalem who assumed that they could claim their houses back or receive rents from them. The answer they got was: 'When King Hussein makes peace with us you can have your property back.' This was very hard on many people who had been living in unsuitable conditions for the past twenty years. A case in point was Dar el Terzibash, the family of the Armenian tailor, who owned four houses in west Jerusalem (two in the Baqa'a and two in Ethiopian Street) and to this day live in one room in the Armenian convent.

As the economy was in the grip of inflation, income from hostel visitors was not enough to cover expenses. To overcome this it was agreed that the college kitchen should close and the domestic side be directed from the hostel. This meant much more work for me – overseeing staff in another building and catering for much larger numbers. To do this I converted a hostel room into a dining-room annexe. I was also made responsible for the college accounts.

After the war the close and hostel went through a gradual change. It was the day and age for tour groups and youngsters seeking cheap accommodation. The word 'hostel' always attracted the latter, who were disappointed to find that it was not the usual establishment for them to doss down in. Formality, now considered stuffy, was swept away and scantily dressed guests appeared in the dining-room. Nevertheless I tried my best to keep up the standards for which the hostel had been well-known in the past.

In March 1974 Archbishop Appleton retired, after five years of painstaking efforts to build peace between Arabs and Jews. He was succeeded by a Vicar-General, Bishop Robert Stopford, former Bishop of London, who had the difficult task of arranging the new constitution for the episcopal church in Jerusalem and the Middle East.

I had now completed twenty years service at St George's, under two bishops and two archbishops, and I decided that it was time for me to move on and give a chance to someone younger and with modern ideas. I regretted that I was leaving the close just when a historic event was about to take place, the consecration of the first Arab bishop in Jerusalem. My resignation caused a stir and pressure was put upon me to change my mind. We had planned to return to England, but were diverted when the Ecumenical Institute for Advanced Theological Studies at Tantur asked me to come and work for them in the same capacity. The contract was to be for two years,

THE 1967 WAR AND ITS AFTERMATH 273

and I accepted the challenge of joining one of the most modern institutions in Jerusalem.

The domestic staff at St George's were deeply disturbed. Over the years a bond had been formed between us: they shared their many problems and relied on me, especially during times of crisis. I received many letters from friends wishing me well, and I quote one from J. B. Wilson, secretary of the Jerusalem and the East Mission of 23 May 1974:

> At the Directors' Meeting on 21st May Bishop Stopford referred to your impending retirement, and I was instructed to write to you and express (or try to express) the shock that this news was, the regret everyone felt at your departure, but more than all else the gratitude for all that you have done for the Mission over the past twenty years. It is not for the Directors to comment on your work done in the garden, your domestic economy measures in the Hostel, or your organ playing qualities, but they do feel deeply beholden to you for the way in which you have looked after their financial interests and disentangled knots that must often have appeared deliberately tied up by us in Warwick Square.
>
> They asked me also to express their gratitude to Monty for all her back-stage help and support, and to give you their good wishes for the future, hoping that you would maintain your links with the Mission and be a bridge over the gap between Tantur and Warwick Square.

It was a very sad day for us when we left St George's. It had been my home for so long, modelled on experience gained from my Armenian relatives and my life at home in the Greek Colony. I showed no emotion but in private I broke down after playing the organ for Matins on my last Sunday at St George's. The instrument, which I knew intimately, had been my friend for so long. I shut the lid on the keyboard and burst into a flood of tears.

At the end of September 1974, after spending two months in England, we returned to our luxury flat at the Ecumenical Institute, Tantur. It took some time to adapt to a modern building run on American lines. Everything was vast, the most up-to-date kitchen, scullery with commercial dishwashers, a parlour for making pastry and icecreams, and a machine churning out ice cubes (a 'must' for

274 ARMENIANS OF JERUSALEM

Americans) 24 hours a day. All this was a far cry from the old world I had been used to at St George's.

The institute, situated on a hilltop between Jerusalem and Bethlehem, was surrounded by extensive grounds, parts of which were wooded. I soon won the confidence of Sheikh Yusef, the gardener, and we formed a happy working relationship. He had escaped from his village, Zakariya, during the 1948 war. Since then he lived with his family in the Dheisheh refugee camp near Bethlehem.

During my time at Tantur I did not visit St George's, adhering to the motto: 'The king is dead. Long live the king.' When I passed the cathedral and close in a bus or car I would turn my face the other way. No one could understand why I behaved like that. On the other hand I was constantly visited by the St George's staff.

In November 1974 Sahag, Malakeh's husband, died of a heart attack during the night while in Jericho. He was 71 years old. Malakeh was on her own and went out to call her neighbour, the Coptic priest Abuna Nahmias, for help. She rang me next morning and asked me to make arrangements for the funeral to be held that afternoon at the Church of the Holy Archangels followed by burial in Pergeech. My mother and her two sisters now had to depend on me alone, since all other members of the family had left Jerusalem in the exodus of 1948.

When my contract at Tantur ended in 1976 we decided to return to England and live in our house in the village of Long Wittenham in Oxfordshire. My mother was already in England with my sister Gertie. This was to be the second time that I had to abandon aunt Isquhie, now in her eighties. Again she had a philosophical approach to my decision, letting it be known that all she wanted was to die in Jerusalem. Her Jewish neighbours in the flat below, Eric and Giti Cohen, with their young children, were of tremendous help to her over the years. Without them to rely on it would have been impossible for aunt Isquhie to be independent and stay on in her own flat. Aunt Malakeh who was in poor health, chose to come with us to England.

To leave Jerusalem, this time for good, was the most difficult step I had ever taken during my life. However, with aunt Isquhie still living there we had the best reason to go out and stay with her every year. This gave her the greatest pleasure and she always maintained that our visits made her live longer.

My mother, Margaret, widowed for 34 years, was the first to die. Like her grandmother, Anna Lüleji Minassian, she gradually failed, and died at the age of 95 in 1985. Eighteen months later Malakeh

THE 1967 WAR AND ITS AFTERMATH 275

also died aged 95 and was buried in the Long Wittenham churchyard. Inscribed on her gravestone are the words: 'Takouhie Gazmararian 1891–1986 Devoted nurse and midwife, Beirut – Aleppo – Jerusalem. *Hanqisd*' (Rest in peace). Isquhie lived on until she was 96, all the while in command of her faculties and household. She had a genius for friendship. Age was no barrier, and talking to her I felt, as did other people, that I was in the presence of a person of my own generation. She always treated me as a young person.

By a sheer stroke of luck Monty and I were staying with her when she fell and broke her hip. She was admitted to the Hadassah Hospital in 'Ain Karim where the surgeons did their best for her. At her age the chance of recovery was slight, and after a long struggle she was moved to the French hospital of St Louis, where she was lovingly nursed until she died on 31 December 1989. The *mukhtar* of the Armenian Quarter, Garabed Hagopian, made all arrangements for the funeral service in the chapel of Etchmiadzin in the Cathedral of Saint James, since the Church of the Holy Archangels was undergoing repairs. Many other *kaghakatsi* friends also helped and supported us during this very difficult time. The service was conducted by a bishop, with three priests and twenty seminarians. Among the many who attended were Armenians, Jews and Arabs. A *kawas* led the procession to Pergeech, where she was laid to rest next to her father, Melkon the barber.

With her death the line of an ancient *kaghakatsi* family in Jerusalem has ended. There are no more Krikorians or Melkonians left, and only one aged member of the Gazmararian family still lives in the Armenian Quarter. The *kaghakatsi* have now been reduced to 300 souls. The twentieth century has brought strife and uncertainty, resulting in emigration of the descendants of a community who arrived centuries ago with great hopes to settle around the Armenian Convent of Saint James in Jerusalem.

MAPS

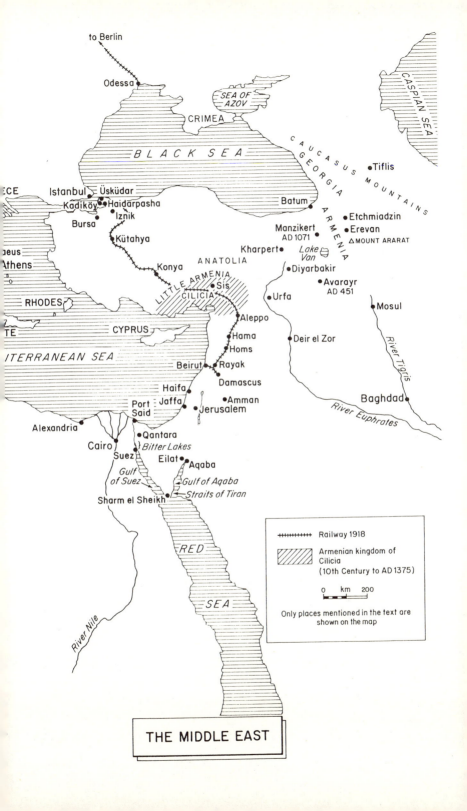

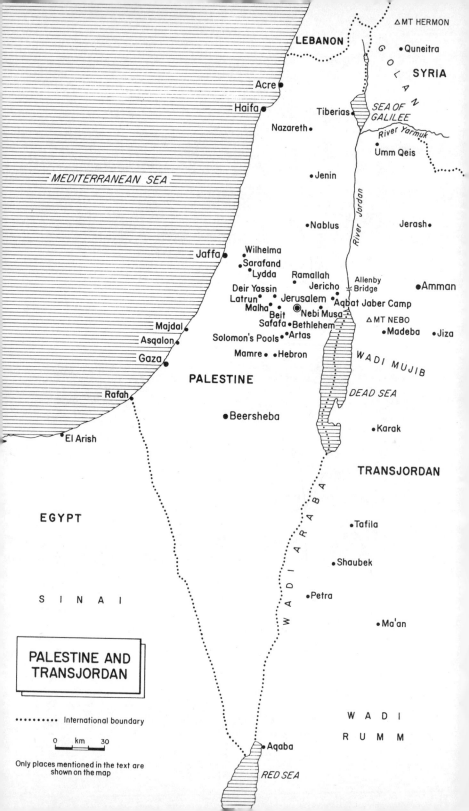

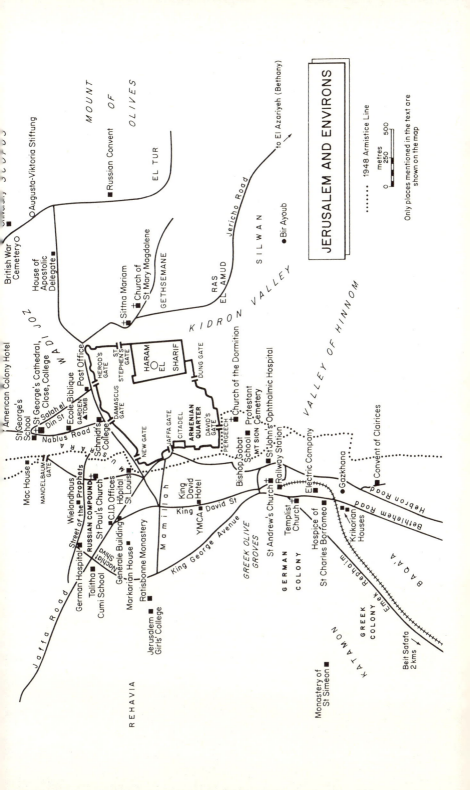

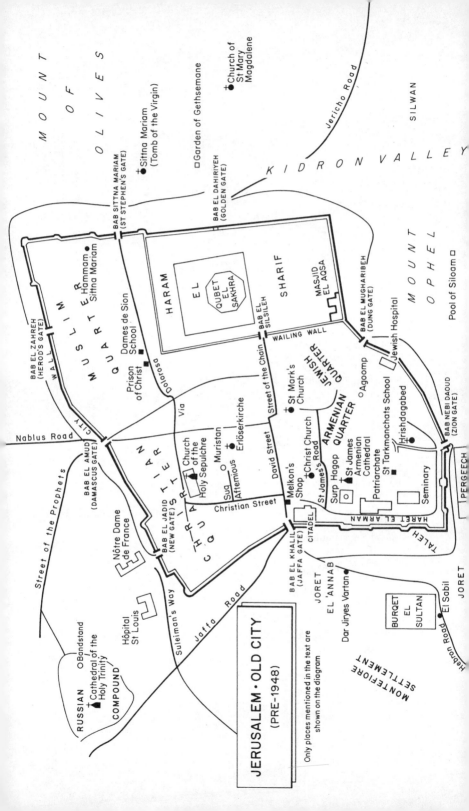

INDEX

Abu Addour 59–60
Abu Fadil, Victoria 55
Abuna Philipos 149
Abu Suan family 182
Aden 49
Adkins, Canon Harold 236, 242,
    254, 262
Afghans 110
Ain Anoub 116, 234–5
Ain Karim 46, 275
el Alami family 78
    Musa bey 241
Aleppo 57–9
    Baron hotel 62, 66
    falls to Allies 65
    military hospital 61, 68
    municipal hospital 57
    Wali of 57, 59
Alexandria 35
Allenby, General Sir Edmund 2,
    63, 83, 115; enters
    Jerusalem 64; opens
    YMCA 145
American University of Beirut 27,
    53
André family 206, 216
Antonius, Mrs George 247, 252
Aplin, Miss A. M. 262
Apostolic Delegate 254
Appleton, Archbishop George
    271–2
Aqaba 147

Arab Higher Committee 153–5,
    201
Arab Legion 197, 215
Arab Rebellion 153
Arabi, Hajj 102–3
Arabic language 6, 100, 140; in
    Braille 127
Armenia, Cilician kingdom of 4;
    King Hethum I of 12
Armenian
    Apostolic Orthodox Church 6
    Brotherhood of St James 4
    Cathedral of St James (Surp
        Hagop) 3, 46
        Etchmiadzin chapel 275
        Kilkhateer 3, 22, 164, 195
        Sunrise Office 40
    Convent of St James 3, 76,
        201
    celebrations at Christmas and
        Easter 8, 9, 81
    clinic 5, 79
    library 12
    schools: St Gayantiants and
        St Tarkmanchats (Holy
        Translators) 74, 198
    seminary 11, 21
    kaghakatsi 2, 5–6, 24, 275
    cemetery (Pergeech) 26, 27,
        158, 159, 275
    characteristics 6–7
    children vowed to the church
        22

284 INDEX

christening and name days 32–3
extended family 5
fasting 9
family names 11–12
languages 6, 17
love of order and beauty 5
mukhtar 5
trades 11, 29
parish church of the Holy
  Archangels (Hrishtagabed) 6, 15, 17, 32
khachkars in 7
registers at 7, 10, 15, 33
patriarchs of Jerusalem
  Apraham 12
  Yessayi Garabedian 31
  Guregh Israelian 198
  Mesrop Nishanian 89
  Elisha Turian 158
pilgrims 3, 4, 81
Quarter of Jerusalem 5, 11, 22
refugees 3
  in Aleppo 61
  boys at St George's school 138
  in 1948 189
Army Base Command Pay Office 160
Artas 63
Ashour 23
Asqalon 146
Audi, Hanna and family 128
Audi, Ibrahim 85
Audi, Isqhuie 184, 218, 267
Augusta-Viktoria Stiftung 79–80
Austrian Post Office 77
Ayyash, Emile 144

Baghdad Pact 241
Bajjalli, Emile 236
Balfour Declaration 65, 114, 153
Balian, Nishan 84
Baly, Denis 146
Baqa'a, Upper 23, 95, 106; in 1948 193–203
Barazani, Ahmad 236
Barclay, Bishop Joseph 132

Bassam, Colonel Maurice 201
Basuto soldiers 167
Bawarshi, Salim 50
Bawarshi, Najib 50, 236
Bayley, Miss M. M. 117
Bayyud, Munir 144
Baz, Canon Ibrahim 137
Bazuzi, George 231, 236, 269
Beersheba 26, 62–3
Begin, Menahem 166
Beidas, Professor Khalil 144
Beirut 23, 55
Beit Duqqu 238
Beit Iksa 20, 102
Beit Mahsir 248
Beit Safafa 95, 101, 215–6
Beit Suriq 238
Bells and clappers 45–6, 188, 201
Bennett, Miss Ruth 117
Berlin 68
Bernadotte, Count Folke 199, 205
Bernstein, Miss 221
Bethany 238, 267
Bir Ayoub 42
Bir el Miscob 38
Birmingham 2, 88, 183, 228
Bir Zeit 237
Bliss, Dr Daniel 53
Bliss, Mrs Daniel 56
Bliss, Dr Howard 53
Blyth, Bishop George Popham 19, 20; Jerusalem bishopric revived by 132
Blyth, Mrs 136
Boehm, Yohanan 227
Bowman, Humphrey 145
Boys' Town, Jericho 78–9
Boyadjian, Haroutiun 138, 141
Brazil 27
Buffam, Elizabeth 86
Bunche, Dr Ralph 212
Buxton, Montagu Lucy 257

Cairo 55; Bab el Luq station 170
Calendar, Julian 8

INDEX

285

Caliphs 12
Call to Prayer 40
  in Jericho 149
  from Sheikh Jarrah 248
Canada Park 241
Carmichael, Dr and Mrs H.
    Kenn 254
Chile 38
Churches
  Christ Church 14, 34
  Church of the Nativity 73, 142
  Dormition Abbey 75–6, 195
  Erlöserkirche 75
  Holy Archangels see Armenian
    parish church
  Holy Sepulchre (Church of the
    Resurrection) 9, 10, 65
    cathedral of Jerusalem 134
    repairs 105
  Holy Trinity Russian cathedral
    74
  St Andrews (Church of
    Scotland) 209
  St George's Collegiate Church
    see St George's
  St Mary Magdalene 240
  St Paul's 92, 191
  Sittna Mariam (Church of the
    Virgin Mary) 76
Church Missionary Society 40,
    55
Clark-Kerr, Rev William 209
Coate, Miss Winifred 116, 132,
    270
Cohen, Albert 215
Cohen, Erik and Giti 274
Convents and monasteries
  of the Clairices 191, 199, 201
  of the Holy Cross 3, 42
  Mar Elias 95
  of St Charles Borromeo 191
  of St James see Armenian
    convent
  of St Mark 4, 44, 247
  of St Simeon, Katamon 182
  Trappist at Latroun 240
Cook, L. D. 143

cookery and food 6, 9, 34, 77,
    151
  in Aleppo 60
  Easter cakes 33
  at St George's Hostel 246
Couasnon, Père 266
Coyle, Father Patrick 211
Cross, Miss Daisy 117
Cub'ain, Bishop and Mrs Najib
    244
cupping 100
Custodian of Enemy Property,
    British 157; Israeli 222,
    229

Dafesh, Miss Adele 127
Dale, Mrs Mary Bliss 54
Damascus 25, 65
Dar Jiyres Vartan 91
Da'uk, Omar 53
Deeb, Mrs Shukri 218
Deir Yassin 185 263
Deir el Zeitouneh see Armenian
    parish church
Djemal pasha, kütchük 20, 137
Dobree, Nicholas 234
Drew, Nancy 257

Efthimios, Archimandrite 94
Egypt 1, 26
Egypt Expeditionary Force 67, 87
Elizabeth, Grand Duchess 240
epidemics 17
  cholera in Hebron 50; in
    Jerusalem 79
  typhus in Aleppo 62
Eppinger, Frau 218
Every, Canon and Mrs Edward
    236–7

fantaziyeh 21, 26, 90
feasts
  Eid el Fitr 18
  Eid el Houriyyeh 76
  Eid el Mughrara 32
  Eid el Salib 16
  Nebi Musa 148
  Sabt el Nur 9, 21, 32, 186

286 INDEX

Sittna Mariam 76–7
Ferguson, Miss Hazel 237, 241
Four Homes of Mercy 252
French Foreign Legion 14
French hospital of St Louis 99, 275
Fulyaneh, Sitt 77

Gaghant Baban 9
Galla slaves 49
gardening *see* plants and trees
Gayane, Saint 11
Gaza 62, 178
Gazmararian family
  Garabed and Heghineh 29
  Malakeh 159
  Movses (Morris) 235
  Sahag 73
Genevisian, Tavid 20
George, Dr Ibrahim 191
Georgian, Kevork 191, 205, 215
German hospital, Jerusalem 42, 48
  in Aleppo 68
  train 66, 69
German Red Cross 62
German Templist colony 24, 38, 93
Ghazawi, Mass'ad 236
Givat Shaul 185
Glazebrook, Dr Otis 66, 137
Glubb, Lady 253
Glubb Pasha 253
Gobat, Bishop Samuel 40
Graf Zeppelin 117
Greek Colony 92, 95
  home in 178
  leaving 188
  in 1948 187
  return to house 207
Greek Orthodox liturgy 10; patriarchs 132
Gregory the Illuminator, Saint 6, 82, 163
Gumri, Wadie' 161
Gurney, Sir Henry 168

Hadassah Hospital, Ain Karim 275
Hadassah Hospital, Mount Scopus 186
Haganah 181; in Greek Colony 193
Hagopian, Garabed *mukhtar* 275
Hagopjian family 21
Haidarpasha 69
Hair Khoren 159
Hair Papken 229
el Halaby, Dar 16
Halaby, Miss Nada 140
Halassa, Senator Jiryes 230
Hannoush, Miss Zahra 140
Harami, Shukri 139, 143
Harris, Mr and Mrs Aylmer 152
Hassan, Hajj 20, 236, 257
Hebron 48, 113
Hill, Hon Richard 249
Hoffman, Christoph 93
Holy Archangels, Chapel of *see* Armenian parish church
Hotels
  American Colony 247, 253
  Fast 66, 80
  Grand, Ramallah 122
  Grand New 23, 29
  Kamnitz, Hebron 49
  King David 162; secretariat destroyed 167–8
  Olivet 66
  Palace 150
  Semiramis 181
Hripsimae, Saint 7
el Husseini family 35
  Abd el Qadir 165
  Haidar 264
  Hajj Amin, Grand Mufti of Jerusalem 151
  Ibrahim efendi, Na'ib el Ashraf 35
  Musa Kazim pasha 165
  Sheikh Taher 76

Imberger, Frau 218
Imwas 241
Irgun Zvai Leumi 166, 167

INDEX 287

Iskander, Dr 59
Istanbul 21, 25, 68

Jaffa 1, 22, 26, 29
 Armenian quarter 53
 Church Missionary Society
  hospital 55
 Collège des Frères 73
 Convent of St Nicholas 229
 government hospital 67
Jaffa oranges 90; dried up groves
 229
Jericho 35–6, 148
 Abuna Philipos 149
 in 1967 267
Jerusalem 1
 in anarchy 182
 divided 202, 239
 localities in
  Akeldama 158
  Bourqet el Sultan 47, 74
  Damascus Gate 79, 266,
   267
  Emek Rephaim 92
  Government House 119
  Haram el Sharif 4, 76, 83,
   148
  Jaffa Gate area 4, 14, 23,
   30, 52, 75
  Jewish Quarter 4
  Mamillah 31, 150
  Mount of Oives 40, 79
  Mount Zion 26, 75
  Musrara 269
  Russian Compound 74
 security zones 178, 205
Jerusalem Armenian Benevolent
 Union 9, 164
Jerusalem Dramatic Society 152
Jerusalem and the East Mission
 233–4, 273
Jerusalem Sports Club 119, 162,
 185
Jewish access to Wailing Wall
 268
Jewish clinic 44
Jewish holocaust in Europe 166
Jewish hospital 79

Kadiköy 69
Kaiser Wilhelm II 75
Kaiserin Augusta–Viktoria 42, 75
Kaiserswerth Diakonissen 40,
 115
Kalebian, Dr 26, 99
Kamal, Daoud efendi 133, 136–7
Kankashian, Sahag 233
Kantara 178
Karakashian, Migerditch 84
Kareklas 184, 186
Katamon 98; battlefield 185;
 taken 187
Kawas, Latifeh 245
Kayyali, Dr 59
Ketchejian, Miss Siranoush 126,
 253
el Khalidi, Yusef efendi 35
Khalil, Mousa 246, 269
Khalil, Yusef 247, 268
Kharpert 4
el Khattab, Omar 12
Khayo, Samir 251, 256
Kitaneh, Issa (Abu Albert) 266
Konya 69
Krikor, Najjar 15, 17
Krikorian family
 Anna 22, 23
 Anna Minassian 14
 Aram 26
 Araxie 26
 Arousiag 17, 19, 20, 26,
  189–90
 Hagop 17, 23–6
 Haiganoush 25–6
 Heghineh 19, 21, 25
 Heghnoug 17, 18, 22, 163,
  164
 Horop 17, 19, 23, 26, 85
 Kegham 22, 23
 Dr Krikor 22, 23, 55, 198,
  202, 203
 Mariam (Mannan) 18; see also
  Melkonian, Mariam
 Movses 17, 27
 Nazouhie 22, 23, 189, 253
 Sirpouhie 17, 20
 Soghmon 17, 21
 Vahan 26, 214

288 INDEX

Vergine 26
Yerevant 22, 23
Yevkineh 26
Krikorian, Yohannes and family 191
Kütahya 158

Landau, Miss Annie 116
Latroun 238, 241
Lawrence of Arabia (film) 62
leeches 30, 39
Lehi 214
leper home 42, 252
Levy, Raphael 224
locusts 83
London Jews Society hospital, Jerusalem 243
Lorenzo family 181–2
Lovedale 49
Lovell, Miss Mary Jane 126
Loya, Sam 144
Lydda, fall of 204

Ma'adi Camp 169, 170
Ma'an 103, 148
Ma'atuk, Fawzi 141
MacInnes, Archbishop Campbell 243, 265
MacInnes, Mrs Campbell 118
MacInnes, Bishop Rennie 66, 145
Madaba 146
Malha 24
Mamluks 13
Mandelbaum Gate 210
Mansur, George (Abu William) 245
Markarian family 166, 168, 181–2
Masterman, Dr 243
Mattar, Mrs 266
Me'ah She'arim 143
Mecca 12
Melkon, Hovhannes (Sapritch Melkon) 28, 54; marriage and children 30–2
Melkonian family
Arousiag 31, 34

Hagop Haroutiun 31
Hovhannes 32, 44
Isquhie 32, 74; *see also* Audi, Isquhie
Macrouhie 32; *see also* Rose, Margaret
Mariam Krikorian 31, 72, 121
Takouhie 32; *see also* Gazmararian, Malakeh
Yughaper 31
Merguerian, Goharig and family 191, 193, 194
Merguerian, John 222
Michaeloff, Mme 78
Michail, Nichola (Abu Najib) 121, 123
Midwifery 15, 17, 68, 70, 72–3, 232
Mildmay Mission 48
Miller, Mr and Mrs Alva 210, 225–6
Minard, Herbert and Marcella 226, 267
Minas el Hindi 14
Minas el Kahwati 14, 54
Montefiore settlement 166
Moore, Miss Elinor 237, 242
Murray, Sir Archibald 63
Musa Dagh 138

Na'ameh 101
Nachlat Shiva 181
Nammar family 192, 270
el Nashashibi, Issam and family 142, 227
Nasir, Miss Elizabeth 252
Nebi Musa 148, 257
Nebi Samwil 102, 257
Nechells Gas Works, Saltley 176

Occupied Enemy Territory Administration (South) 83, 90
Odessa 69
Ohannessian, Mary and Vahé 206
Ohannessian, Tavid 84, 158

INDEX 289

Operation Polly 168, 182
Ottoman Bank 237, 252

Palestine 1, 4, 12, 65, 71, 83
British Mandate in 2, 33, 106;
ends 179, 193
divided 212
education in 115
Greeks in 94
martial law in 83
Palestine, British High
Commissioners in
Sir Alan Cunningham 193
Sir Harold MacMichael 141,
160, 246–7
Lord Plumer 145
Sir Herbert Samuel 90
Sir Arthur Wauchope 119, 163
Palestine Broadcasting Service
150, 153
Palestinians 1, 1456
assist British 65
attached to land 181
curfews on 154
general strike in 1936 by 153
misunderstood by British 169
send 'Messages to Families'
225
under foreign rule 165
vendors and tradesmen 110–11
villagers 30, 109, 114, 154,
241
Paterson, Dr Alexander 48,
66–7, 83
Paterson, Mrs May 49
Paul VI, Pope 254–6
Pedretti, Colonel and Mrs 203,
221
Peel Commission 154
Père Marcel 240
Pergeech see Armenian cemetery
Perowne, Stewart 236, 238,
239–40
Persian peepshow 75, 112
Petra 147
Petrie, Sir Flinders 141
Pilgrims
Armenian see Armenian pilgrims

Coptic 149
Greek 9
Russian 38
Pilz, Schwester Charlotte 41, 42
Plants and trees
in gardens and courtyards 5,
16, 45
in Aleppo 60
at Apostolic Delegate's
254–6
in Baqa'a 24, 209
in Greek Colony 98
in Jericho 35–6, 148
in Ramallah 126
at St George's 20, 247
at Talitha Cumi 41
in the wild by Greek Colony
109
round Ramallah 129–30
near Jericho 149
in east Jordan 147
Postgate, Mr O. O. 160
Poston, Ralph 150
Public Works Department 90, 91
Putnam, J. Leslie and Rena 226

el Qawukji, Fawzi 165
Quakers (Society of Friends) 122

Ramadan 18, 59, 151, 248
Ramallah 67, 122
Ramat Rahel 185, 202
Ramleh 62, 204
Red Crescent and Cross Society
centre 189, 192, 203
Red Crescent Society Maternity
Hospital 232
Red Cross, International
Committee of the 203,
225
Reynolds, K. L. 135, 138
Rittel, Mrs 236
Roberts, Hannah Maria 86
Rose family
Dorothy (Dolly) 87, 173
Gertrude Dorothy 100, 150,
177
Harold Victor 71, 86; marries

290 INDEX

88; at PWD 91; builds
organ 104; revisits
England 171; leaves
Palestine 182, 183
John Harold 92; leaves school
160; visits England 173;
returns to Jerusalem 177;
leaves Greek Colony for
Baqa'a 188–9; crosses to
Jordan 232; 20 years at St
George's Hostel 272
Hilda 87, 174
Leslie 87, 174
Margaret (Mrs H. V. Rose) 71,
90, 177; widowed 228
Margaret 2, 71, 90, 99, 116,
150, 159–60
rose-water 24
Russell & Company 161, 185,
217, 225

Saba, Iskander 191, 210
Safieh, Emile 237
St George's Anglican Boys'
School 26, 132, 135;
reopened in 1918 137; in
1967 261, 262
St George's Close 20
and College 252, 262
and Hostel 234, 238; warden
of 243
St George's Collegiate Church
65
consecration 134
Kaiser's visit 76
St John of Jerusalem Ophthalmic
Hospital 219, 251
Salah el Din 12
Salomon, Karl and Edith 150
Samu' 260
Sanjak of Jerusalem 21, 35
Sarafand 169
Sarafian, Haiganoush 25; see also
Krikorian, Haiganoush
Save the Children Fund 239
el Sawabini, Dar 20
Schick, Konrad 40
Schurr, Simon 204

Schneller, Johan Ludwig 84
Schools and colleges
Bishop Gobat School 23, 40;
in 1948 195, 243
Bishop's School, Amman 233
Collège des Frères 26
Dar el Awlad 252
Evelina de Rothschild 116
Friends' Boys School, Ramallah
67, 122
Friends' Girls School, Ramallah
122–3
Jerusalem Girls' College 26;
British Section 116
Rawdat el Zuhur 252
St Gayantiants and St
Tarkmanchats see
Armenian schools
St George's School see St
George's in main index
Schneller's Orphanage 53, 84,
111, 161, 252
Sisters of Sion 35
Syrian Protestant College,
Beirut 53
Talitha Cumi 41, 75, 251
Terra Sancta College 211
Scrimegour, Colonel 66
seder 52
Selim I, Sultan 13
Seychelles 155
Sharm el Sheikh 261
Sharp, Mr and Mrs Colin 233
Sharp, Mr H. B. 141
Sheikh Jarrah 186, 202
Shepherd, Miss Phyllis 234
Siksik, Mrs George 252
Silwan 46, 185
Simon, Joshua 201, 215
Simon the tanner 21
Sis 4
Smith, Mrs Theophilus 53
Spinney, Mr A. R. 107
State of Israel proclaimed 194;
property laws in 222
Stepan, Kevork 29, 34
Stepanian, varbed Christine 35
Stern, Avraham 166

INDEX

Stern Gang 166, 205
Stewart, Bishop W. H. and Mrs 161, 210, 243, 238
Stopford, Bishop Robert 272
Storrs, Colonel Ronald 65, 83, 90
Suez Crisis 241
Suleiman the Magnificent 4, 47
Suleiman, Omar and family 248, 262, 263, 267–8
Supreme Moslem Council 150, 239, 265; plan Arab university 151
Surp Hagop see Armenian Cathedral of St James
Sutton, James 210, 215
Swift, Emma Elizabeth 86
Swift, Samuel and Florrie 174
Swift, William and Ada 174–5
Syria and Palestine Relief Fund 83, 115
Syrian Protestant College in Beirut 56

el Tal, Colonel Abdullah 198
Tantur, Ecumenical Institute at 272
Tegart forts 241
Tekoa 145
Templist German community 19, 93, 157
el Terzibash, Dar 18, 272
Thaddeus, Archimandrite 96, 184
Thomas Cook & Sons 29, 34, 75
Thompson, Miss Mary 236, 242
Thornton-Duesbery, Rev J. P. 139, 175
Thornton-Duesbery, Miss Jean 139
Toon family 170, 175
Turkey, massacres of Armenians in 3, 4, 11, 127, 164
Turkish baths 47

Turkish coffee 14, 15
Turkish fliers 26

Umm, Qeis 232
United Free Church of Scotland 49
United Nations
  Mixed Armistice Commissions 212, 239
  Relief and Works agency (UNRWA) 213
    Aqbat Jaber camp 248, 268
  vote to partition Palestine 179
Üsküdar 69

Valero family 84
Valine, Mme Sonia 227, 270
Van Zandt, Miss Jane E. 54, 59
Vartan, Miss 50
Viennese Tearoom 162, 185
Voskerichian, Haigazoun 34

Wa'ariyeh 24
Waddell, Miss Jean 259
Waddy, Canon Stacy 238
Wadi Mujib 147, 162
Wadi Qelt 37, 146, 247, 257
Wadi Shu'eib 257
Walker, Miss Grace Kerr 51
War
  in 1914–18 1, 11, 20, 60, 83
  in 1939–45 153, 156
  in 1948 4, 101, 164, 205
  in 1967 236
Warburton, Miss M. 115
Weisenberg, Judy 150, 153
Wilson, J. B. 273
Wilson, Mr and Mrs Tug 245
Wordsworth, John, Bishop of Salisbury 134
World Council of Churches 237

YMCA 145, 152, 163, 242
YWCA 251

Zimmerman, Canon and Mrs John D. 250–1, 263